WEB SEARCH: PUBLIC SEARCHING OF THE WEB

Information Science and Knowledge Management

Volume 6

The titles published in this series are listed at the end of this volume.

WEB SEARCH: PUBLIC SEARCHING OF THE WEB

by

AMANDA SPINK

University of Pittsburgh, U.S.A.

and

BERNARD J. JANSEN

The Pennsylvania State University, U.S.A.

KLUWER ACADEMIC PUBLISHERS

DORDRECHT / BOSTON / LONDON

A C.I.P. Catalogue record for this book is available from the Library of Congress.

ISBN 1-4020-2268-9 (HB)
ISBN 1-4020-2269-7 (e-book)

Published by Kluwer Academic Publishers,
P.O. Box 17, 3300 AA Dordrecht, The Netherlands.

Sold and distributed in North, Central and South America
by Kluwer Academic Publishers,
101 Philip Drive, Norwell, MA 02061, U.S.A.

In all other countries, sold and distributed
by Kluwer Academic Publishers,
P.O. Box 322, 3300 AH Dordrecht, The Netherlands.

Printed on acid-free paper

Contents

SECTION IV: CONCLUSION

Preface

This book brings together results from the Web search studies we conducted from 1997 through 2004. The aim of our studies has been twofold: to examine how the public at large searches the Web and to highlight trends in public Web searching. The eight-year period from 1997 to 2004 saw the beginnings and maturity of public Web searching. Commercial Web search engines have come and gone, or endured, through the fall of the dot.com companies. We saw the rise and, in some cases, the demise of several high profile, publicly available Web search engines.

The study of the Web search is an exciting and important area of interdisciplinary research. Our book provides a valuable insight into the growth and development of human interaction with Web search engines. In this book, our focus is on the human aspect of the interaction between user and Web search engine. We do not investigate the Web search engines themselves or their constantly changing interfaces, algorithms and features. We focus on exploring the cognitive and user aspects of public Web searching in the aggregate. We use a variety of quantitative and qualitative methods within the overall methodology known as transaction log analysis.

Our studies examined large datasets of keywords, queries and search sessions provided by commercial Web search engine companies, but these companies provided limited or no access to the demographics of the individual or aggregate of Web search engines users. Our studies do not include analysis of query data from Web search engines where the data was unavailable to us. We are very grateful to commercial Web search engine companies who were generous enough to provide large query data sets for academic analysis, including Excite.com, AskJeeves.com, AlltheWeb.com and AltaVista.com. Their support for our research is an outstanding example of the beneficial cooperation that can occur between industry and academia.

The authors have contrasting backgrounds. This contrast contributed greatly to the interdisciplinary nature of our studies. The first author (Spink) is an information scientist who has worked with, taught and researched human interaction with information systems and search engines since 1980. The second author (Jansen) is a computer scientist who has worked with, taught and researched information systems, information retrieval, Web content design, and search engines since 1986. The authors started working jointly on researching public Web searching when Excite.com offered a large dataset of Web queries to attendees at the 1997 Association of Computing Machinery Special Interest Group on Information Retrieval Conference (ACM-SIGIR) in Philadelphia.

PURPOSE AND APPROACH

Our book has three objectives. First, we provide an overview and synthesis of Web searching research within a broad theoretical framework. Second, we offer in-depth analysis of Web searching within several topical domains. Third, we provide an overview and synthesis of our research findings on public Web searching and highlight trends in public Web searching.

The book is organized in four sections to reflect these objectives:

Section I: The Context of Web Search
Section II: How People Search the Web
Section III: Subjects of Web Search
Section IV: Trends and Future Directions

Thus, Section I describes the broad framework and context for research examining public Web searching, including the technological, social, organizational, human information behavior and human computer interaction levels of analysis. This section also describes the research designs used in our studies. Section II focuses on providing an overview and synthesis of public Web searching. In particular we focus on users' search terms and topics, querying and search sessions. Section III discusses the major subjects of Web searching in four areas: e-commerce, medical health, sexual search, and multimedia search. Section IV discusses the key findings of our studies, the trends in public Web search we observed, including the growth of more complex search behaviors, and future research directions.

Each section contains one or more chapters relating to the broader topic area of the section. Each chapter is stand-alone, in respect of presenting a complete picture of the particular topic, including its own reference list. The chapters are also cross-referenced where appropriate to illustrate how that topic meshes with the broader area of Web search.

AUDIENCE

This book is a valuable resource for Web searching researchers, educators, and practitioners. The primary audience is researchers and students in the fields of information science, computer science, information systems, cognitive science, and related disciplines. The book is a valuable research resource for those investigating Web searching. This book is an appropriate text for undergraduate, graduate and doctoral level courses in areas of information and Web retrieval, online information management, information science, human information behavior, digital libraries, Web content structuring, and management information systems.

Web consultants, search engine optimization specialists, Web masters, providers of online content and services, and those working within Web search engine companies would find this book useful for research-based insights into how people seek and search for electronic information. In addition, anyone who searches the Web will find the book a fascinating and enlightening read.

ACKNOWLEDGMENTS

A good portion of this book is a result of many previous studies conducted by the authors, often with other researchers and students. We would like to thank Tefko Saracevic from Rutgers University for helping to launch this major research project, and Dietmar Wolfram from the University of Wisconsin-Milwaukee who contributed to the data analysis and key publications.

We also thank Jan Pedersen from Alta Vista, Per Gunan from AlltheWeb.com, and Jack Xu and Doug Cutting from Excite@home.com, for generously providing the large datasets of Web queries that formed the initial basis of our research. We also acknowledge our colleagues Seda and Huseyin Cenk Ozmutlu from Uludag University (Turkey) who analyzed some of the transaction logs and co-authored publications.

We also thank our students and other researchers who collaborated on the query analysis and co-authored publications, including Mohammad Abbas,

Judy Bateman, Carol Chang, Abby Goodrum, Alice Goz, Okan Guner, Shaoyi He, Ali Hurson, Daniel Lorence, Stephanie Milchak, Pirkko Nyganen, Minsoo Park, Anthony Pfaff, Megan Pomeroy, Andrew Koricich, Michelle Sollenberger, and Yin Yang. We would also like to acknowledge the following people for their reviews of our book chapters – James Wang, Magy Sief El-Nasr, Dongwon Lee, Praseniit Mitra, Karen Jansen and Peter Spink.

Amanda Spink
School of Information Sciences
University of Pittsburgh

Bernard J. Jansen
School of Information Sciences and Technology
The Pennsylvania State University

Foreword

As regards speed of global adoption and scale of effects, the World Wide Web is a phenomenon unlike any other in the history of technology. It spread worldwide in an amazingly short period of time. Tim Berners-Lee created the Web in 1991 while at CERN (Conseil European pour la Recherché Nucleaire) in Geneva. This provided a relatively straightforward mechanism for sharing online information. Marc Andreessen and Eric Bina created Mosaic, a graphic interface-browser for the Web later to become Netscape, in 1993 while at NCSA (National Center for Supercomputing, University of Illinois). This made the Web easy and interesting to use for the masses. Within two years the number of Web sites reached a million. Within a decade the Web was a part of our social fabric – it affected every human activity in some way or other. Society-at-large has adopted and adapted it.

The obvious question that one can ask is "Why did all this happen so fast and so far?" Answers are forthcoming from a number of disciplines and viewpoints. From the technological point of view, the Internet, as the underlying technology for the Web, was already solidly in place and gaining an ever-wider presence – the Web was the most successful piggyback of this technology. Socially, global connections were accelerating at a rapid pace and the Web fit into that mode seamlessly – it even significantly accelerated the acceleration. Economically, the Web was a natural fit for the information society. And so on. But the real underlying reason is the people.

People flocked to the Web in massive numbers for a variety of reasons. The Web is intuitive, relatively easy to learn and use. Even the creation of one's own Web site is not that difficult. The Web became a huge and rich depository of all kinds of information, with a complex structure of links and ever-changing content. Additionally, the content of the Web is value-neutral

– anything goes. The variety, dynamics, and neutrality of content, coupled with ease of use, became prime factors responsible for the Web's popularity and astonishing growth in use.

However, the Web also became a jumble, an unmapped space. Disorganization is inherent to the Web – high and progressive entropy seem to be a natural state. Metaphors abound depicting this feature of the Web as terra incognita, sailing an ocean without a compass, uncharted, bewildering, and so on. A Web paradox emerged: as the Web (or to be more precise, Web content) became potentially more and more useful to a wider and wider population of users, it became more and more difficult to use. Navigating, browsing, and searching became a serious problem – and still is to a large degree.

Enter search engines as a solution. A few Internet search engines were created in the pre-Web era. Following their experiences, the first genuine Web search engines were World Wide Web Wanderer, created by Matthew Gray, and ALIWEB, created by Martin Koster in 1993, followed in rapid succession by many others. The first big successful engine, Yahoo!, was launched in early 1994, by Jerry Yang and David Filo of Stanford University, and Google, the present (as of 2004) search engine superpower, was launched in 1999 by Larry Page and Sergey Brin, also from Stanford. While a few large search engines dominate the scene, search engines also went global. In 2003, Search Engine Worldwide listed 3,105 search engines in 211 countries.

Search engines are used massively. They must have hit upon a real human information need. Millions of searches are conducted every single day around the clock and the world. Not surprisingly, interesting questions arise:

How are people going about the Web?

How are they getting to wherever they are intending on going?

How are they going about finding selecting, identifying, and obtaining potentially relevant information?

These are not just research questions about human information behavior on the Web that are of academic interest, but also questions of a practical nature, critical for evaluating effectiveness and efficiency of Web searching, for a variety of uses, not least for improvement of performance and education. There may be serious organizational and societal issues that should be addressed.

As yet, we have limited understanding of the Web's nature and possibilities in a formal way. Research on human information behavior on the Web is in its infancy – we have just begun to chart this area of studies. This outstanding book deals in territory with a very short history and not that many studies. It provides a valuable and insightful synthesis of pioneering research. It provides insights, challenges and guidance for both students and practitioners of the Web. And, as any good research book does, it raises more questions than it answers. In summary, this book is Web terra less incognita.

Tefko Saracevic, PhD   February 2004
Professor II at the School of Communication,
Information and Library Studies,
Rutgers University,
New Brunswick, NJ, USA

Section   I

THE CONTEXT OF WEB SEARCH

Chapter 1

TECHNOLOGICAL, SOCIAL AND ORGANIZATIONAL CONTEXT

1. INTRODUCTION

The first section briefly focuses on the technology context and trends associated with Web search – the trends and growth in Web users, searches, search engines and websites. One can view the public searching of the Web from many different and often overlapping levels and contexts. This chapter discusses technological trends associated with how the public searches the Web.

Figure 1.1 shows the general theoretical framework we use in the book for understanding Web search trends and issues.

2. WEB SEARCH TECHNOLOGY CONTEXT

Some people compare the Web to a library. In this book, we make a distinction between the terms Web and Internet. The term Web is used to describe all hypermedia-based information sources available through the Internet. The term Internet encompasses all services available through this communication medium including the Web, email, ftp, telnet, streaming video, etc.

The Internet was developed in the 1960s by the U.S. Defense Department's Advanced Research Project Agency (DARPA) to provide a military communication infrastructure. Internet technologies are largely used for interpersonal communications such as sending and receiving emails, and obtaining information for work and hobbies (Gunter, Russell, Withey and Nicholas, 2003; Kraut, Mukhaopadhyay, Szczypula, Kiesler and Scherlis, 2000).

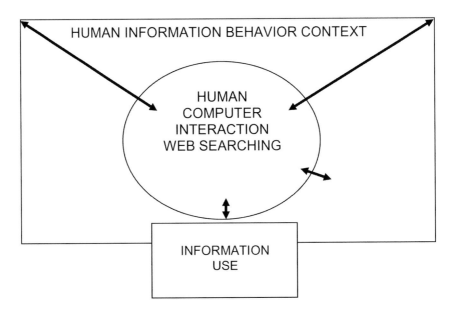

Figure 1-1. Framework for Web Search

Today, many people see the Web as a computer network or a way to link information systems (Berners-Lee, 1989; Berners-Lee, Cailliau, Luotonen, Nielsen and Secret, 1994). The growth of the Web has been phenomenal and its immense size is difficult to estimate, and it is the Web search engines that have been critical to navigating this huge resource. Web search engines come in two broad forms. Web directories, such as Yahoo.com <http://www.yahoo.com>, provide a hierarchical human-compiled directory of Web sites. Web search engines, such as Alta Vista <http://www.altavista.com> and Google <http://www.google.com>, match the user's terms with indexed Web pages. Web meta-search engines, such as Dogpile <http://www.dogpile> and Metacrawler <http://metacrawler.com>, query several Web search engines concurrently and provide collated results

(Selberg and Etzioni, 1997). Web search engines are becoming mass consumer products that process thousands of user queries per second.

Even as the major Web search engines continue to expand their coverage of the Web, it is estimated that at best they only covered from a high of 34% to a low of 3% of the documents on the Internet in 1998 (Lawrence and Giles, 1998) with the highest percentage dropping to 16% in 1999. Combining multiple search engines in a given search can increase the likelihood of finding the information desired by a factor of 3.5 or more.

3. WEB SEARCH ENGINES

3.1 Overview

A portal is a Web site that provides specialized access to Web services and information. A wide range of portals exists. A portal may provide access to a specific collection of materials to support activities in a particular discipline (e.g., law, travel, research articles). For example, within the legal domain, there are several portals providing legal information, including associations <http://www.abanet.org/>, government <http://www.uscourts. gov/>, <http://www.fedworld.gov/>, and commercial <http://www.law.com/ lawfirmcentral/papers/>.

Web search engines are an important class of portals whose primary purpose is to support searches on a wide variety of topics across a comprehensive range of Web sites. Web search engines are a special form of information retrieval (IR) systems designed specifically for the hypermedia environment of the Web. They are the major portals for users of the Web, with 71% of Web users accessing Web search engines to locate other Web sites (Neilsen Media, 2000). As such, it is important to have an understanding of their impact and effect on how people search for information on the Web. In the next sections, we review some of the commonly used search engines, the architecture of Web search engines in general and typical Web search functionality.

3.2 The Web Search Engine Landscape

There are more than 3,200 search engines on the Web (Sullivan, 2000b), with a very small number of these dominating in terms of usage. The dominant search engines usually have a mix of reliable technology for searching, a reasonable business model, and broad recognition within the Web audience. The top five search engines in terms of audience reach in January 2003 were Google (29.5%), Yahoo (28.9%), Microsoft Search

(MSN) (27.6%), America Online (AOL) (18.4%), and AskJeeves (9.9%) (Sullivan, 2002a, b). Audience reach is the estimated percentage of U.S. home and work users using the service during that particular month.

There are currently several major Web search engines, including Google, Alta Vista, Yahoo, AlltheWeb.com, Ask Jeeves, Overture, Teoma, and MSN. Over the last five years, there has been a great consolidation and activity in the Web search engine marketplace with corporations buying many formerly independent search engines. AOL purchased Netscape (Junnarkar and Clark, 2003). Google entered the scene in 1998 (Brin, 1998). Excite sold various parts of its search engine and portal organization to Infospace, iWon, and AT&T (Singer, 2003).

Overture purchased AltaVista (Morrissey, 2003) and AlltheWeb.com (Kane, 2003). Yahoo purchased Inktomi and Overture (Berkowitz, 2003). Additionally, Microsoft announced that it is formally entering the search engine market with the introduction of its own search engine (Bowman and Olsen, 2003). Yahoo then purchased Overture. This consolidation of Web search engines will lead to the emergence of three major consumer Web search engines and portals – Google, Yahoo and MSN.

Let's look at the three most popular Web search engines – America Online (AOL), Google and Microsoft's MSN. Popularity, using the number of unique visitors, is a standard metric for Web site traffic. A unique visitor is based on the Internet Protocol (IP) address of the client computer visiting a Web site within a certain time period, typically one month.

AOL is America Online's search engine. Since August of 1999, AOL has utilized third parties for its backend document collection, first using Excite, then Inktomi, and then Google. AOL currently has access to over 3 billion documents from the Google database. AOL received 90,031,000 unique visitors in August 2002 (Neilsen Netrating, 2002),

Google is a full-featured Web searching tool. In addition to possessing a searchable database of over 3 billion HTML documents, Google has indexed 700,000,000 USENET messages, 35,000,000 non-HTML documents, and 390,000,000 images. Google reports approximately 150 million search queries per day. In March 2002, Google received 31,901,000 unique visitors (Neilsen Netrating, 2002).

As of 2003, *MSN* uses the Inktomi Gigadoc database and the LookSmart directory service as its backend content collection. LookSmart reports its service indexes over 2,500,000 unique uniform resource locators (URLs) in 250,000 categories (Looksmart, 2002). Inktomi reports having a master database containing over two billion URLs (Inktomi, 2002). In March 2002, MSN received 97,426,000 unique visitors (Neilsen Netrating, 2002).

3.3   How Web Search Engines Work

The major Web search engines currently provide information from typically massive content collections in response to specific queries from millions of users worldwide in a matter of seconds. In addition to the massive increase in scale relative to earlier computerized IR systems, there are forces that intentionally attempt to subvert search engine efforts via spam and other hacking techniques. It is an overall daunting task that few, if any, previous IR systems have had to face. So, how do they do it?

There are many sources of information that provide a detailed look at the functionality and architecture of Web search engines; two articles are Liddy (2001) and Arasu, Cho, Garcia-Molina, Paepcke and Raghavan (2001). Here we provide a concise overview using the architecture described in Arasu, Cho, Garcia-Molina, Paepcke and Raghavan (2001). Although there is other terminology one can use, the major components are generally the same.

A Web search engine comprises four essential modules: (1) a crawler, (2) an indexer, (3) a query engine, and (4) a page repository, as displayed in Figure 1.2.

Web search engines basically match terms in queries submitted by searchers against an inverted file that the Web search engine creates. The inverted file is an index consisting of the words in each document along with pointers to the locations of these words within all the Web documents in the search engine's content collection. How do search engines get these documents?

Every Web search engine relies on one or more *crawlers* (also called softbots or agents) to provide the content for its operation. Crawlers are computer programs that browse the Web on the search engine's behalf in a manner similar to the way a person follows links to reach different pages. The crawlers use a starting set of uniform resource locators (URL). The crawler retrieves (i.e., copies and stores) the content on the sites specified by the URLs. The crawlers extract URLs appearing in the retrieved pages and visit some or all of these URLs, thus repeating the retrieval process. Each Web search engine follows its own unique timetable for re-crawling the Web and updating its content collection. The Web search engines store the Web content they retrieve during the crawling process in a page repository.

The *indexer* takes all the words from each document in the page repository and records the URL where each word occurred. The result is generally a very large database providing the URLs that point to pages where a given word occurs. In this area, search engines have much in common with traditional IR systems in terms of the techniques they employ to organize their content. Given the hypermedia aspects of much of the Web content, however, the database may also contain other structural information such as links between documents, incoming URLs to these documents, formatting aspects of the documents, and location of terms with respect to other terms.

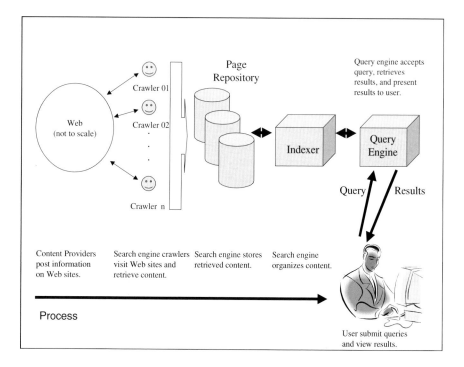

Figure 1-2. Basic Web Search Engine Architecture and Process

The use of this information can lead to fairly sophisticated applications. For example, the niche Web search engine CiteSeer (Giles, Bollacker and Lawrence, 1998), indexes computer science literature automatically and calculates the citation relationships among these documents.

The Web *query engine* receives the search requests from users. It takes the query submitted by the user, splits the query into terms, and searches the database built by the indexer to locate the terms and hence the Web documents referred by the stored URLs. The Web query engine then retrieves the documents that match the terms within the query and returns these documents to the user. The user can then click on one or more of the URLs of the presented Web documents.

The Web search engine typically ranks documents when presenting them to the user by calculating a similarity score between the query and each document. The higher the similarity score, the higher the ranking for a particular document. Different ranking algorithms can produce very different document rankings. These ranking algorithms are extremely important to both search engines and users, as research shows the effectiveness of the ranking generally improves the user's perceptions of system performance (Witten, Moffat and Bell, 1994).

Although matching and ranking algorithms vary among Web search engines, there are some generally applied techniques used by most Web search engines. The exact details of the algorithms used by a specific Web search engine are generally regarded as proprietary and thus cannot be examined in detail.

For more technical information about Web systems, engines, algorithms, crawling, and interfaces, consult monographs by Arasu, Cho Garcia-Molina, Paepcke and Ragha (2001), Baldi, Frasconi and Smyth (2003), Brin and Page (1998), Chakrabarti (2002), Kobayashi and Takeda (2000), and Rasmussen (2003).

3.4 Methods of Document Ranking

The underlying approach to matching and ranking used by Web search engines is simply to take the terms in the query and locate items that contain at least some of the same terms. There are many variations on this basic approach; a great deal of experimental research has been devoted to evaluating their effectiveness. Most of the research published in this area has involved small experimental collections, although there is an increasing amount of work involving much larger collections. Some of the techniques commonly used in matching and ranking algorithms include:

3.4.1 Click Through Analysis

Click through analysis utilizes data concerning the frequency with which users chose a particular page as a means of future ranking. Click through analysis consists of logging queries and the URLs searchers visit for those queries. The URLs that are visited most often by searchers in response to a particular query or term are ranked higher in future results listings.

3.4.2 Link Popularity

Link popularity is an examination of the links pointing to a Web document. Most Web search engines use some type of link analysis as part of their ranking algorithm. Link analysis is a method for determining which pages are good for particular topics based on both the quantity and quality of links pointing to that document. Authority documents are those with many incoming high quality links.

3.4.3   Term Frequency

Term frequency is a numerical evaluation of how frequently a term appears in a Web document. Generally, a higher frequency of occurrence indicates a greater likelihood that the document is related to the query. Overall, and within special domains such as law, documents use a small subset of terms quite often and a large subset of terms very infrequently.

Additionally, there is usually a set of words occurring quite frequently in documents that have little to do with document content (e.g., the, is, a, etc.). Web search engines may maintain a stop list of such words, which are excluded from both indexing and searching.

3.4.4   Term Location

Term location many times indicates its significance to the document. Therefore, most Web search engines give more weight to certain terms (e.g., those occurring in titles, lead paragraphs, image captions, special formatting such as bold, etc.) than terms occurring in the body of the document or even in a footnote.

3.4.5   Term Proximity

Term proximity is the distance between two or more query terms within a document. The rationale is that it is more likely that the document is relevant to the query if the terms appear near each other. Given that most Web queries are short (i.e., one or two terms), term proximity is many times of little value. However, in certain situations, term proximity can be of great value. Name searching is one such area.

3.4.6   Text Formatting

Text formatting is the use of specific HTML codes in their ranking algorithms. Although several schemes exist (e.g., bold terms, emphasis tags, etc.), the most successful of these is the use of anchor tags. When an information provider produces a Web page, the document will many times contain links to other Web documents or links to specific locations in the document. Readers of the documents see these links as clickable text. This clickable text is called the anchor text. Search engine designers have discovered that these anchor texts and tags are valuable sources of metadata about the document at the address specified by the link.

4. WEB SIZE

The size of the Web and the number of Websites continues to grow. In 1999 Lawrence and Giles (1999) estimated that 800 million documents are publicly available on the Web. By July 2003, Jan Pedersen (2003) of Overture estimated the size of the Web as 50 terabytes of data or several billion pages. Document growth on the Web may be doubling every year.

The Online Computer Library Center (OCLC) Office of Research Web Characterization Project (2003) estimated the size of the "public" Web has grown from 1.5 million Web sites in 1998 to 3,080,000 Web sites. By June 2002 only 35% of the Web or 1.4 billion Web pages was accessible by the public via Web search engines. They also point to a slowdown in the growth of the public Web pages from 1998 to 2002 (O'Neil, Lavoie and Bennett, 2003) and that IP address volatility led to the consolidation of 51 per cent of Web sites in 2001.

OCLC (2003) report little change in the origin of Web sites from 1999 to 2002 with approximately half the world's Web sites originating in the United States. The distribution of languages on Web sites changed little from 1999 to 2002 with consistently three-quarters of all Web sites in English. The proportion of Web sites using META tags to describe the content of the Web site increased from 70% in 1998 to 87% in 2002

5. WEB SEARCHES

Kobayashi and Takeda (2000) report that some 85% of the Web users they surveyed claimed using Web search engines to find information. Two-thirds to three-quarters of all users cite finding information as one of their primary uses of the Web. Two-thirds to three-quarters of all users cite the inability to find the information they seek as one of their primary frustrations (second only in frustration to slowness of response).

The number of Internet users is measured as "audience reach" or the percentage of United States' home and work Internet users estimated to have searched on each site at least once during the month through a Web browser or some other "online" means. Because of this, the average time spent by visitors in a given month can be a useful way to determine which sites may be more popular, when it comes to search.

In early 2002, the average America Online user spent 10 to 11 minutes when searching. By October 2002, the average minutes more than tripled. Web search engines generate 7% to 8% of traffic to Web sites. Nine of ten Web users visit a search engine, portal or community site each month. They also revisit frequently, nearly five times per month (Nielsen//NetRatings,

May 2002). People looking for products on the Web are far more likely to type the product name into a search engine's search box (28%) than browse shopping "channels" (5%) or click on ads (4%).

In January 2003, there were an estimated 134 million active Internet users at home and at work in the United States. By July 2003, Jan Pedersen (2003) from Overture estimated the total of World Wide Web searches per day at 400 million and a significant portion of these searches were generated in the United States.

6.   SOCIAL WEB CONTEXT

In this section, we examine the social level trends of public use of the Web. Trends in the social impact of the Web on different publics and communities are also highlighted by Sawyer and Eschenfelder (2002).

Some studies have examined the social aspect of the Web, but few specifically focus on Web searching. Mowshowitz and Kawagichi (2001) point to the biases of various Web search engines. DiMaggio, Hargittai, Neumann and Robinson (2001) examine the social implications for the Internet. Bar-Ilan (2001) and Introna and Nissenbaum (2000) call for the development of Web search engines that are not driven by profit considerations. Introna and Nissenbaum (2000) view the Web as a public good, but see dangers in the use of commercial Web search engines that are driven by market forces.

6.1   Internet Use at Home

A growing body of studies is examining Web use in the home. A major study of home Web use is the HomeNet project at Carnegie Mellon University (Kraut, Scherlis, Mukhopadhyay, Manning and Kiesler, 1996; Kraut, Patterson, Lundmark, Kiesler, Mukhopadhyay and Scherlis, 1998). Using a variety of data including logs, questionnaires, help requests, and interviews with families, the research group measured how people integrated electronic communication and information resources on the Internet and how Internet services affected their lives.

Cummings and Kraut (2002) found that a significant trend has been towards the domestication of the Internet. In 1995, the National Science Foundation found that one in five Americans had home Internet access. However by 2002, home access increased to 59.3% (UCLA CCP, 2003). Cummings and Kraut (2002) suggest that Internet use is now in both the home and workplace. Home use of the Internet has increased with the growth in the availability of broadband services.

Haythornthwaite and Wellman (2002) identify trends in the impact and uses of the Internet in people's everyday lives. In their book, *The Internet in Everyday Life* (2002), they include many studies that demonstrate the Internet is embedded in everyday life and the home use of the Internet is increasing. They studied the use and impact of the Internet at home, including the effect on domestic relations, community, civil involvement, alienation, activities, and work

Anderson and Tracey (2002) provide an impact model of Internet access and suggest that usage is not a valuable explanatory tool. They suggest that future research is needed to provide a deeper understanding of the home Web use.

Haythornthwaite and Kazmer (2002) examined the views of adult distance learners about their Internet use. They found that both home and work environments are extended by Internet use. Nie, Hillygus, and Erbring (2002) found that home Internet use had a strong negative impact on time spent with friends and family. Internet use at work decreased social spent with colleagues, but had little impact on social time spent with friends and family.

Another large-scale research project of home environments is the HomeNetToo project at Michigan State University (Jackson, Barbatsis, Biocca, Zhao and von Eye, 2002), which used server logs, surveys, and interviews to focus on Internet use by low-income adults. Their results revealed that while half of the participants never used email at all, their main Internet activity was finding information on the Web. The participants incorporated the Internet into their ongoing lives as a communication device and an information resource: however, they noted that the Internet was still an uncomfortable environment as participants persisted in feelings of novelty and felt that user skills were too difficult to develop.

Rieh (2004) studied how 12 people used the Internet, through home-based interviews and search activity diaries. Users engaged in a more diverse range of Internet use patterns in the home than in work environments. Findings indicated that the home, indeed, provided a distinct information use environment in which the subjects interpreted the Web in various ways, using it not only as an IR system but also as a tool for information recording, sharing, disseminating, and communication.

Based on Rieh's (2004) empirical findings, the relationships of the home environment, Web context, and interaction situation were identified with respect to user goals and information seeking behaviors. She suggests that there are differences between work and home Web usage. Rieh (2004) found that people conducted Web searches incrementally, involving intervals of hours or days with little time pressure.

The ongoing Pew studies use large-scale surveys to determine the usages and impact of the Internet on everyday lives (Pew Internet and American Life Project, 2002b). This is a valuable and ongoing research project that is investigating many aspects of Web access, usage, commitment, and domestication. The Pew Internet and American Life Project (2002a) found that approximately 24 million Americans, or 21% of all Internet users, had high-speed Internet connections at home. The number of home high-speed users had increased form from 6 million to 24 million in 2002.

The British Life and Internet Project (Gunter, Russell, Withey and Nicholas, 2003) is exploring the way people in Britain use the Internet. Using survey data, the project is investigating people's history and patterns of Internet use. So far the project results show that people in Britain use the Internet mainly for email, obtaining news and searching for information for home and work use. Study participants reported reducing activities, such as television viewing and shopping, in favor of Internet use.

7.   ORGANIZATION WEB

An important area of study is the trends in the organizational level use the Web. The organizational view explores the impact of Web search on organizational functions and effectiveness. Choo, Detlor and Turnbull (2000) provide a key book in this area that discusses the organizational Web, understanding organizational Web use and the Intranet as infrastructure for knowledge work.

Recent books by Anandarajan and Simmers (2002, 2004) provide an analysis of the impact of Internet and Web use in the workplace. They examine the social, ethical, legal, management, human resources and personal usage aspects of the Web use in organizations.

8.   CONCLUSION

This chapter focused on the broader context of the Web search environment, including the nature, growth, and structure of the Web. Specifically, we presented an overview of the technological and social context, and a brief discussion of the organizational context and trends for Web search.

An overwhelming number of studies continue to focus on the technical and algorithmic aspects of the Web. Further research is needed to fully extend our understanding of Web use at the social and organizational level.

9. REFERENCES

Anandarajan, M. and Simmers, C. A. (2002). *Managing Web Usage in the Workplace: A Social, Ethical and Legal Perspective*. Hershey: Idea Group, Inc.

Anandarajan, M. and Simmers, C. A. (2004). *Personal Web Usage in the Workplace: A Guide to Effective Human Resources Management*. Hershey: Idea Group, Inc.

Anderson, B and Tracey, K. (2002). Digital Living: The Impact or Otherwise of the Internet on Everyday British Life. In B. Wellman and C. Haythornthwaite Eds., *The Internet in Everyday Life* pp. 139–163. Oxford, UK: Blackwell.

Arasu, A., Cho, J., Garcia-Molina, H., Paepcke, A. and Raghavan, S. (2001). Searching the Web. *ACM Transactions on Internet Technology, 1*, 2–43.

Baldi, P, Frasconi, P. and Smyth, P. (2003). *Modeling the Internet and the Web: Probabilistic Methods and Algorithms*. New York: John Wiley & Sons.

Bar-Ilan, J. (2001). Data Collection Methods on the Web for Informetric Purposes: A Review and Analysis. *Scientometrics, 50*(1), 7–32.

Berners-Lee, T. (1989). *Information Management: A Proposal*. <http://www3.org/History/1989/proposal.html>.

Berners-Lee, T., Cailliau, R., Luotonen, A., Nielsen, H. F. and Secret, A. (1994). The World Wide Web. *Communications of the ACM, 37*(8), 76–82.

Berkowitz, B. (2003). Yahoo! to Buy Overture in $1.63 Bln Deal. In *Reuter*. Los Angeles, CA, USA.

Bowman, L. M. and Olsen, S. (2003) *Microsoft Increases Search Focus*. Accessed on 17 September 2003 on the World Wide Web at <http://www.pandia.com/sw-2003/24-msn.html>.

Brin, S. (1998). Extracting Patterns and Relations From the World Wide Web. *Proceedings of the World Wide Web and Databases*, Valencia, Spain, 172–183.

Brin, S. and Page, L. (1998). The Anatomy of a Large-Scale Hypertextual Web Search Engine. *Proceedings of the 7th International World Wide Web Conference*.

Chakrabarti, S. (2002). *Mining the Web: Analysis of Hypertext and Semi Structured Data*. San Francisco: Morgan Kaufmann.

Choo, C. W., Detlor, B. and Turnbull, D. (2000). *Web Work. Information Seeking and Knowledge Work on the World Wide Web*. Kluwer Academic Publishers.

Cummings, J. and Kraut, R. (2002). Domesticating Computers and the Internet. *Information Society, 183*, 221–232.

DiMaggio, P., Hargittai, E., Neumann, W. R. and Robinson, J. P. (2001). Social Implications of the Internet. *Annual Review of Sociology, 27*, 307–336.

Giles, C. L., Bollacker, K. and Lawrence, S. (1998). CiteSeer: An Automatic Citation Indexing System. *Proceedings of the 3rd ACM Conference on Digital Libraries*, Pittsburgh PA, 89–91.

Gunter, B. C., Russell, R., Withey, N. D. and Nicholas, D. (2003). The British Life and Internet Project: Inaugural Survey Findings. *Aslib Proceedings: New Information Perspectives, 55*(4), 203–216.

Haythornthwaite, C. and Kazmer, M. M. (2002). Bringing the Internet Home: Adult Distance Learners and Their Internet, Home, and Work Words. In B. Wellman and C. Haythornthwaite Eds., *The Internet in Everyday Life* (pp. 431–463). Oxford, UK: Blackwell.

Haythornthwaite, C. and Wellman, B. (2002). The Internet in Everyday Life: An Introduction. In B. Wellman and C. Haythornthwaite Eds., *The Internet in Everyday Life* (pp. 3–41). Oxford, UK: Blackwell.

Inktomi. (2002) *Refocused Inktomi Seeks to Monetize Search.* Accessed on 20 December 2002 on the World Wide Web at <http://www.inktomi.com/company/news/>.

Introna, L. D. and Nissenbaum, H. (2000). Shaping the Web: Why the Politics of Search Engines Matter. *The information Society, 16,* 169–180.

Jackson, L. A., Barbatsis, G., Biocca, F., Zhao, Y., von Eye, A., and Fitzgerald, H. E. (2002). Home Internet Use in Low-Income Families: Frequency, Nature and Correlates of Early Use in the HomeNetToo Project. *Paper Presented at the 11th International World Wide Web Conference.*

Junnarkar, S. and Clark, T. (2003). *AOL buys Netscape for $4.2 billion.* Accessed on 17 September 2003 on the World Wide Web at <http://news.com.com/2100-1023-218360.html?legacy=cnet>.

Kane, M. (2003, 23 February). *Overture to buy search services* [Electronic Journal]. CNET News.com. Retrieved 1 March, 2003, from the World Wide Web: <http://rss.com.com/2100-1023-985850.html?type=pt&part=rss&tag=feed&subj=news>.

Kobayashi, Mei and Takeda, K. (2000). Information Retrieval on the Web. *ACM Computing Surveys, 322,* 144–173.

Kraut, R., Mukhopadhyay, T., Szczypula, J., Keisler, S. and Scherlis, B. (2000). Information and Communication: Alternative Uses of the Internet in Households. *Information Systems Research, 10,* 287–303.

Kraut, R., Patterson, M., Lundmark, V., Kiesler, S., Mukophadhyay, T. and Scherlis, W. (1998). Internet Paradox: A Social Technology That Reduces Social Involvement and Psychological Well-Being? *American Psychologist, 539,* 1017–1031.

Kraut, R., Scherlis, W., Mukhopadhyay, T., Manning, J. and Kiesler, S. (1996). The HomeNet Field Trial of Residential Internet services. *Communications of the ACM, 39*(12), 55–65.

Lawrence, S. and Giles, C. L. (1998). Searching the World Wide Web. *Science, 280*(5360), 98–100.

Lawrence, S. and Giles, C. L. (1999). Accessibility and Distribution of Information on the Web. *Nature, 400*(6740), 107–109.

Liddy, E. (2001). How a Search Engine Works. *Searcher: The Magazine for Database Professionals, 9,* 38–45.

LookSmart. (2002). *LookSmart Search: About Us.* Accessed on 1 February 2002 on the World Wide Web at <http://aboutus.looksmart.com/about.jhtml;$sessionid$MFR0PZY AAACADLAQQBTSOJQ?dir=profile&page=about>.

Morrissey, B. (2003, February 18, 2003). *Overture to Buy AltaVista* [Web site]. Internet Advertising Report. Retrieved 16 May, 2003, from the World Wide Web: <http://www.internetnews.com/IAR/article.php/1587171>.

Mowshowiski, A. and Kawagichi, A. (2001). Assessing Bias in Search Engines. *Information Processing and Management, 38,* 141–156.

Nie, N. H, Hillygus, D. S. and Erbring, L. (2002). Internet Use, interpersonal Relations, and Sociability: A Time Diary Study. In B. Wellman and C. Haythornthwaite Eds., *The Internet in Everyday Life,* pp. 215–243. Oxford, UK: Blackwell.

Nielsen Media. (2000). *Search Engines Most Popular Method of Surfing the Web.* Accessed on 30 August 2000 on the World Wide Web at <http://www.commerce.net/news/press/0416.html>.

Nielsen Netrating. (2002). *Top Web Properties March 2002.* Accessed on 27 September 2002 on the World Wide Web at <http://www.nielsen-netratings.com>.

Online Computer Library Center (OCLC). (2003). *Office of Web Characterization Project.* <http://www.oclc.org>.

O'Neil, E., Lavoie, B. F. and Bennett, R. (2003). Trends in the Evolution of the Public Web. *D-Lib Magazine, 9*(4).

Pedersen, J. (July 2003). Web IR Workshop. *ACM SIGIR 2003*. Toronto, Canada.

Pew Internet and American Life Project. (2002a). *The Broadband Difference*. Retrieved December 31, 2002 from <http://www.pewinternet.org/reports/toc.asp?Report=63>.

Pew Internet and American Life Project. (2002b). *Counting on the Internet*. Retrieved January 6, 2003 from <http://www.pewinternet.org/reports/toc.asp?Report=80>.

Rasmussen, E. (2003). Indexing and Retrieval From the Web. *Annual Review of Information Science and Technology, 37*, 91–124.

Rieh, S-Y. (2004). On the Web at Home: Information Seeking and Web Searching in the Home Environment. *Journal of the American Society for Information Science and Technology*.

Sawyer, S. and Eschenfelder, K. (2002). Social Informatics: Perspectives, Examples and Trends. *Annual Review of Information Science and Technology, 36*, 427–465.

Selberg, E. and Etzioni, O. (1997 January–February). The Metacrawler Architecture For Resource Aggregation on the Web. *IEEE Expert*, 11–14.

Singer, M. (2003). *Excite At Home Selling Its Portal*. Internetnews.com. Retrieved 3 August, 2003, from the World Wide Web: <http://www.internetnews.com/xSP/article.php/8_921261>.

Sullivan, D. (2000a). *Search Engine Sizes*. Retrieved 30 August, 2000, from the World Wide Web: <http://searchenginewatch.com/reports/sizes.html> .

Sullivan, D. (2000b). *Search Watch*. Accessed on 1 June 2000 on the World Wide Web at <http://searchenginewatch.com/>.

Sullivan, D. (2002a). *Nielsen/NetRatings Search Engine Ratings* [website]. SearchEngine Watch.com. Retrieved 6 January, 2002, from the World Wide Web: <http://www.searchenginewatch.com/reports/netratings.html>

Sullivan, D. (2002b). *Nielsen/NetRatings Search Engine Ratings*. Accessed on 21 October 2002 on the World Wide Web at <http://www.searchenginewatch.com/reports/netratings.html>.

UCLA Center for Communication Policy. (2003). *Surveying the Digital Future: The UCLA Internet Report Year Three*. Retrieved May 1, 2003 from <http://www.ccp.ucla.edu>.

Wellman, B and Haythornthwaite, C. Eds. (2002). *The Internet in Everyday Life*. Oxford, UK: Blackwell.

Witten, I., Moffat, A. and Bell, T. C. (1994). *Managing Gigabytes: Compressing and Indexing Documents and Images*. New York, NY: Van Nostrand Reinhold.

Chapter 2

HUMAN INFORMATION BEHAVIOR AND HUMAN COMPUTER INTERACTION CONTEXT

1. INTRODUCTION

This chapter provides an overview of studies that have examined Web search within various informational contexts. People search the Web in many different types of information environments, such as their home, libraries, and institutional, organizational or work settings.

Researchers from many diverse disciplines including information science, computer science, cognitive science, educational psychology, information systems, human computer interaction, and business have studied Web searching. Recent papers by Jansen and Pooch (2001), Bar-Ilan (2004), Kobayashi and Koichi (2000), and Hsieh-Yee (2001) also provide a valuable discussion of Web search studies from information and computer science perspectives.

2. HUMAN INFORMATION BEHAVIOR CONTEXT

Many Web search studies at the human information behavior level explore the factors that influence Web search within the context of human information seeking. For millennia, humans have sought, stored and used information as they learned and evolved patterns of human information behaviors to resolve problems related to survival, work and everyday life (Spink and Cole, 2001; forthcoming).

The broader focus of Web search research looks at the user in an information world engaged in a whole range of *human information behavior* (HIB). HIB includes both (1) purposive and (2) non-purposive information seeking. People's information behaviors are embedded with an information environment that includes channels of information and communication, as well as the full panoply of social micro-cultures or small worlds (Spink & Cole, 2001; Savolainen, 1999).

Much research in this area examines the impact of broader human information behavior on the Web search process and the impact of Web search on human information behaviors (Spink, 2002). Other studies focus on identifying the psychological factors that affect Web search, such as personality, gender and attitudes towards computers (Roy, Taylor and Chi, 2004).

3.   HUMAN COMPUTER INTERACTION CONTEXT

The human computer interaction (HCI) aspects of Web searching have become more important as Web search engine use continues to grow. Human computer interaction studies model the interaction between humans and Web search engines. Many HCI Web studies focus on interactive variables, such as Web search terms, strategy and tactics, search duration and other human–computer interaction variables.

The next section briefly discusses the research methods used in the Web searching studies. A more detailed discussion of this topic is provided in Chapter 3 of this book.

4.   RESEARCH METHODS

Web researchers have used varied methodologies, both quantitative and qualitative approaches, depending upon the research questions addressed (Hsieh-Yee, 2001). Popular research methods have included surveys (e.g., Spink, Bateman and Jansen, 1999), questionnaires (e.g., Spink, 2002), analysis of verbal protocols (e.g., Hoelscher and Strube, 2000), observing search behavior in experimental or natural settings (e.g., Wang, Hawk and Tenopir, 2000), Web query log analysis (e.g., Spink, Jansen, Wolfram and Saracevic, 2002), and the use of multiple methods (e.g., Spink, 2002).

Hsieh-Yee (2001) and Bar-Ilan (2004) also provide an overview of the research designs, and data collection and analysis methods used in Web search studies.

5.   WEB SEARCH STUDIES

This section discusses the current state of Web search studies within the following categories:

- Web search behavior, including cognitive abilities, variables, and attitudes that effect Web search behavior
- Single Web site search studies
- Information foraging studies
- Children's Web search behavior
- Web search training and learning
- Web search evaluation

Some studies may fall into multiple categories. The next section discusses Web search studies in chronological order to examine the progress and trends in such studies since the middle 1990s.

The Web search studies conducted by the book's authors from 1997 to 2004 are discussed in Chapters 4 to 11 of this book, and also briefly in Spink (2003), and Spink and Xu (2000). E-commerce Web searching is discussed in Chapter 7, medical and health Web searching in Chapter 8, sexually-related Web searching in Chapter 9, and multimedia Web searching in Chapter 10.

6.   WEB SEARCH BEHAVIOR STUDIES

Web search behavior studies investigate why and how people search the Web and their use of Web search tools. The findings from Web search behavior studies from 1995 to 2004 include models of Web search, and provide an increasing understanding of the elements and patterns of Web search. Overall, many Web search behavior studies use small user sample sizes and their findings are not replicated. Access to large-scale complex data about Web searching, beyond Web query transaction logs, is problematic and costly to collect.

6.1   Web Search Behavior Studies 1995 to 1998

The earliest studies of Web search behavior were conducted during the mid-1990s, as Web search engine and Web browser use was growing, particularly in academic environments. From 1997, we also see the first large-scale Web transaction log studies, such as those by the authors of this book and Silverstein, Henzinger, Marais and Moricz (1999).

Many early studies began to examine elements of the Web search process, including who searched, how they searched, identification of search variables and how to measure search effectiveness. Kellogg and Richards (1995) first examined users' Web experience as a search factor. Catledge and Pitkow (1995) analyzed the browsing patterns of adult Web searchers using Web browsers and found that they relied mainly on hyperlink structure.

Tillotson, Cherry and Clinton (1995) studied gender as a Web search behavior variable and found that by 1995 males formed 75% of Internet users, and 46% of study participants claimed to be able to find information on the Internet. He and Jacobson (1996) found similar results to Tillotson, Cherry and Clinton (1995), when they identified gender as a factor in Internet use and resources retrieved.

By 1997, Web search behavior studies began to identify further patterns in Web search behavior. Tauscher and Greenberg (1997) found that people repeatedly returned to the same Web pages and conducted short searches. Chen, Wang, Proctor and Salvendy (1997) identified that users conduct short searches using Web browsers.

Yee, Hsieh-Yee, Thompson, Karn and Weaver (1998) show that the cognitive ability to navigate a maze was not significantly related to Web search performance. They also identified a relationship between level of Web experience and Web search success. Hsieh-Yee (1998) also conducted a major study of Web query reformulation as a feature of some Web searches.

Nahl (1998) found that for novices Web searchers, affective goal or information need influenced search actions. In addition, Nahl (1998) identified that Web search engine usefulness was affected by quick and easy search engine access. Huberman, Pirolli, Pitkow and Lukose (1998) found regularities in Web surfing. Hill and Hannafin (1997) found that more experienced searchers performed more sophisticated Web search strategies.

These early Web search behavior studies laid the groundwork for further and more extensive research.

6.2   Web Search Behavior Studies 1999 to 2001

This section provides an overview of Web search behavior studies from 1999 to 2001. By 1999, the Web was emerging as a mainstream business and lifestyle tool. The dot.com companies were in full force and Web search studies were a growing interdisciplinary research area. As the Web proliferated, the study of user interaction with Web search interfaces became more important. Byrne, John, Wehrie and Crow (1999) found that Web users made little use of graphical user interfaces (GUIs), but preferred to scroll, waiting for responses, visually searching and reading.

By 1999, more studies were identifying factors in Web search performance. Hawk and Wang (1999) examined Web searching for factual answers and identified ten strategies during the Web search process, including exploring, link following, back and forward moving, engine seeking and using, shortcut seeking, and surveying or scanning Web pages. Navarro-Prieto, Scaife and Rogers (1999) found that experienced users are more systematic in their search planning and execution. Novice searchers adopted haphazard strategies and were more affected by the external presentation of the information presented.

Choo, Detlor and Turnbull (1999) developed one of the first behavioral models of Web interaction, including searching and browsing. Their model depicts how users translate their information need into search strategies and tactics. Alternatively, Wang, Hawk and Tenopir (2000) developed a multi-dimensional model of user–Web interaction, consisting of users, the interface and the Web.

As more people began to access the Web, researchers began to compare the characteristics of Web search novices and experts (Lazonder, Biemans and Wopereis, 2000). Hoelscher and Strube (2000) found that domain experts who were also novice Web searchers relied on terminology rather than query formatting. Alternatively, low domain knowledge expert searchers used more formatting tools. Palmquist and Kim (2000) studied the effect of cognitive style on search performance. Hawking, Craswell, Bailey and Griffith (2001) identify four Web information groups based on the level of information needed – very short, single document, selection of documents and high recall searches for all documents.

As Web searching became popular, studies of search patterns and performance became more frequent. Rieh and Xie (2001) identified some patterns and sequences of query reformulation during interaction with the Excite Web search engine. They show that during query reformulation most users make parallel movements, e.g., they change their query from "American Airlines" to "Delta Airlines". Jansen (2000) found that increasing the complexity of Web queries has little effect on search results. Moukdad and Large (2001) show that many Web searchers do not use advanced or Boolean search features, and interact with the Web as if it was another person. Montgomery and Faloutsos (2001) identified Web search browsing patterns.

Further studies examined the impact of gender and personality on Internet use. Schumacher and Morahan-Martin (2001) highlight the impact of gender differences in Internet and computer attitudes and experiences. Swickert, Hittner, Harris and Herring (2001) discuss the relationship between Internet use, personality and social support.

Following the growth of the Web from 1999 to 2001, more outlets for Web search behavior research emerged, including conferences such as the World Wide Web, IEEE ITCC, and journals such as *Internet Research* and *World Wide Web Journal.*

6.3   Web Search Behavior Studies 2002 to 2003

This section provides an overview of Web search studies from 2002 to 2003. By 2002 we see more: (1) larger-scale studies of Web search behavior and (2) further research that identified the cognitive variables related to Web search performance, such as personality, cognitive styles and users' experience levels.

Amichai-Hamburger (2002) argues that personality is a common factor that is ignored in Web research. Hills and Argyle (2002) found that gender and age influence Internet use which is also a form of displacement activity when users' had nothing else to do or their current task was less attractive to them that Internet use. Hargiattai (2002) argues that Web search is a complex task with many different possible search strategies.

White and Iivonen (2002) show that users regard closed or predictable topics as easy to search, and open or unpredictable topics as difficult to search on the Web. Ford, Miller and Moss (2002) found that Web search effectiveness was related to best match searching, not the use of Boolean search operators. Eastman and Jansen (2003) identify that Web query operator use has no significant effect on coverage, relative precision or ranking. However, the effect of Web operator use varied depending upon the Web search engine.

Rieh (2002) found that the topic interest, and information authority and quality affect users' acceptance of a Web document. Dennis, Bruza and McArthur (2002) identified that browsing through a Web directory search engine was less effective than keyword searching. Slone (2003) shows that novice Web searchers rely more on uniform resource locators (URL) and Web browsers rather than Web search engines.

Kim (2001) found that a Web search engine user's level of experience and cognitive style affects search performance. Liaw and Huang (2003) show that individual computer experience, quality of the Web search engine, user motivation and perceptions of technological acceptance affect individual feelings to use Web search engines.

By 2002, we see more longitudinal, cognitive (Kim and Allen, 2002) and consumer-oriented studies. Cothey (2002) used a longitudinal study to determine that over time Web searchers adopt browsing as opposed to searching strategies as their level of experience increased. Hodkinson, Kiel and McColl-Kennedy (2000), and Hodkinson and Geoffrey (2003) specifically model consumer Web search behavior, including personal demographic, behavioral, use and experience variables. Their papers provide a good overview of research in this area of study.

Our overview of studies from 1995 to 2004 highlights the growing and interdisciplinary nature of Web search behavior studies. Further studies are needed that utilize larger sample sizes and attempt to replicate results.

7. SINGLE WEB SITE SEARCH STUDIES

Some studies have conducted a longitudinal analysis of users' interaction with one Web site. Hert and Marchionini (1998) studied the users' information seeking behavior on statistical Websites. Wang, Berry and Yang (2003) studies the transaction log of the University of Tennessee's Website for a four-year period as logged by the SWISH search engine. They found that queries averaged 2 words or 13 characters, the quantity of queries and the vocabulary used grew over time, users' vocabulary was relatively small, and included a large number (26%) of misspelled words and personal names. Search topics and search behavior varied little over the four-year period.

Further single Web site studies are needed to replicate and extend the previous studies.

8. WEB INFORMATION FORAGING STUDIES

Using the metaphor of foraging rather than seeking or searching, Pirolli and Card (1999) relate information foraging to the design of Web environments for diverse groups of users. Web information searching is highlighted in Pirolli and Card's (1999) as information foraging, which is based on optimal foraging theory (OFT) from evolutionary ecology. OFT is concerned with the "searching efficiency" of cognitive systems, both human and non-human, for food and mating opportunities in the environment. Natural selection penalizes any cognitive system whose searching deviates from the optimal design for their environment. Consequently, cognitive systems, both human and non-human, "evolve toward stable states that maximize gains of valuable information per unit cost" (Pirolli and Card, 1999).

Similar to cues in non-human foraging, the human information forager uses what Pirolli and Card call "the proximal perception of information scent" to assess profitability of an information source in relation to other potential sources (Card, Pirolli, Van Der Wege, Morrison, Reeder, Schraedley and Boshart, 2001; Pirolli and Card, 1999). If the scent is strong, the information forager can make the correct choice; if there is no scent, the forager will have to perform a "random walk" through the Web environment. The forager's perception of which direction offers the optimal information source/patch is changed by sniffing for scent activities; so the forager is constantly adapting decision-making and direction – in the Pirolli and Card ACT-IF model, this is called "adaptive control of thought in information foraging" (ACT-IF).

Choo, Detlor and Turnbull (2000) and Spink and Cole (forthcoming) further discuss the information foraging in relation to information seeking and human information behavior studies.

9.   CHILDREN'S WEB SEARCH STUDIES

This section provides an overview of the studies into children's Web search behavior from 1997 to 2004. Most Web search studies focus on adult behavior. However, since 1997, a growing set of studies has investigated children's Web search behavior.

Pioneering studies by Kafai and Bates (1997), and Wallace and Kupperman (1997) studied Web searching by school-age children. Schacter, Chung and Dorr (1998) found that children use different search strategies for different information task types and prefer browsing to analytical search techniques. Fidel, Davies, Douglass, Hopkins, Kushner, Miyagishimo and Toney (1999), Large, Beheshti and Moukdad (1999), Large and Beheshti (2000), and Large, Beheshti and Rahman (2002a) also examined the way children seek information on Web search engines. Bilal (2000; 2002) specifically studied children's use of the Web and Yahooligans, a part of the Yahoo Web search engine.

Wallace, Kuppermann, Krajcik and Soloway (2000), and Vansickle and Monaco (2000) found that students did not demonstrate much Web search sophistication.

Roy, Taylor and Chi (2003) identified that boys performed significantly better than girls during Web search in gaining target-specific and target-related information. In a later study, Roy and Chi (2003) show that boys tend to employ a different search pattern from girls that related to the pattern of Web search performance outcome. Large, Beheshti and Rahman (2002) found that boys were more active in their Web searching. MaKinster, Beghetto and Plucker (2003) show that students with lower domain knowledge had difficulty conducting effective Web searches.

Studies focused on children's Web search behavior have found some interesting gender differences that need further exploration. Further research is also need to explore how children learn to search and the cognitive, human information behavior and human computer interaction factors that influence their search performance.

10.   TRAINING AND LEARNING STUDIES

This section discusses the small number of studies investigating the learning and training aspects of Web searching. Lucas and Topi (2002) show that query operator errors and incorrect usage, or non-use, negatively affect search results. Lucas and Topi (2003) found that even limited training in basic Boolean logic could improve users' performance on Web search engines. Users who accessed assisting interfaces experienced improvements in search performance over simple interfaces. Topi and Lucas (2003) claim that an assisted search tool and Boolean logic training can positively affect Web search quality. Lucas and Topi (2003) conclude that the quality of Web search interfaces and level of user training affects users' performance.

Overall, studies suggest that information task complexity and the quality of search terms affects search performance. Further studies are needed to model how people learn how to search Web search engines, how to improve Web search interfaces and techniques.

11.   WEB SEARCH EVALUATION STUDIES

This section provides an overview of the studies evaluating human interaction with Web search engines, including the usability and effectiveness of Web search tools. Many evaluation studies have used small queries and search numbers, dichotomous relevance judgments, precision and recall measures, and in general do not use real user relevance judgments (Leighton and Srivastava, 1999; Losee and Paris, 1999). Rasmussen (2003), Bar-Ilan (2002; 2004), and Oppenheim, Morris, McKnight and Lowley (2000) also provide overviews of the Web evaluation literature.

Recent studies have produced valuable insights into Web search engine performance. In a large-scale study, Lawrence and Giles (1998) found that individual Web search engines generally do not cover a majority of Web sites. A recent study by Gordon and Pathak (1999) identifies two forms of Web search engine evaluations – testimonials or industry assessments, and shootouts in laboratory settings, and provide a valuable comparison of previous search engine evaluation studies. They also found: (1) absolute retrieval effectiveness is fairly low, (2) differences in Web search engine retrieval and precision, and (3) a lack of overlap in retrieval by Web search engines.

Many aspects of Web search engine performance have been studied, including bias (Mowshowitz and Kawaguchi, 2001), quality measures (Henzinger, Heydon, Mitzenmacher and Najork, 1999, 2000; Henzinger, Motwani and Silverstein, 2002; Introna and Nissenbaum, 2000; Zhu and Gauch, 2000), and number of links (Brin and Page, 1998). Radev, Libner and Fan (2002) found that commercial Web search engines could retrieve at least one correct answer to a factual question.

Su (2003a, b) takes a traditional information retrieval approach to Web search engines evaluation based on precision and relative recall, user satisfaction, search time, comprehensiveness, utility, number of good links provided and valuation of results as a whole measures. The study gathered users' impressions after their Web search engines interactions and identified that the Excite (which no longer exists) and AltaVista (now part of Yahoo) Web search engines performed significantly better than the other Web search engines in the evaluation.

Spink (2002) developed a new heuristic user-centered approach to Web search engine evaluation, including the effectiveness measure *information problem shift. Information problem shift* is a measure based on the impact of users' interactions on their information problem and information seeking stage. Unlike traditional search engine evaluation studies, Spink (2002) collected data before and after users' Web search engine interactions and measured the impact of the Web search engine interaction on the user's information problem.

Using the Inquirus Web search engine, Spink (2002) found that: (1) all users experienced some level of shift or change in their information problem, information seeking, and personal knowledge due to their Inquirus interaction, (2) different users experienced different levels of change or shift, and (3) the search metric precision did not correlate with other user-based measures. Some users experienced major changes or shifts in various user-based variables, such as information problem or information seeking stage with a search of low precision and vice versa. Bar-Ilan (2004) describes Spink's (2002) approach as a promising one for further studies that enhance Web search evaluation.

12. CONCLUSION AND FURTHER RESEARCH

Overall, from 1995 to 2004, Web search behavior studies have proliferated in number and complexity, and are becoming more international and interdisciplinary in nature. The range of studies has diversified to include cognitive and behaviors studies using transaction log, experimental, and single Web site and longitudinal studies. Fewer studies have used experimental study methods.

Web search evaluation studies are moving to consider more user-centered approaches, but training and learning issues have produced few studies. In addition to viewing Web search behavior from a human information behavior perspective based on information seeking, the information foraging approach is growing in significance.

Major issues for research in the Web search behavior field include the lack of large-scale and in-depth studies using at least hundreds, if not thousands, of subjects. Also, most studies tend to focus on one or two aspects or variables associated with Web search within a short temporal span instead of taking a more longitudinal and holistic approach.

Further funding and Web industry collaboration is sorely needed to assure that the human aspects of Web search do not continue to be overshadowed by the technical and algorithmic perspectives.

13.   REFERENCES

Amichai-Hamburger, Y. (2002). Internet and Personality. *Computers in Human Behavior, 18*, 1–10.

Bar-Ilan, J. (2002). Methods For Measuring Search Engine Performance Over time. *Journal of the American Society for Information Science and Technology, 54*, 308–319.

Bar-Ilan, J. (2004). The Use of Web Search Engines in Information Science Research. *Annual Review of Information Science and Technology, 38*, 231–288.

Bilal, D. (2000). Children's Use of the Yahooligans! Web Search Engine: I. Cognitive, Physical, and Affective Behaviors on Fact-Based Search Tasks. *Journal of the American Society for Information Science, 5*, 646–665.

Bilal, D. (2002). Perspectives on Children's Navigation of the World Wide Web: Does the Type of Search Task Make a Difference? *Online Information Review, 26*(2), 108–177.

Brin, S. and Page, L. (1998). The Anatomy of a Large-Scale Hypertextual Web Search Engine. *Proceedings of the 7th International World Wide Web Conference.*

Byrne, M. D., John, B. E., Wehrie, N. S. and Crow, D. C. (1999). The Tangled Web We Wove: A Taskonomy of WWW Use. In: M. G. Williams, M. W. Altom and W. Newman (Eds.), *CHI'99: Conference Proceedings* (pp. 544–551). New York: ACM.

Card, S. K., Pirolli, P., Van Der Wege, M., Morrison, J. B., Reeder, R. W., Schraedley, P. K., and Boshart, J. (2001). Information Scent as a Driver of Web Behavior Graphs: Results of a Protocol Analysis Method for Web Usability. *CHI 2001: ACM Conference on Computer–Human Interaction, 3*(1), 498–505.

Catledge, L and Pitkow, J. (1995). Characterizing Browsing Strategies in the World Wide Web. *Proceedings of the 3rd International World Wide Web Conference, Darmstadt, Germany.* <http://www.igd.fhg.de/www/www95/papers>.

Chen, B., Wang, H., Proctor, R. W. and Salvendy, G. (1997). *A Human-Centered Approach For Improving World Wide Web Browsers.* Retrieved May 1, 2000 from <http://palette.ecn.purdue.edu/~behen/project/paper.html>.

Choo, C. W, Detlor, B. and Turnbull, D. (2000). *Web Work: Information Seeking and Knowledge Work on the World Wide Web.* Boston: Kluwer Academic Publishers.

Cothey, V. (2002). A Longitudinal Study of World Wide Web Users' Information Searching Behavior. *Journal of the American Society for Information Science and Technology, 53*(2), 67–78.

Dennis, S., Bruza, P. and McArthur, R. (2002). Web Searching: A Process-Oriented Experimental Study of Three Interactive Search Paradigms. *Journal of the American Society for Information Science and Technology, 53*, 120–133.

Eastman, C. and Jansen, B. J. (2003). Coverage, Relevance and Ranking: The Impact of Query Operators on Web Search. *ACM Transactions on Information Systems, 21*(4), 383–411.

Fidel, R., Davies, R. K., Douglass, M. H., Holder, J. K., Hopkins, C. J., Kushner, E. J., Miyagishimo, B. K. and Toney, C. D. (1999). A Visit to the Information Mall: Web Searching Behavior of High School Students. *Journal of the American Society for Information Science, 50*, 24–37.

Ford, N., Miller, D., and Moss, N. (2002). Web Search Strategies and Retrieval Effectiveness: An Empirical Study. *Journal of Documentation, 58*(1), 30–48.

Gordon, M. and Pathak, P. 1999. Finding Information on the World Wide Web: The Retrieval Effectiveness of Search Engines. *Information Processing and Management, 35*(2), 141–180.

Hargiattai, E. (2002). Beyond Logs and Surveys: In-Depth Measures of People's Web Use Skills. *Journal of the American Society for Information Science and Technology, 53*(14), 1239–1244.

Hawk, W. B. and Wang, P. (1999). Users' Interaction With the World Wide Web; Problems and Problem Solving. In L. Woods (Ed.), *Proceedings of the 62nd American Society for Information Science Annual Meeting* (pp. 256–270). Medford, NJ: Information Today.

Hawking, D., Craswell, N., Bailey, P. and Griffith, K. (2001). Measuring Search Engine Quality. *Information Retrieval, 4*, 33–59.

He, P. W. and Jacobson, T. E. (1996). What Are They Doing With the Internet? A Study of User Information Seeking Behaviors. *Internet Reference Services Quarterly, 1*, 31–51.

Henzinger, M. R., Heydon, A., Mitzenmacher, M. and Najork, M. (1999). Measuring Index Quality Using Random Walks on the Web. *Proceedings of the 8th International World Wide Web Conference.*

Henzinger, M. R., Heydon, A., Mitzenmacher, M. and Najork, M. (2000). On Near Uniform URL Sampling. *Proceedings of the 9th International World Wide Web Conference.*

Henzinger, M. R., Motwani, R. and Silverstein, C. (2002). Challenge in Web Search Engines. *ACM SIGIR Forum.*

Hert, C. and Marchionini, G. (1998). Information Seeking Behavior on Statistical Websites: Theoretical and Design Implications. In C. M. Preston (Ed.), *Proceedings of the 61st American Society for Information Science Annual Meeting*, pp. 303–314. Medford, NJ: Information Today.

Hill, J. R. and Hannafin, M. J. (1997). Cognitive Strategies and Learning From the World Wide Web. *Educational Technology Research and Development, 45*, 37–64.

Hills, P. and Argyle, M. (2002). Use of the Internet and Their Relationships With Individual Differences in Personality. *Computers and Human Behavior, 19*, 59–70.

Hodkinson, C. and Geoffrey K. (2003). Understanding Web Information Search Behavior: An Exploratory Model. *Journal of End User Computing, 15*(4), 27–48.

Hodkinson, C., Kiel, G. and McColl-Kennedy, J. R. (2000). Consumer Web Search Behavior: Diagrammatic Illustration of Wayfinding on the Web. *International Journal of Human-Computer Interaction, 52*, 805–830.

Hoelscher, C. and Strube, G. (2000). Web Search Behavior of Internet Experts and Newbies. In *Proceedings of the Ninth International World Wide Web Conference* (pp. 337–346).

Hsieh-Yee, I. (1998). Search Tactics of Web Users in Searching For Texts, Graphics, Known Items and Subjects: A Search Simulation Study. *Reference Librarian, 60*, 61–85.

Hsieh-Yee, I. (2001). Research on Web Search Behavior. *Library and Information Science Research* 23: 167–185.

Huberman, B. A., Pirolli, P. L., Pitkow, J. E. and Lukose, R. M. (1998). Strong Regularities in World Wide Web Surfing. *Science, 280*(5360), 94–97.

Introna, L. D. and Nissenbaum, H. (2000). Shaping the Web: Why the Politics of Search Engines Matter. *The Information Society, 16*, 169–180.

Jansen, B. J. (2000). The Effect of Query Complexity on Web Searching Results. *Information Research, 6*(1).

Jansen, B. J. and Pooch, U. (2001). Web User Studies: A Review and Framework for Future Work. *Journal of the American Society of Information Science and Technology, 52*(3), 235–246.

Kafai, Y. and Bates, M. J. (1997). Internet Web-Searching Instruction in the Elementary Classroom: Building a Foundation For Information Literacy. *School Library Media Quarterly, 25*, 103–111.

Kellogg, W. A. and Richards, J. T. (1995). The Human Factors of Information on the Internet. In J. Neilsen (Ed.), *Advances in Human–Computer Interaction 5*, 1–36. Norwood, NJ: Ablex.

Kim, K-S. (2001). Information Seeking on the Web: Effects of User and Task Variables. *Library and Information Science Research, 23*, 233–255.

Kim, K-S. and Allen, B. (2002). Cognitive and Task Influences on Web Searching Behavior. *Journal of the American Society of Information Science and Technology, 53*(2), 109–119.

Kobayashi, M. and Koichi T. (2000). Information Retrieval on the Web. *ACM Computing Surveys, 322*, 144–173.

Large, A. and Beheshti, J. (2000). The Web as a Classroom: Reactions From Users. *Journal of the American Society for Information Science, 51*(12), 1069–1080.

Large, A., Beheshti, J. and Moukdad, H. (1999). Information Seeking on the Web: Navigational Skills of Grade-Six Primary School Students. In L. Woods (Ed.), *Proceedings of the 62nd American Society for Information Science Annual Meeting* (pp. 84–97). Medford, NJ: Information Today.

Large, A., Beheshti, J., and Rahman, T. (2002a). Design Criteria for Childrens' Web Portals: The User Speaks Out. *Journal of the American Society of Information Science and Technology, 53*(2), 79–94.

Large, A., Beheshti, J. and Rahman, T. (2002b). Gender Differences in Collaborative Web Searching Behavior: An Elementary School Study. *Information Processing and Management, 38*, 427–443.

Lawrence, S. and Giles, L. (1998). Searching the World Wide Web. *Science, 280*(5360) 98–100.

Lazonder, A. W., Biemans, H. J. A. and Wopereis, I. G. J. H. (2000). Differences Between Novice and Experienced Users in Searching Information on the World Wide Web. *Journal of the American Society of Information Science, 51*, 576–581.

Leighton, H. V. and Srivastava, J. (1999). First 20 Precision Among World Wide Web Search Services (Search Engines). *Journal of the American Society for Information Science, 50*(10), 870–881.

Liaw, S-S. and Huang, H-M. (2003). An Investigation of User Attitudes Toward Search Engines as an Information Retrieval Tool. *Computers and Human Behavior, 19*(6), 751–765.

Losee, R. M., & Paris, L. H. (1999). Measuring Search-Engine Quality and Query Difficulty: Ranking with Target and Freestyle. *Journal of the American Society for Information Science, 50*(10), 882–889.

Lucas, W. and Topi, H. (2002). Form and Function: The Impact of Query Terms and Operator Usage on Web Search Results. *Journal of the American Society for Information Science and Technology, 53*(2), 95–108.

Lucas, W. and Topi, H. (2003). Training For Web Search: Will it Get You in Shape? *Information Processing and Management*.

MaKinster, J. G., Beghetto, R. A. and Plucker, J. A. (2003). Why Can't I Find Newton's Third Law: Case Studies of Students' Using of the Web as a Science Resource. *Journal of Science Education and Technology*.

Montgomery, A. and Faloutsos, C. (2001). Identifying Web Browsing Trends and Patterns. *IEEE Computer, 34*(7), 94–95.

Moukdad, H. and Large, A. (2001). Users' Perceptions of the Web as Revealed By Transaction Log Analysis. *Online Information Review, 25*(6), 349–358.

Mowshowitz, A. and Kawaguchi, A. (2001). Assessing Bias in Search Engines. *Information Processing and Management, 38*, 141–156.

Nahl, D. (1998). Ethnography of Novices First Use of Web Search Engines: Affective Control in Cognitive Processes. *Internet Reference Services Quarterly, 3*, 51–72.

Navarro-Prieto, R., Scaife, M. and Rogers, Y. (1999). *Cognitive Strategies in Web Searching*. http://zing.ncsl.nist.gov/hfweb/proceedings/navarro-prieto/index.html.

Oppenheim, C., Morris, A., McKnight, C. and Lowley, S. (2000). The Evaluation of WWW Search Engines. *Journal of Documentation, 56*(2), 190–211.

Palmquist, R. A. and Kim, K-S. (2000). The Effect of Cognitive Style and Online Search Experience on Web Search Performance. *Journal of the American Society for Information Science, 51*, 558–567.

Pirolli, P. and Card, S. K. (1999). Information Foraging. *Psychological Review, 106*, 643–675.

Radev, D. R., Libner, K. and Fan, W. (2002). Getting Answers to Natural Language Questions on the Web. *Journal of the American Society for Information Science and Technology, 53*, 359–364.

Rasmussen, E. (2003). Indexing and Retrieval from the Web. *Annual Review of Information Science and Technology, 37*, 91–124.

Rieh, S. Y. (2002). Judgment of Information Quality and Cognitive Authority in the Web. *Journal of the American Society for information Science and Technology, 53*, 145–161.

Rieh, S. Y. and Xie, H. (2001). Patterns and Sequences of Multiple Query Reformulations in Web Searching: A Preliminary Study. *Proceedings of the 64th American Society for Information Science Annual Meeting* (pp. 246–255). Medford, NJ: Information Today.

Roy, M and Chi, M. T. H. (2003). Gender Differences in Patterns of Searching the Web. *Journal of Educational Computing Research, 29*(3), 335–348.

Roy, M. Taylor, R. and Chi, M.T.H. (2003–2004). Searching For Information On-Line and Off-Line: Gender Differences Among Middle School Students. *Journal of Educational Computing Research, 29*(2), 229–252.

Savolainen, R. (1999). The Role of the Internet in Information Seeking: Putting the Networked Services in Context. *Information Processing and Management, 35*, 765–782.

Schacter, J., Chung, G. K, W. K. and Dorr, A. (1998). Childrens' Internet Searching on Complex Problems: Performance and Process Analyses. *Journal of the American Society for Information Science, 49*, 840–849.

Schumacher, P. and Morahan-Martin, J. (2001). Gender, Internet and Computer Attitudes and Experiences. *Computers in Human Behavior, 17*, 95–110.

Silverstein, C., Henzinger, M., Marais, H., & Moricz, M. (1999). Analysis of a very large web search engine query log. *SIGIR Forum, 33*(1), 6–12.

Slone, D. J. (2003). Internet Search Approaches: The Influence of Age, Search Goals and Experience. *Library and Information Science Research, 25*, 403–418.

Spink, A. (2002). A User-Centered Approach to Evaluating Human Interaction With Web Search Engines; an Exploratory Study. *Information Processing and Management, 38*, 401–426.

Spink, A. (2003). Web Search: Emerging Patterns. *Library Trends, 52*(2), 299–306.

Spink, A., Bateman, J. and Jansen, B. J. (1999). Searching the Web: Survey of Excite Users. *Internet Research: Electronic Networking Applications and Policy, 9*(2), 117–128.

Spink, A. and Cole, C. (2001). Everyday Life Information Seeking Research. *Library and Information Science Research, 23*(4), 301–304.

Spink, A. and Cole, C. (Forthcoming). *Human Information Behavior: Integrating Information Use and Various Approaches.*

Spink, A., Jansen, B. J., Wolfram, D. and Saracevic, T. (2002). From E-Sex To E-Commerce: Web Search Changes. *IEEE Computer, 35*(3), 133–135.

Spink, A. and Xu, J. (2000). Selected Findings From the Excite Web Searching Study. *Information Research*, October. <http://www.shef.ac.uk/~is/publications/infers>.

Su, L. T. (2003a). A Comprehensive and Systematic Model of User Evaluation of Web Search Engines. I. Theory and Background. *Journal of the American Society for Information Science and Technology, 54*(13), 1175–1192.

Su, L. T. (2003b). A Comprehensive and Systematic Model of User Evaluation of Web Search Engines. II. An Evaluation By Undergraduates. *Journal of the American Society for Information Science and Technology, 54*(13), 1193–1223.

Swickert, R. J., Hittner, J. B., Harris, J. L. and Herring, J. A. (2001). Relationships Among Internet Use, Personality and Social Support. *Computers in Human Behavior, 18*(4), 437–451.

Tauscher, L. and Greenberg, S. (1997). How People Revisit Web Pages: Empirical Findings and Implications for the Design of History System. *International Journal of Human–Computer Interaction, 47*, 97–137.

Tillotson, J., Cherry, J. M. and Clinton, M. (1995). Internet Use Through the University of Toronto Library: Demographics, Destinations and Users' Reactions. *Information Technology and Libraries, 14*, 190–198.

Topi, H. and Lucas, W. (2003). Searching the Web: Operator Assistance Required. *Information Processing and Management.*

Vansickle, S. and Monaco, M. (2000). *Tenth Graders' Search Knowledge and Use of the World Wide Web*. Unpublished doctoral dissertation, Georgia State University.

Wallace, R., Kuppermann, J., Krajcik, J. and Soloway, E. (2000). Science of the Web: Students Online in a Sixth-Grade Classroom. *The Journal of the Learning Sciences, 9*(1), 75–104.

Wang, P., Berry, M. and Yang, Y. (2003). Mining Longitudinal Web Queries: Trends and Patterns. *Journal of the American Society for Information Science and Technology, 54*(8), 743–758.

Wang, P, Hawk, W. B. and Tenopir, C. (2000). Users' Interaction with World Wide Web Resources: An Exploratory Study Using a Holistic Approach. *Information Processing and Management, 36*, 229–251.

White, M. D. and Iivonen, M. (2002). Assessing Level of Difficulty in Web Search Strategies. *Library Quarterly, 72*(2), 205–233.

Yee, P. L., Hsieh-Yee, I., Pierce, G. R., Grome, R. and Schantz, L. (2004). Self-Evaluative Intrusive Thoughts Impede Successful Searching on the Internet. *Computers and Human Behavior, 20*(1), 85–101.

Yee, P., Hsieh-Yee, I., Thompson, E., Karn, M and Weaver, D. (1998). Individual Differences in Search Behavior on the WWW. Unpublished manuscript.

Zhu, X. and Gauch, S. (2000). Incorporating Quality Metrics in Centralized/Distributed information Retrieval on the World Wide Web. *Proceedings of the 2000 ACM SIGIR Annual Information Conference on Research and Development in Information Retrieval,* 288–295.

Chapter 3

RESEARCH DESIGN

1. INTRODUCTION

This chapter discusses the methods of data collection and analysis used in our Web searching studies that are presented in the remainder of this book. We first define and discuss transaction log analysis, which is widely used when studying user interaction on Web search systems. Second, we outline the nature, structure and characteristics of the specific Web query data sets that we analyzed in this research. Three, we outline the quantitative methods used for in-depth analysis of portions of our large-scale Web query analyses. Finally, we describe the qualitative methods used to gain further insight into the nature of Web search.

2. WEB QUERY TRANSACTION LOG ANALYSIS

Given the ubiquitous nature of the Web, there is considerable interest in investigating how people locate information using Web search engines. Studying the interaction between users and Web information retrieval (IR) systems can be a challenging task. People seeking information have the ability to access the Web content and Web search engines from a nearly endless variety of locations. Directly and unobtrusively observing Web searchers, in the manner of observing library patrons using online catalogues, is difficult. Electronic surveys are viable; however, electronic surveys, like all survey data collection, have significant self-selection and other issues (Spink, Bateman and Jansen, 1999).

Laboratory studies combined with analytical methods, such as interviews and verbal protocol analysis (Ericsson and Simon, 1984) of small Web user groups, can also provide valuable information and test specific Web search variables. However, laboratory studies have numerous disadvantages, including getting a population sample that mirrors the Web user population. Additionally, it is difficult to recreate the dynamic and complex Web environment in a controlled lab study.

Elements of this complex environment include: (1) continual additions to the content collection, (2) constant deletions from the content collection, (3) rapid algorithms and indexing changes to the Web IR systems, (4) the effect of paid placement on retrieval results, and (5) directed efforts by certain content providers to subvert the effectiveness of the retrieval process. Given these factors, transaction log analysis has emerged the primary method to study the interactions between Web search engines and the users of these Web search engines, along with users of Web services and content sites (Ivory and Hearst, 2002; Stout, 1997).

A *transaction log* is an electronic record of interactions that have occurred between a user and a system, in this research, between a searcher and a Web search engine. Given the current nature of the Web, transaction logs appears to be the most reasonable and non-intrusive means of collecting user–system interaction data during the information searching process from a large number of Web users.

Transaction log analysis is the use of data collected in a transaction log to investigate a particular research question concerning the user, the system or the content. The goal of transaction log analysis is to gain a clearer understanding of the interactions among searcher, content and Web search engine or the interactions between two of these system elements. From this understanding, we hopefully achieve some objective, such as improved system design, advanced searching assistance, or identified user information searching behavior.

Transaction logs are a common method of capturing characteristics of user interactions with IR systems by researchers and practitioners. One can employ transaction logs in conjunction with other methods of data collection. Researchers have used transaction logs for analyzing a variety of Web systems (Croft, Cook, and Wilder, 1995; Jones, Cunningham, and McNab, 1998; Wang, Berry, and Yang, 2003). Web search engines companies use transaction logs to research trends and system improvements (c.f., Google <http://www.google.com/press/zeitgeist.html>). Peters (1993) provides a review of transaction log analysis in library and experimental information retrieval systems.

The research questions define what information one must collect in a transaction log. However, collecting data from real users pursuing needed information while interacting with real systems on the Web impacts the type of data that one can realistically assemble. The method of data monitoring and collecting cannot interfere with the information seeking process in such an environment. In addition to the loss of potential customers, a data collection method that interferes with the information seeking process may unintentionally alter that process. Transaction logs provide a good balance between collecting a robust set of data and unobtrusively collecting that data.

The process of recording the data in the transaction log is relatively straightforward. Web servers record and store the interactions between searchers (i.e., actually a browser on a particular computer) and search engines in a log file of interactions (i.e., the transaction log) on the server. Major Web search engines execute millions of these interactions per day. The server can record various types of data depending on the file formats that the server supports. Typical transaction log format are access log, referrer log, or extended log. A widely employed file type is the extended file format, which contains data such as client computer's Internet Protocol (IP) address, user query, search engine access time, and referrer site, among other fields.

Once the server collects the data, one must analyze it in order to obtain beneficial information. Web *transaction log analysis* is the use of these transaction logs to answer research questions related to the interactions among searchers, Web search systems, and Web content. A variety of researchers use transaction log analysis (Drott, 1998), but it typically focuses on either issues of system performance, information structure, or measurements of user interactions. The research presented in these studies focuses primarily on user interactions. Within this user context, transaction log analysis uses the data in transaction logs to discern attributes of the search process, such as the searcher's actions, the interaction between the user and the system, and the evaluation of results by the searcher.

Peters (1993) defines transaction log analysis more specifically as: the study of electronically recorded interactions between on-line IR systems and the people who search for the information found in these systems. Transaction log analysis lends itself to a grounded theory approach (Glaser and Strauss, 1967) in that one examines the characteristics of searches in order to isolate trends and identify typical interactions between searchers and the system. Researchers and practitioners have used transaction log analysis extensively to evaluate library systems, traditional IR systems, and more recently Web systems.

3.   STRENGTHS AND WEAKNESSES OF WEB TRANSACTION LOG ANALYSIS

It is important to understand the strengths and limitations of Web transaction log analysis. First, transaction log analysis provides a method of collecting data from a great number of users. One can easily collect data on hundreds of thousands to millions of interactions, depending on the traffic of the Web site. Second, one can collect this data fairly inexpensively. The costs are basically the software and storage. Third, the data collection is unobtrusive, so the interactions represent the unaltered behavior of searchers. Finally, transactions log are, at present, the only method for obtaining significant amounts of data within the complex environment that is the Web (Dumais, 2002).

There are limitations of transaction log analysis, as with any methodology. First, there may be certain types of data not in the transaction log, individuals' identities being the most common example. An IP address or cookie typically represents the "user" in a transaction log. Since more than one person may use a computer, an IP address is an imprecise representation of the user. However, there are several sources for demographic data on the Web population based on observational and survey data. From these data sources, one can get reasonable estimations of needed demographic data. Second, a transaction log does not record the reasons for the search, the searcher motivations, or other qualitative aspects of use. In the instances where one needs this data, one should use transaction log analysis in conjunction with other data collection methods.

Third, the logged data may not be complete due to caching of server data on the client machine or proxy servers. This is an often mentioned limitation. In reality, this is a relatively minor concern for Web search engine research due to the method with which most search engines dynamically produce their results pages. For example, a user accesses the page of results from a search engine using the Back button of a browser. This navigation accesses the results page via the cache on the client machine. The Web server will not record this action.

However, if the user clicks on any uniform resource locator (URL) on that results page, functions coded on the results page redirects the click first to the Web server, from which the Web server records the visit to the Web site. Finally, there are privacy concerns with transaction logging. In practice, search engine organizations make considerable effort to respect the privacy of individual searchers, focusing generally on aggregate data.

With respect to these shortcomings, transaction log analysis by itself is limited (Peters, 1993), and one should, when possible, combine transaction log analysis with other data collection methods or other research results to improve the robustness of the analysis. However, transaction log analysis by itself can provide significant insights into user–system interactions, and it complements other methods of analysis by overcoming the limitations inherent in these methods.

For further dialogue on this area, Kaske (1993) and Kurth (1993) discuss the strengths and weaknesses of transaction log analysis, although advances in transaction logging software, standardized transaction log format, and improved data analysis has addressed many of these shortcomings. Sandore and Kaske (1993) reviews methods of applying the results of transaction log analysis. For a historical review of transaction log analysis, see Peters (1993) and Borgman, Hirsch, and Hiller (1996).

4.   WEB SEARCH LOGS

To address the research objectives and arrive at the research results that this book presents, query transaction logs from three major Web search engines, Excite, AlltheWeb.com and AltaVista were analyzed. Additionally, we present data analysis from AskJeeves, which utilized Excite as a surrogate. These transaction logs contained actual queries submitted by real users to these real-world information systems. Standard relational database and spreadsheet packages (i.e., Access and Excel), along with statistical analysis software packages (i.e., SPSS) were used as the basic analysis tools. There are also transaction log analysis packages available on the market (Stout, 1997).

The Web searching environment is one of continual modification and incremental changes. Although the overall interaction between Web users and Web IR systems appears relative stable, one must anchor any analysis within the specific searching rules, customer attraction, user demographics, and document collection of a particular Web IR system at the time of data collection.

Our analysis is beneficial for understanding the system itself and the user interactions during the "real" search process. The research analysis in this chapter centers on the interactions between user and Web search engine. Interaction has several meanings in information searching, although the definitions generally encompass query formulation, query modification, and inspection of results list, among other actions. In the broader information retrieval (IR) context, Bates (1990) presents four levels of interaction, which are move, tactic, stratagem, and strategy. Using this classification and Bates' definitions, this research primarily focuses on levels one and two (move and tactic) and glimpses of level three (stratagem). Viewing the entire information-seeking process as consisting of five entities (Saracevic, Kantor,

Chamis, and Trivison, 1988), transaction log analysis can only deal with the searcher's interactions during information searching.

To understand how the analysis was conducted, this section discusses the three Web search engines, presenting their marketing and algorithmic characteristics at the time of data collection. A standard set of metrics used in Web transaction log analysis, along with a discussion of their definitions and impact, is then presented. The chapter then discusses the data collection methods, Web searching environment, and analysis techniques for each set of Web transaction logs. The data collection methods for each transaction log for each Web search engine were similar.

For each Web query transaction log, each user's initial query was located and the chronological series of actions during each user session recreated, including: *User Identification*: an anonymous user code assigned by Web server; *Time of the day*: second, minute, hour, day, month and year are given in adjacent format; *Query terms*: the terms entered by the users.

5.   ALTAVISTA

In 2002, AltaVista (<http://www.altavista.com>) was the 9th most popular search engine with a significant content collection of Web pages and multimedia files (Sullivan, 2000, 2002). AltaVista supported several query operators including AND, OR, NOT, NEAR, MUST APPEAR, MUST NOT APPEAR, and PHRASE (AltaVista, 2003). AltaVista displayed results in ranked relevance order. Overture Services purchased AltaVista in 2003 (Morrissey, 2003), and Yahoo! subsequently purchased Overture Services (Stevens, 2003). Overall, AltaVista offers a full range of searching options, has an extremely large content collection, and millions of unique visitors per month.

We used queries that Web users submitted to AltaVista on Sunday, 8 September 2002. This set of queries spanned a 24-hour period. The AltaVista server recorded the queries in four transaction logs (e.g., general, audio, image, and video), each representing a portion of the searches executed on the Web search engine on this particular date. AltaVista used multimedia radio buttons for audio, image and video searches. AltaVista processes queries submitted via these radio buttons to the respective independent index content collections, separate from the content collection for the general search box. Each of the multimedia collection has its own indexing and retrieval algorithm. The original general transaction log contains approximately 3,000,000 records from the main AltaVista search page. The audio, image, and video transaction logs each contain approximately fifty thousand records.

6.   EXCITE

Excite (<http://www.excite.com>) was the second most popular Web site in 1997 (Munarriz, 1997), and was the fifth most popular in 1999 and 2001 as measured by number of unique visitors (Cyber Atlas, 1999, 2001). Excite supported several query operators and searching features including AND, OR, NOT, NEAR, MUST APPEAR, MUST NOT APPEAR, PHRASE, and MORE LIKE THIS (Jansen, Spink, Bateman, and Saracevic, 1998). Infospace purchased Excite in 2001 (Singer, 2001). Infospace re-launched Excite as a meta-search portal in 2002 (Goodman, 2002). At the time of the data collection, Excite offered a variety of searching features, had a large content collection, and served millions of unique visitors per month.

Excite had some very advanced searching features and capabilities, which require some discussion. Excite searches were based on the exact terms that a user entered in the query, however, capitalization was disregarded, with the exception of logical commands AND, OR, and AND NOT. Stemming was not available. Excite also used an online thesaurus and concept linking method called Intelligent Concept Extraction (ICE) to find related terms in addition to terms entered. It provided search results in ranked relevance order.

As for searching logic, a user could implement AND, OR, AND NOT, and PHRASE operators, but the Boolean operators must appear in ALL CAPS and with a space on each side. When using Boolean operators, ICE (concept-based search mechanism) is not used. Excite also implemented the MUST APPEAR and MUST NOT APPEAR operators. A page of search results contains ten answers on a page that are relevance ranked. For each site, Excite provided the title, URL (Web site address), and a summary of its contents. The user could also display results by site and titles only. In addition, there was a clickable option MORE LIKE THIS option, which was a relevance feedback mechanism to find similar sites.

Queries that Web users submitted to Excite on three separate dates over a four year period were used. Each transaction log holds a large and varied set of queries (approximately one million queries in each set). The transaction log spanned several hours of user searching on the following dates: 16 September 1997 (Tuesday, midnight to 8 a.m.), 1 December 1999 (Wednesday, 9 a.m. to 1 p.m.), and 30 April 2001 (Monday, midnight to midnight).[1] Each record within the Excite transaction log contains the four fields: (1) *Time of Day*, (2) *User Identification*, (3) *Query Terms, and (4) Results Page.*

---

[1] Times are Pacific Time as recorded by the Excite Web server.

7.   ALLTHEWEB.COM

A highly regarded Web search engine (Sullivan, 2003), AlltheWeb.com had a large content collection (Sullivan, 2000) and millions of queries per day. AlltheWeb.com provided the ability to search for news stories, pictures, video clips, MP3 and FTP files. It supported over 49 different languages. AlltheWeb.com provided the AND, OR, NOT, MUST APPEAR, MUST NOT APPEAR, PHRASE and RANK query operators.

Most users of AlltheWeb.com Web search engine were from Norway and Germany, according to AlltheWeb.com personnel. The FAST Corporation purchased AlltheWeb.com in 2003 Corporation (Kane, 2003) and that company was later purchased by Yahoo! (Stevens, 2003).

The queries examined for this study were from searchers using AlltheWeb.com on Tuesday, 6 February 2001 and Tuesday, 28 May 2002, with each transaction log spanning a 24-hour period. The queries represent a portion of the searches executed on the Web search engine on these particular dates. The transaction log hold a large and varied set of queries (over one million records). Each record within the transaction log contained five fields: (1) *Time of Day,* (2) *User Identification, (3) Query Terms, (4) Language, and (5) Page Viewed.*

8.   WEB QUERY LOG FIELDS

In order to facilitate valid comparisons and contrasts with other analysis, a standard terminology and set of metrics was used (Jansen and Pooch, 2001). Each record was classified as a *searching episode*. Each *searching episode* was of the following format, although not all transaction logs contained all the fields listed.

1. *Time of Day*: measured in hours, minutes, and seconds from midnight of each day as recorded by the search engine server.
2. *User Identification*: an anonymous user code assigned by the search engine   server representing the IP address of the client's computer. We attempted to   exclude   sessions   from   softbots   using   numerical limitation. However, currently, there is no way to precisely identify all of these automated searches (Silverstein,   Henzinger, Marais, and Moricz, 1999).
3. *Query Terms*: terms exactly as entered by the given user.
4. *Results Page*: a numerical code representing a set of result abstracts and URL returned by the search engine in response to a query. Some refer to the results   page as the SERP (Search Engine Results Page). Within the results page, there are, or can be, several subsections. These include the

sponsored links (i.e., those URL for which someone is paying for placements), of which there are several favors. Another section is the organic results (the most common name) or the hit list. These are the results for which no one is specifically paying for placement, although some URLs may take the user to sites that also have sponsored links.

5. *Language:* the user preferred the language of the retrieved Web pages.
6. *Page Viewed*: the URL that the searcher visited after entering the query.

9. ANALYSIS LEVELS

Analyses were conducted at multiple levels, including the *term*, *query*, *session* and *page view*, and *click-through* levels. These metrics are defined as:

1. *Term Level:* A *term* is a string of characters separated by some delimiter such as a space or some other separator. A blank space is used as the separator.
2. *Query Level:* A *query* is defined as a string list of zero or more terms submitted to a search engine. This is a mechanical definition as opposed to an information seeking definition (Korfhage, 1997). The first query by a particular searcher is as an *initial query*. A subsequent query by the same searcher that is identical to one or more of the searcher's previous queries is an *identical query*. A subsequent query by the same searcher that is different than any of the searcher's initial query is a *modified query*. There can be several occurrences of modified queries.

   A *unique query* refers to a query that is different from all other queries in the transaction log, regardless of searcher.

   At the *query* level of analysis, *query length*, *query complexity*, and *failure rate* were examined:
   - *Query length* was measured by counting the number of terms in the query.
   - *Query complexity* examines the query syntax, including the use of advanced searching techniques such as Boolean and other query operators.
   - *Failure rate* is a measure of the deviation from the published rules of the search engine. The use of query syntax that the particular IR system does not support, but may be common on other IR systems, is *carry over*.
3. *Session Level:* The *session* is the entire sequence of queries entered by a searcher with a given data sampling period. This is similar to the definition of a unique visitor that is used by commercial search engines and by organizations to measure Web site traffic. The number of queries

per searcher is the *session length*. Each searcher is given a unique identifier within the Web query transaction log, which the transaction log software usually bases on the IP address of the client machine.

Session duration is the total time the user spent interacting with the search engine including the time spent viewing the first and all subsequent Web documents, except the final document. Session duration can therefore be measured from the time the user submits the first query until the user departs the search engine for the last time (i.e., does not return). This final viewing time is not available since the Web search engine server records the time stamp. Naturally, the time between visits from the Web document to the search engine may not have been entirely spent viewing the Web document.

4. *Results Pages Viewed Level*: A results page is the list of results, either sponsored or organic, returned by a Web search engine in response to a query. The result page viewing patterns of Web searchers are analyzed, focusing on the number of results pages viewed.

5. *Click-through Level:* From the results page, a searcher may click on a URL, (i.e., visit) one or more results from the listings on the result pages. This page viewing behavior of Web searchers is analyzed. Some researchers and practitioners refer to this type of analysis as page view analysis.

A *Web document* is the Web page referenced by the URL on the search engine's results page. A Web document may be text or multimedia and, if viewed hierarchically, may contain a nearly unlimited number of sub-Web documents. A Web document may also contain URLs linking it to other Web documents or other Web documents containing URLs linking to it. We measure *document viewing duration* as the time from when a searcher clicks on a URL on a results page to the time that searcher returns to the search engine.

10.   QUANTITATIVE ANALYSIS

Using the three fields of *Time of Day*, *User Identification*, and *Query Terms*, common to all Web transaction logs, the *initial query* is located and then the chronological series of actions in a session is recreated. The Web query transaction logs contain searches from both human users and agents. For the most part, we were interested in only those queries submitted by humans. From the Web transaction log, a sub-set of queries was culled that were deemed likely to have been submitted by humans. To do this, all sessions with less than 101 queries were separated into an individual transaction logs that were used for this research. A session of 101 queries or more was chosen because it is almost 50 times greater than the reported mean search session for human Web searchers.

Given that there is no way to accurately identify human from non-human searchers (Silverstein, Henzinger, Marais, and Moricz, 1999; Sullivan, 2001), most researchers relying on Web transaction log for data collection must either ignore it (Cacheda and Viña, 2001) or assume some temporal or interaction cut-off (Montgomery and Faloutsos, 2001; Silverstein, Henzinger, Marais, and Moricz, 1999). Using a cut-off of 101 queries, we were satisfied that this subset of the transaction log contained queries submitted primarily by human searchers in a non-common user terminal, but it is also broad enough not to introduce bias by too low a cut-off threshold.

When a searcher submits a query, then views a document, and returns to the search engine, the server logs this second visit with the identical user identification and query, but with a new time (i.e., the time of the second visit). This is beneficial information in determining how many of the retrieved *results pages* the searcher visited from the search engine, but unfortunately it also skews the results in analyzing how the user searched on system.

To address the *sessions*, *queries*, and *term* analyses, the transaction logs were collapsed by combining all identical queries submitted by the same user to give the *unique queries* in order to analyze sessions, queries and terms, and pages of results viewed. The complete un-collapsed sessions were utilized in order to obtain an accurate measure of the temporal length of sessions and the number of *pages viewed* in the transaction log where this field was available.

Table 3.1 shows the basic data from the six Web transaction studies we compared in our research.

Table 3-1. Overall Data From AlltheWeb.com, Excite, and AltaVista Transaction Logs

Search Engine	Excite	Excite	AlltheWeb	Excite	AlltheWeb	AltaVista
Data Collection	Tuesday 16 September 1997	Wednesday 1 December 1999	Tuesday 6 February 2001	Monday 30 April 2001	Tuesday 28 May 2002	Sunday 8 September 2002
Sessions	210,590	325,711	153,297	262,025	345,093	369,350
Queries	545,206	1,025,910	451,551	1,025,910	957,303	1,073,388
Terms	1,224,245	1,500,500	1,350,619	1,538,120	2,225,141	3,132,106

Figure 3.1 shows the Entity–Relation (ER) diagram for the relational database used to store and analysis the data from the transaction logs.

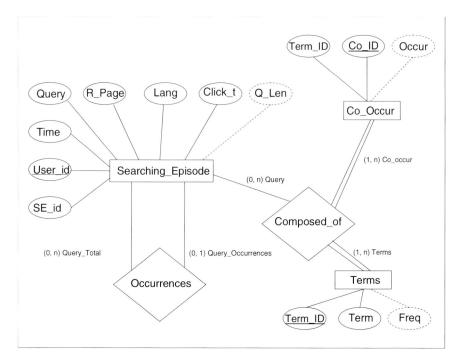

Figure 3-1. ER Scheme Diagram For the Transaction Log Databases

Table 3-2. Legend for Naming of Scheme Constructs

Construct Name	Construct
Searching_Episode	main table
Time	time of day
User_id	user identification
Query	query terms
R_Page	Results page
Lang	language
ClickT	page viewed
Q_Len	query length
Terms	table with terms and frequency
Term_ID	term identification
Term	term from the query set
Freq	number of occurrences of term in the query set
Co_Occur	table term pairs and the number of occurrences of those pairs
Term_ID	term identification
CO_ID	the combined term identification for a pair of terms
Occur	number of occurrences of pair in the query set

An ER diagram models the concepts and user perceptions of the data and displays the conceptual schema for the database. Standard ER notation is used as outlined in (Elmasri and Navathe, 1989).

Table 3.2 presents the legend for the schema constructs names.

11.   QUALITATIVE METHODS

11.1   Web Query Classification

The desire to better understand the information seeking and Web searching processes is a primary motivation for our studies. We primarily used content analysis based on grounded theory approaches and inductive methods to find evidence of the empirical connection between the data in the transaction logs and inferences from the data (Krippendorf, 1980), concerning the interaction between the systems and users. Content analysis was used to group together data when there were similar characteristics in a particular field or fields of the transaction log.

This methodology had the advantage of providing insights into large amounts of Web data to develop hypotheses or research questions for further testing. The methodology used in our qualitative studies is outlined below, with the caveat that qualitative analysis also has limitations especially in terms of external validity because the findings of this study may not be generalizable to a larger group of users.

In each analysis or classification of Web queries, at least two evaluators were used. Each evaluator classified each query by judging the query intent and deriving strong evidence of such intent from the query log. For example, during the analysis of sexual queries, the evaluators judged queries as related to sexual (including pornographic) needs if the queries explicitly requesting sexual information, visual images or textual descriptions of sexual behavior (Spink, Koricich, and Jansen, 2004; Spink, Ozmutlu, and Lorence, 2003).

To check coding consistency, each evaluator recoded a set of queries previously classified by the other researcher. The researchers met in order to make final decision about the classifications. The two or more evaluators discussed each disputed query until they reach a classification consensus for that query.

11.2   Topical Analysis

For each transaction log, a topical analysis of queries was conducted. In these cases, typically about 2,500 random queries were selected. Two or more evaluators (in one case over twenty) then reviewed and categorized each record in a self-building set of categories. The evaluators would then meet and resolve any discrepancies, a version of the Delphi technique (Cline, 2000).

11.3   Topical Relevance

Performance evaluation of the Web search engines was conducted using topical relevance based on queries in the transaction log. In these cases, we either randomly selected a set or selected a stratified set of records, typically approximately 500 queries. Using an automated submission script, we submitted these queries to major search engines and retrieved the top ten results from the results listings. Independent evaluators, usually three, then viewed the results abstract or the actual Web page and assigned a numerical evaluation of relevance, using a scale from 0 (i.e., no relevance) to 3 (i.e., total relevance). The inter-rater agreement for each evaluation is then calculated. Where click through data was available, we used the same technique to evaluate the Web site denoted by the URL in the transaction logs for each of the approximately 500 selected queries.

12.   STRENGTH AND LIMITATIONS

As with any research study and corresponding analysis, there are strengths and limitations.

This stream of research contributes to the Web searching literature in several important ways. First, the data comes from real users with real information needs submitting real queries to working IR systems in order to satisfy those information needs. Accordingly, it provides a realistic glimpse into how Web users search, without the self-selection issues or altered behavior that can occur with lab studies or survey data. Second, the sample is quite large, with hundreds of thousands of searchers, millions of queries, hundreds of thousands of results pages. The data are fairly robust. Third, all six transactions logs are analyzed using the exact same terminology and methods; therefore, the analysis does not suffer from change in methods over time. In preparation for this book, we completely re-analyzed all datasets to ensure consistent of methods. This allows valid comparisons among studies.

Third, we obtained data from three major and very popular Web search engines, as measured by both document collection and number of unique visitors, to ensure that our results were generalizable. Fourth, analysis at multiple levels of granularity and subject domain are provided. Finally, this research involves multiple analyses over multiple systems all conducted by the same set of researchers, which helps ensure consistency of analysis and metrics. From this consistency, one can better distinguish which searching behaviors carry over from system to system, one of the challenges of transaction log analysis identified by Kurth (1993).

As with any research, there are *limitations* that one should recognize. The sample data comes from three major Web search engines, introducing the possibility that the queries do not represent the interactions of the broader Web searching population. However, Jansen and Pooch (2001) have shown that characteristics of Web sessions, queries, and terms are very consistent across Web search engines. Other potential limitations are that we do not have information about the demographic characteristics of the users who submitted queries, so we must infer their characteristics from the demographics of Web searchers as a whole.

Also, the data was collected on specific dates, introducing the possibility of bias due to these particular dates not being representative. However, a comparison of the collected body of Web transaction log research (Abdulla, Liu, and Fox, 1998; Cacheda and Viña, 2001; Hölscher and Strube, 2000; Jansen and Spink, forthcoming; Jansen, Spink, and Pedersen, forthcoming; Montgomery and Faloutsos, 2001; Selberg and Etzioni, 1997; Spink, Jansen, Wolfram, and Saracevic, 2002) shows a great deal of similarity among Web searchers, indicating particular dates have little effect on session lengths, query lengths, Boolean usage, etc. However, particular dates do have an effect on the usage of popular terms (Wolfram, 1999).

13.   CONCLUSION

Our use of Web transaction log analysis, in addition to other research methods and analysis techniques, provided valuable insights into Web search. As the use of agents and automated submission software increases, one may need to combine transaction log with the data collected from cookies or other client software to shed more light on users and usage. Presently, with results of Web transaction log analysis properly reported and knowledgeably interpreted, transaction logs and their analysis can provide meaningful statistical indicators of searcher–system interaction.

14.   REFERENCES

Abdulla, G., Liu, B. and Fox, E. (1998). Searching the World-Wide Web: Implications from Studying Different User Behavior. In *Proceedings of the World Conference of the World Wide Web, Internet, and Intranet*, pp. 1–8. Orlando, FL.

Bates, M. J. (1990). Where Should the Person Stop and the Information Search Interface Start? *Information Processing and Management.*, 26(5), 575–591.

Borgman, C. L., Hirsh, S. G. and Hiller, J. (1996). Rethinking Online Monitoring Methods for Information Retrieval Systems: From Search Product to Search Process. *Journal of the American Society for Information Science, 47*(7), 568–583.

Cacheda, F. and Viña, Á. (2001). Experiences Retrieving Information in the World Wide Web. In *Proceedings of the 6th IEEE Symposium on Computers and Communications*, pp. 72–79. Hammamet, Tunisia. July.

Cline, A. (2000, 12 May). *Prioritization Process Using Delphi Technique*. Carolla Development. Retrieved 3 August, 2003, from the World Wide Web: <http://www.carolla.com/wp-delph.htm>.

Croft, W., Cook, R. and Wilder, D. (1995). Providing Government Information on the Internet: Experiences with Thomas. In *Proceedings of the Digital Libraries Conference*, pp. 19–24. Austin, TX. 11–13 June.

Cyber Atlas. (1999). *U.S. Top 50 Internet Properties December 1999 at Home/Work Combined*. Cyber Atlas. Retrieved 1 July, 2000, from the World Wide Web: <http://cyberatlas.internet.com>.

Cyber Atlas. (2001). *U.S. Top 50 Internet Properties, May 2001, at Home/Work Combined* [Website]. CyberAtlas. Retrieved 15 February, 2002, from the World Wide Web: <http://cyberatlas.internet.com>.

Drott, M. C. (1998). Using Web Server Logs to Improve Site Design. In *Proceedings of the 16th annual international conference on Computer documentation*, pp. 43–50. Quebec, Quebec, Canada.

Dumais, S. T. (2002, 7–11 May). *Web Experiments and Test Collections* [Presentation]. Retrieved 20 April, 2003, from the World Wide Web: <http://www2002.org/presentations/dumais.pdf>.

Elmasri, R. and Navathe, S. B. (1989). *Fundamentals of Database Systems*. Redword City, CA., USA: Benjamin/Cummings Publishing Company.

Ericsson, K. A. and Simon, H. A. (1984). *Protocol Analysis: Verbal Reports as Data*. Cambridge, MA: M.I.T Press.

Glaser, B. and Strauss, A. (1967). *The Discovery of Grounded Theory: Strategies for Qualitative Research*. Chicago, IL: Aldine Publishing Co.

Goodman, A. (2002, 11 May). *Excite Metasearch Serves up Equal Doses of Innovation and Monetization* [Web site]. Traffick.com. Retrieved 3 August, 2003, from the World Wide Web: <http://www.traffick.com/article.asp?aID=83>.

Hölscher, C. and Strube, G. (2000). Web Search Behavior of Internet Experts and Newbies. *International Journal of Computer and Telecommunications Networking, 33*(1–6), 337–346.

Ivory, M. Y. and Hearst, M. A. (2002). Improving Web Site Design. *IEEE Internet Computing, (IEEE)*(March/April), 56–63.

Jansen, B. J. and Pooch, U. (2001). Web User Studies: A Review and Framework for Future Work. *Journal of the American Society of Information Science and Technology, 52*(3), 235–246.

Jansen, B. J., and Spink, A. (forthcoming). An Analysis of Web Searching by European Alltheweb.Com Users. *Information Processing and Management*.

Jansen, B. J., Spink, A., Bateman, J. and Saracevic, T. (1998). Real Life Information Retrieval: A Study of User Queries on the Web. *SIGIR Forum, 32*(1), 5–17.

Jansen, B. J., Spink, A. and Pedersen, J. (forthcoming). A Trend Anaysis of AltaVista Web Searching. *Journal of the American Society for Information Science and Technology*.

Jones, S., Cunningham, S. and McNab, R. (1998). Usage Analysis of a Digital Library. In *Proceedings of the Third ACM Conference on Digital libraries*, pp. 293–294. Pittsburgh, PA. June 1998.

Kane, M. (2003, 23 February). *Overture to Buy Search Services* [Electronic Journal]. CNET News.com. Retrieved 1 March, 2003, from the World Wide Web: <http://rss.com.com/2100-1023-985850.html?type=pt&part=rss&tag=feed&subj=news>.

Kaske, N. K. (1993). Research Methodologies and Transaction Log Analysis: Issues, Questions, and a Proposed Model. *Library Hi Tech, 11*(2), 79–86.

Korfhage, R. (1997). *Information Storage and Retrieval*. New York, NY: Wiley.

Krippendorf, K. (1980). *Content Analysis: An Introduction to Its Methodology*. Beverly Hills, CA.: Sage Publications.

Kurth, M. (1993). The Limits and Limitations of Transaction Log Analysis. *Library Hi Tech, 11*(2), 98–104.

Montgomery, A. and Faloutsos, C. (2001). Identifying Web Browsing Trends and Patterns. *IEEE Computer, 34*(7), 94–95.

Morrissey, B. (2003, February 18, 2003). *Overture to Buy Altavista* [Web site]. Internet Advertising Report. Retrieved 16 May, 2003, from the World Wide Web: <http://www.internetnews.com/IAR/article.php/1587171>.

Munarriz, R. A. (1997, 12 August 1997). *How Did It Double?* The Motley Fool. Retrieved 10 November, 2002, from the World Wide Web: <http://www.fool.com/DDouble/1997/DDouble970812.htm>.

Peters, T. (1993). The History and Development of Transaction Log Analysis. *Library Hi Tech, 42*(11), 41–66.

Sandore, B. F. and Kaske, N. K. (1993). A Manifesto Regarding the Future of Transaction Log Analysis. *Library Hi Tech, 11*(2), 105–111.

Saracevic, T., Kantor, P., Chamis, A. Y. and Trivison, D. (1988). Study of Information Seeking and Retrieving: I. Background and Methodology. *Journal of the American Society for Information Science, 39*(3), 161–176.

Selberg, E. and Etzioni, O. (1997). The Metacrawler Architecture for Resource Aggregation on the Web. *IEEE Expert, 12*(1), 11–14.

Silverstein, C., Henzinger, M., Marais, H. and Moricz, M. (1999). Analysis of a Very Large Web Search Engine Query Log. *SIGIR Forum, 33*(1), 6–12.

Singer, M. (2001, 12 November). *Excite at Home Selling Its Portal*. Internetnews.com. Retrieved 3 August, 2003, from the World Wide Web: <http://www.internetnews.com/xSP/article.php/8_921261>.

Spink, A., Bateman, J. and Jansen, B. J. (1999). Searching the Web: Survey of Excite Users. *Internet Research: Electronic Networking Applications and Policy, 9*(2), 117–128.

Spink, A., Jansen, B. J., Wolfram, D. and Saracevic, T. (2002). From E-Sex to E-Commerce: Web Search Changes. *IEEE Computer, 35*(3), 107–111.

Spink, A., Koricich, A. and Jansen, B. J. (2004). Sexual Searching on Web Search Engines. *Cyber-psychology and Behavior, 40*(1), 113–123.

Spink, A., Ozmutlu, H. C. and Lorence, D. P. (2003). Web Searching for Sexual Information: An Exploratory Study. *Information Processing and Management*.

Stevens, J. (2003, 14 July). *Yahoo! To Acquire Overture* [Web site]. Overture Press Release. Retrieved 14 July, 2002, from the World Wide Web: <http://www.corporate-ir.net/ireye/ir_site.zhtml?ticker=OVER&script=410&layout=0&item_id=430830>.

Stout, R. (1997). *Web Site Stats: Tracking Hits and Analyzing Web Traffic*. Berkeley, CA.: Osborne Publishing.

Sullivan, D. (2000). *Search Engine Sizes*. Retrieved 30 August, 2000, from the World Wide Web: <http://searchenginewatch.com/reports/sizes.html>.

Sullivan, D. (2001, 6 November). *Spiderspotting: When a Search Engine, Robot or Crawler Visits* [Website]. SearchEngineWatch.com. Retrieved 5 August, 2003, from the World Wide Web: <http://www.searchenginewatch.com/webmasters/article.php/2168001>.

Sullivan, D. (2003, 29 April). *The Major Search Engines and Directories* [Web site]. Searchenginewatch.com. Retrieved 5 August, 2003, from the World Wide Web: <http://www.searchenginewatch.com/links/article.php/2156221>.

Wang, P., Berry, M. and Yang, Y. (2003). Mining Longitudinal Web Queries: Trends and Patterns. *Journal of the American Society for Information Science and Technology, 54*(8), 743–758.

Wolfram, D. (1999). Term Co-Occurrence in Internet Search Engine Queries: An Analysis of the Excite Data Set. *Canadian Journal of Information and Library Science, 24*(2/3), 12–33.

Section II

HOW PEOPLE SEARCH THE WEB

Chapter 4

SEARCH TERMS

1. INTRODUCTION

This chapter reports results from an analysis of the search terms submitted to Web search engines – AlltheWeb.com, AltaVista and Excite. Terms are the basic building blocks through which a Web searcher expresses their information problem when searching on a Web search engine. Single or multiple term and operators form a Web query. What are the subjects of Web users' search terms? Where do the search terms come from? Why does a user select one term instead of another? What influences a searcher's decisions?

Major findings suggest: (1) the topic interests of Web search engine users has shifted to commercial and informational from the sexual and technology domains, (2) the information problems of Web search engine users are becoming increasingly more diverse, (3) there is a notable increase in non-English terms, numbers, and acronyms used as Web search terms, (4) a set of approximately 20% of search terms are used with great regularity while approximately 10% of the terms are used only once, and (5) major news events and holidays influence search term usage.

Many researchers view Web search as a communication process in which there is a dialog or discourse occurring between the searcher and the Web search engine (Jansen, 2003; Spink, 1997). A dialog is a communication exchange about a certain topic between a user and a Web search engine that includes thinking on the part of the user. Iivonen and Sonnenwald (1998) note that when selecting search terms, searchers appear to navigate a variety of dialogs. Searchers evaluate and synthesize information among these dialogs in order to select search terms.

Hsieh-Yee (1993) reports that the level of a user's search experience and domain knowledge affects the searchers' selection of search terms. Along with domain knowledge and searching experience, Spink and Saracevic (1997) identified three other sources of search terms pertinent to Web searching, namely (1) the users' level of domain knowledge of their search topic, (2) the Web systems output, and (3) a thesaurus or related terms. They noted that search terms from the user's domain and the system's output were the terms that helped the most in retrieving relevant documents.

Researchers have also investigated reformulation (Dennis, Bruza and McArthur, 2002) and search term weighting in order to improve performance. The underlying assumption is that not all terms in a query are of equal importance. The most well known case being that of stop words (Fox, 1990), which are query terms that occur so frequently that they are deemed of little content value (e.g. *and, or, the*). Some Web search engines automatically remove stop words from queries unless the user specifically tells the search engine (via query operators such as PHRASE or MUST APPEAR) to keep them in the query. Members of some communities refer to stop words as filter words (WebMasterWorld.com, 2004), in which case stop words refer to terms in Web documents that cause a Web search engine spider to stop indexing.

The idea behind term weighting is that the terms with the most importance should have more effect on the retrieval process. Budzik, Hammond, and Birnbaum (2001) use a version of term weighting in an application to automatically formulate queries. Some Web search engines have attempted to implement term weighting automatically using click-through data from query transaction logs (Schaale, Wulf-Mathies and Lieberam-Schmidt, 2003).

In a similar vein, the term co-occurrence approach attempts to identify terms that are similar to those that previous searchers have specified. The idea with term co-occurrence is that the search engine or searcher can use these similar terms to augment the current query and improve retrieval performance. Several researchers have examined term co-occurrence in transaction logs in order to locate common terms that may be related (Pu, Chuang and Yang, 2002; Wolfram, 1999). This is a tricky area, however, because frequently occurring terms tend to discriminate poorly between relevant and non-relevant documents. If the identified terms occur too frequently they do little and often nothing to improve the effectiveness of the query (Peat and Willett, 1991).

This brief literature review highlights the importance of term selection for the Web searching process. Given the significance of terms and term selection in Web search engines addressing the searchers' information problems, it is vital that we understand how Web searchers are using search terms.

The next section investigates the search terms that Web searchers use and how they use them. This important area of research can affect Web search engine design, Web site development, and production of online content.

The investigation of search terms used on Web search engines examined results from transaction logs from three major Web search engines – AlltheWeb.com, AltaVista, and Excite. This analysis identified trends that can be seen across all Web search engines, related to the frequency of term occurrence, term co-occurrence and topic of search terms for the three Web search engines. Results show consistent trends across multiple Web search engines.

The next section first presents trends across all three Web search engines, the aggregate data for the three Web search engines, then specific analysis for each Web search engine and finally general conclusions and possible future directions for Web term usage.

2. WEB SEARCH TERM TRENDS

One of the most telling trends in Web search terms is the shifting of topic interest by Web search engine users. Figure 4.1 shows a stacked column chart compares the percentages of each value to the total of all categories across Web search engines (EX – Excite, ATW – AlltheWeb.com, and AV – AltaVista) and time. The categories *People, places or things* (PPT), *Sex or pornography* (SEX), and *Commerce, travel, employment, or economy* (CTEE) experienced significant changes over the course of the studies.

For all the Web search engines, searching for *Sex or pornography* has decreased while searching for information on *People, places or things* has increased. Searching for *Commerce, travel, employment, or economy* topics steadily rose on Excite. However, the percentage searching for this topic on AlltheWeb.com and AltaVista is lower. It may be an indication that Web searchers do not use these Web search engines as much for this topic domain. One should not interpret this as implying that interest in pornography is necessarily decreasing. These issues are further discussed in more detail in Chapters 7 and 9 of this book and in Spink, Jansen, Wolfram and Saracevic (2002).

The decrease in sexual searching may be due to the ease and effectiveness of other means to locate Web pornography (Fox, 2002b). What these topic trends suggest is that Web searching is moving from an entertainment medium to a more commercial and business medium.

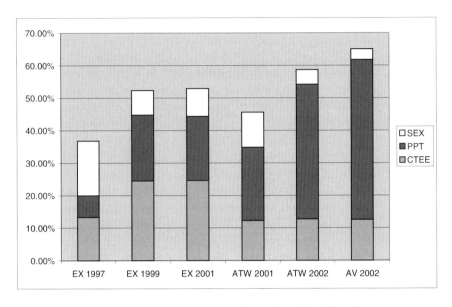

Figure 4-1. Contribution of Three Categories to Total Searching

3.   AGGREGATE DATA BY WEB SEARCH ENGINES

The next section examines search term usage on each of the three Web search engines – AlltheWeb.com, AltaVista and Excite.

3.1   AlltheWeb.com

Table 4.1 presents the aggregate results from the analysis of two AlltheWeb.com data sets from 2001 and 2002.

Overall, a slight increase in variability of terms occurred. The number of unique terms increased (from 12% to 15%) and the percentage of terms not repeated in the data set increased from 7% in 2001 to 10% in 2002. There was a corresponding decrease in the percentage of usage represented by the top 100 most frequently occurring terms, dropping from 15% to 14%. Taken together, these results may indicate a broadening of topic interests by AlltheWeb.com users.

Table 4-1. Comparative Results Statistics for AlltheWeb.com Data Sets

	AlltheWeb.com 2001		AlltheWeb.com 2002	
Sessions	153,297		345,093	
Queries	451,551		957,303	
Terms				
Unique	180,998	13%	340,711	15%
Total	1,350,619	100%	2,225,141	100%
Terms not repeated in data set	100,649	7%	212,040	10%
Use of 100 most frequently occurring terms	196,390	15%	303,176	14%

3.2   AltaVista

Table 4.2 shows the aggregate results for the AltaVista analysis. For comparison the results from a previously published AltaVista study by Silverstein, Henzinger, Marais and Moricz (1999) are also presented.

Table 4-2. Aggregate Results for Data Analysis of 1998 and 2002 AltaVista Data Sets

	AltaVista 1998	AltaVista 2002	
Sessions	285,474,117	369,350	
Queries	993,208,159	1,073,388	
Terms			
Unique		297,528	9.5%
Total		3,132,106	100%
Terms not repeated in data set		176,196	5.6%
Use of 100 most frequently occurring terms		592,699	18.9%

Notes: For the 1998 study, percentage and figures use the 575,244,993 non-empty queries.
The 1998 data from this and other tables is from or calculated from data reported in
    (Silverstein, Henzinger, Marais, & Moricz, 1999).

The differences based on the term analysis cannot be presented, since the 1998 study presented little term analysis results. Using the 2002 results and comparing to other published research, the unique terms (9.5%) and the terms not repeated in the data set (6%) is lower than that of AlltheWeb.com users (Spink, Ozmutlu, Ozmutlu and Jansen, 2002) and Excite users (Spink, Jansen, Wolfram and Saracevic, 2002). The use of the top most frequently occurring terms (19%) is similar to that reported for users of Excite (Spink, Jansen, Wolfram and Saracevic, 2002) and AlltheWeb.com users (Spink, Ozmutlu, Ozmutlu and Jansen, 2002), although again lower.

3.3   Excite

Table 4.3 presents the aggregate results for the three Excite transaction logs.

The use of unique terms held steady during the entire five-year period, hovering at 11% to 12%. The use of unique terms and terms not repeated in the data set is similar to that of AlltheWeb.com and higher than AltaVista searchers. The use of the top one hundred most frequently occurring terms is about twice of AlltheWeb.com searchers and higher than AltaVista searchers. The higher term variability, and therefore topic interests, may be due to the popularity, as measured by number of unique visitors, of Excite during the data collection period.

Table 4-3. Comparative Statistics of Excite Data Sets From 1998, 1999, and 2001

	Excite Study 1997		Excite Study 1999		Excite Study 2001	
Sessions	210,590		325,711		262,025	
Queries	545,206		1,025,910		1,025,910	
Terms						
Unique	139,398	11.4%	171,789	11.5%	184,323	12.0%
Total	1,224,245	100.0%	1,500,500	100.0%	1,538,120	100.0%
Terms not repeated in data set	86,303	6.8%	105,994	7.1%	113,875	7.4%
Use of 100 most frequently occurring terms	228,720	17.9%	289,597	19.3%	338,386	22.0%

4. IN-DEPTH ANALYSES BY WEB SEARCH ENGINE

4.1 AlltheWeb.com

4.1.1 Most Frequently Occurring Terms

Table 4.4 shows a term analysis identifying the most frequently utilized terms from the AlltheWeb.com transaction logs.

From both Web transaction logs, a rank frequency ordering of all terms, then removing the terms without content (i.e., stop words such as: *and*, *or*, *de*, *la*, *le*, etc.) was generated. The top 25 remaining terms from each year were examined. For better identification of trends, if a term appeared in one list and not the other, it was added to those terms and the frequency of occurrence of those terms to the other list. This resulted in a combined list of thirty-four terms for the two years. Table 4.4 presents the combined list. The table was ordered by frequency of occurrence in the 2002 data set and calculated the percentages using the number of total terms from each data set.

Three trends present themselves from the term level of analysis. First, all of the top terms are English language terms, despite AlltheWeb.com being primarily a European Web search engine. Second, technology terms dominate the top term usage list, with terms such as *Internet*, *Linux*, *software*, *Web*, *Windows*, and *XP*. These types of terms certainly seem to stand out as indicators of a major topic interest for AlltheWeb.com searchers. Third, another topical area for AlltheWeb.com searchers is entertainment, with terms such as *CD*, *games*, *MP3*, *lyrics*, *music*, and *video*. These topic areas have remained constant over the two analysis periods.

4.1.2 Term Co-occurrence

Although a term analysis is useful, it is sometimes difficult to determine the specific usage of a term intended by a searcher within the framework of a particular query. In these cases, a term co-occurrence is more helpful (Leydesdorff, 1989; Wolfram, 1999). A term co-occurrence analysis was conducted on each AlltheWeb.com data set.

Table 4.5 shows the top ten term co-occurrence pairs for the 2001 data set in a correlation matrix fashion.

From the term co-occurrence analysis, the predominance of technical searching is even clearer. Nearly half of the top occurring term pairs are technology-related (e.g., *windows mac*, *windows os*, and *bug fixes*).

Table 4-4. AlltheWeb.com Top Occurring Terms and Frequencies

	Term	Frequency			
		AlltheWeb.com 2001	%	AlltheWeb.com 2002	%
1	free	8,583	0.6%	9,691	0.4%
2	sex	4,513	0.3%	6,784	0.3%
3	download	5,566	0.4%	5,997	0.3%
4	software	2,031	0.2%	3,838	0.2%
5	uk	3,534	0.3%	3,549	0.2%
6	windows	2,216	0.2%	3,252	0.1%
7	new	2,240	0.2%	2,994	0.1%
8	hotel	2,433	0.2%	2,991	0.1%
9	mp3	2,303	0.2%	2,909	0.1%
10	video	1,574	0.1%	2,793	0.1%
11	crack	1,660	0.1%	2,731	0.1%
12	nude	2,439	0.2%	2,689	0.1%
13	pictures	3,539	0.3%	2,552	0.1%
14	web	1,336	0.1%	2,513	0.1%
15	home	939	0.1%	2,235	0.1%
16	world	1,304	0.1%	2,192	0.1%
17	online	1,438	0.1%	2,189	0.1%
18	internet	1,341	0.1%	2,133	0.1%
19	cd	1,420	0.1%	2,113	0.1%
20	music	1,612	0.1%	2,041	0.1%
21	girls	1,449	0.1%	2,005	0.1%
22	canada	905	0.1%	1,928	0.1%
23	photo	1,208	0.1%	1,876	0.1%
24	how	1,415	0.1%	1,871	0.1%
25	car	1,025	0.1%	1,852	0.1%
26	pics	2,110	0.2%	1,848	0.1%
27	xp	17	0.0%	1,815	0.1%
28	map	1,574	0.1%	1,705	0.1%
29	games	1,307	0.1%	1,639	0.1%
30	school	1,470	0.1%	1,615	0.1%
31	lyrics	1,901	0.1%	1,503	0.1%
32	university	1,551	0.1%	1,193	0.1%
33	history	1,370	0.1%	1,072	0.0%
34	linux	1,413	0.1%	894	0.0%
	Total	70,736	5.2%	91,002	4.1%

Table 4-5. Frequency of Term Co-Occurrence For Top 25 AlltheWeb.com Terms For 2001

	alternative(s)	bug	cell(s)	fix	fuel (s)	hat	me	microsoft	ms	nt	operating	power	windows
alternative(s)	-												
bug		-											
cell(s)			-										
fix		564		-									
fuel (s)	1054		1380		-								
hat						-							
me							-						
microsoft								-					
ms									-				
nt										-			
operating											-		
power	459			690								-	
windows						410	1041	642	632	420			-

Table 4.6 shows the top ten term co-occurrence pairs from the 2002 data set in a correlation matrix fashion.

Table 4.6 does not show the clustering of term pairs that Table 4.5 showed for the 2001 data set. This diversity reinforces the findings with the initial term analysis that these Web users are searching for an increasingly variety of topics. Business and entertainment term pairs have replaced technology as the predominant grouping.

In order gain more insight into the interest of AlltheWeb.com searchers, a topic analysis was conducted.

4.1.3   Topic Trends

A random sample of approximately 2,500 English language queries each from the 2001 (2,503 queries) and 2002 (2,525 queries) data sets were classified into 11 non-mutually exclusive, general topic categories previously derived by Spink, Wolfram, Jansen and Saracevic (2001).

Table 4.7 shows the results of this classification.

Table 4-6. Frequency of Term Co-Occurrence for Top 25 AlltheWeb.com Terms for 2002

	2000	cup	download	estate	for	Free	job	pics	real	resume	sale	sex	skills	windows	world
2000	-														
cup		-													
download			-												
estate				-											
for					-										
free			611			-									
job							-								
pics						499		-							
real				1162					-						
resume							1059			-					
sale					995						-				
sex			619			552						-			
skills								482					-		
windows	583													-	
world		714													-

Table 4.7 was ordered by categories percentages in the 2002 transaction log. *People, places or things* category remained the top ranked category with a large percentage increase from 2001 to 2002. Percentage drops occurred in several other categories, most noticeably *Computers or internet* and *Sex or pornography*. The category rankings changed somewhat. The *Sex or pornography* category, for example, dropped from 4th to 6th place.

Table 4-7. Comparison of AlltheWeb.com General Topic Categories

Rank	Categories	AlltheWeb. com 2001	AlltheWeb. com 2002	% Increase / Decrease
1	People, places or things	22.50%	41.50%	84.4%
2	Computers or Internet	21.80%	16.30%	−25.2%
3	Commerce, travel, employment, or economy	12.30%	12.70%	3.3%
4	Entertainment or recreation	9.10%	9.50%	4.4%
5	Health or sciences	7.80%	4.90%	−37.2%
6	Sex or pornography	10.80%	4.50%	−58.3%
7	Government	2.70%	2.60%	−3.7%
8	Unknown or Other	0.60%	2.50%	316.7%
9	Education or humanities	2.90%	2.30%	−20.7%
10	Society, culture, ethnicity or religion	4.80%	2.10%	−56.3%
11	Performing or fine arts	4.70%	1.10%	−76.6%

This decrease in sexual searching as a percentage of overall Web searching parallels that reported in studies of US searching (Spink, Jansen, Wolfram and Saracevic, 2002). This analysis also confirms that reported by Spink, Ozmutlu, Ozmutlu and Jansen (2002) who found less European commercial Web searching compared to the large shift to e-commerce searching in the US. This finding also parallels the increase in non-sexual content on the Web (Lawrence and Giles, 1999) and reports from survey data (Fox, 2002b).

The next section reports results from a similar analysis using an AltaVista data set.

4.2 AltaVista

4.2.1 Most Frequently Occurring Terms

Table 4.8 shows a term analysis identifying the most frequently utilized terms from the 2002 AltaVista Web transaction log.

Term analysis was not available for the 1998 data set. From the general transaction log the top terms were extracted, removing the terms without content (*and*, *or*, *de*, *la*, *le*, etc.). Table 4.8 presents the top 34 terms representing those terms that appeared at least 0.1% of the time. Some interesting aspects present themselves from the term level of analysis.

First, even the most frequently occurring terms represent a small percentage of overall term usage. The most frequently used term (*free*) accounted only for approximately 0.6% of all term usage. Second, the occurrence of sexual terms (*sex*, *nude*, *porn*) was lower than some might expect. Although, searching for sexual information has decreased, it is still, usually, a popular topic. Third, there were a significant variety of terms, indicating a diverse set of information needs of AltaVista users. Similar to AlltheWeb.com, the top terms from AltaVista represent a small (5%) of the total terms.

Silverstein, Henzinger, Marais and Moricz (1999) did not report a direct term analysis. However, they do report the occurrences of the top twenty-five queries. Removing the one non-ASCII query, these queries represent 2% (8,734,653 queries) of the 575,244,993 queries in the database. Three of the remaining 24 queries are two term queries (*september 11*, *spice girls*, and *animal sex*). If one splits these three queries by term and disregards capitalization, there are twenty terms representing 9,304,270 occurrences. Of these twenty terms from the 1998 study, only three (*nude, porn, sex*) appear in the top terms in 2002.

Table 4-8. Top Occurring Terms and Frequencies for the AltaVista 2002 Data Set

	Term	Frequency	%
1	free	18,404	0.6%
2	sex	7,771	0.2%
3	pictures	7,713	0.2%
4	new	7,468	0.2%
5	nude	5,363	0.2%
6	music	5,358	0.2%
7	school	5,160	0.2%
8	how	5,148	0.2%
9	lyrics	5,006	0.2%
10	home	4,872	0.2%
11	pics	4,788	0.2%
12	download	4,715	0.2%
13	online	4,365	0.1%
14	american	4,206	0.1%
15	state	4,179	0.1%
16	county	4,109	0.1%
17	university	3,765	0.1%
18	car	3,762	0.1%
19	texas	3,644	0.1%
20	real	3,587	0.1%
21	games	3,527	0.1%
22	software	3,495	0.1%
23	art	3,493	0.1%
24	map	3,434	0.1%
25	florida	3,417	0.1%
26	world	3,412	0.1%
27	college	3,405	0.1%
28	video	3,374	0.1%
29	city	3,355	0.1%
30	history	3,299	0.1%
31	search	3,188	0.1%
32	web	3,149	0.1%
33	porn	3,118	0.1%
34	sale	3,082	0.1%
Total		160,131	5.00%

4.2.2   Term Co-occurrence

Table 4.9 shows the top ten most frequent term co-occurrences pairs for the 2002 AltaVista data set in a correlation matrix fashion.

Table 4-9. Frequency of Term Co-Occurrence for the AltaVista 2002 Dataset

	11	Estate	free	high	los	new	pics	porn	puerto	real	school	september	sex	state(s)
11	-													
estate		-												
free			-											
high				-										
los					-									
new						-								
pics		1098					-							
porn		1037						-						
puerto									-					
real		2927								-				
school			1925								-			
september	827											-		
sex													-	
state(s)														-
stories													893	
united														1127
vegas					950									
york						2782								

The term co-occurrence analysis shows that the predominance of searching clustered around *free* is apparent. All of the occurrences of *free* appear to be cost related. Other than this, there was no noticeable clustering of term pairs, other than the cluster around temporal issues (e.g., *september 11*). This pair diversity reinforces this finding with the term and the query analyses that these Web users are searching for an increasing variety of topics. In a study of Excite users, Wolfram (1999) notes high clustering of several term pairs around entertainment that is not seen in this analysis.

Silverstein, Henzinger, Marais and Moricz (1999) report the co-occurrence of the top 10,000 terms from approximately 313,000,000 million queries. They then followed this with co-occurrence of phrases within queries and noted the highest correlated terms pairs are portions of phrases, even when the Web searcher did not use the PHRASE operator. In addition, there were some high interest topics that skewed the analysis, most notably the interest in the then popular television show *Buffy the Vampire Slayer* along with fashionable female entertainers of the period, such as *Cindy Crawford* and *Pamela Anderson*. They also noted that the query term *the* was correlated with long queries, indicating the possibility of natural language queries.

In order to gain more insight into the interest of AltaVista searchers, a topic analysis was conducted.

4.2.3   Topic Trends

A random sample of 2,603 queries from the AltaVista 2002 data set was classified into 11 non-mutually exclusive, general topic categories developed by Spink, Wolfram, Jansen and Saracevic (2001). Two independent evaluators manually classified each of the queries independently. The evaluators then met and resolved discrepancies.

Table 4.10 displays the classification results.

Table 4-10. Comparison of AltaVista General Topic Categories for 2002

Rank	AltaVista 2002	Percentage
1	People, places or things	49.27%
2	Commerce, travel, employment or economy	12.52%
3	Computers or Internet or technology items	12.40%
4	Health or sciences (physics, math)	7.49%
5	Education or humanities	5.07%
6	Entertainment or recreation (music, TV, sports)	4.57%
7	Sex or pornography	3.26%
8	Society, culture, ethnicity or religion	3.11%
9	Government (or military)	1.57%
10	Performing or fine arts (i.e., ballets, plays, etc)	0.69%
		100.00%

Queries for *People, place or things* account for nearly half of the queries, with *Commerce, travel, employment or economy* and *Computers, internet or technology* accounting for another 25% of the queries.

The other eight categories account for the remaining 25%. Combined with the evidence from the term and term co-occurrence results, this analysis extends survey data that the Web is now a major information source for most people (Cole, Suman, Schramm, Lunn, and Aquino, 2003; Fox, 2002a), the move toward the use of the Web as an economic resource and tool (Lawrence and Giles, 1999; Spink, Jansen, Wolfram and Saracevic, 2002), and that people use the Web for an increasingly variety of information tasks (Fox, 2002a; National Telecommunications and Information Administration, 2002). This finding also confirms the continued drop in *Sex and pornography* as a major topic for search engine users.

Silverstein, Henzinger, Marais and Moricz (1999) did not conduct a topic analysis. However, the top twenty-five queries that they do report can be used and classified into corresponding categories. Of the twenty queries, 14 (56%) concerned *Sex or pornography*, 6 (24%) are *Entertainment or recreation*, 4 (16%) are *Computers or Internet or technology items*, and 1 (4%) is *Other* (i.e., queries containing non-ASCII characters). Comparisons of these percentages to those from the 2002 data set also show the decline of sexual searching and the increase in commercial searching.

The next section reports the results of a similar analysis using three Excite data sets.

4.3   Excite

4.3.1   Most Frequently Occurring Terms

Table 4.11 presents an analysis of the most frequently occurring terms for the 1997, 1999, and 2001 Excite data sets.

From the general transaction logs, the top most frequently occurring terms were extracted after removing the terms without content (*and*, *or*, *de*, *la*, *le*, etc.). All terms were then combined into one list, duplicates removed, and the frequency of all terms for all years reported. The resulting list contains thirty seven terms, reports the occurrences from all terms from all years, and is displayed by Table 4.9.

There are a number of terms that represent sexuality (*sex, nude, porn, xxx, naked*) and education (*school, university, college*). The high rank of terms like *diana* and *christmas* reflect the temporal interest of certain topics for certain data sets. For example, Princess Diana died in 1997, and the term *diana* is a frequently occurring term in that data set. Another example shows that for the 1999 transaction log in December of 1999, the term *christmas* is the most highly occurring term.

4.3.2   Term Co-occurrence

Table 4.12 shows the ten most frequently occurring term co-occurrences pairs for the 1997 data set in a correlation matrix fashion.

Table 4-11. Excite Top Occurring Terms and Frequencies From the 1997, 1999, and 2001 Data Sets

	Term	Excite 1997	%	Excite 1999	%	Excite 2001	%
				Frequency			
1	free	9710	0.9%	12,277	1.2%	11,472	1.1%
2	sex	10,757	1.0%	7,859	0.8%	4,851	0.5%
3	pictures	5,939	0.6%	4,882	0.5%	4,311	0.4%
4	new	3,109	0.3%	4,617	0.5%	3,918	0.4%
5	nude	7,047	0.7%	5,732	0.6%	3,417	0.3%
6	pics	3,815	0.4%	4,158	0.4%	3,025	0.3%
7	school	2,176	0.2%	2,174	0.2%	2,619	0.3%
8	music	2,490	0.2%	3,345	0.3%	2,563	0.2%
9	download	1,381	0.1%	1,599	0.2%	2,523	0.2%
10	university	4,383	0.4%	3,271	0.3%	2,405	0.2%
11	state	2,010	0.2%	2,467	0.2%	2,248	0.2%
12	lyrics	1,735	0.2%	1,532	0.1%	2,226	0.2%
13	home	2,150	0.2%	2,085	0.2%	2,099	0.2%
14	games	1,904	0.2%	3,153	0.3%	2,064	0.2%
15	software	1,908	0.2%	1,960	0.2%	2,007	0.2%
16	american	1,961	0.2%	2,013	0.2%	2,006	0.2%
17	stories	1,958	0.2%	2,432	0.2%	1,965	0.2%
18	porn	2,400	0.2%	2,919	0.3%	1,947	0.2%
19	college	2,043	0.2%	2,012	0.2%	1,923	0.2%
20	county	1,533	0.1%	1,396	0.1%	1,870	0.2%
21	car	1,195	0.1%	1,784	0.2%	1,843	0.2%
22	women	3,211	0.3%	2,405	0.2%	1,835	0.2%
23	city	1,222	0.1%	1,763	0.2%	1,807	0.2%
24	web	1,366	0.1%	1,674	0.2%	1,794	0.2%
25	online	1,813	0.2%	2,024	0.2%	1,712	0.2%
26	adult	3,385	0.3%	2,153	0.2%	1,588	0.2%
27	girls	2,732	0.3%	1,878	0.2%	1,563	0.2%
28	gay	2,187	0.2%	1,961	0.2%	1,503	0.1%
29	recipes	1,381	0.1%	2,098	0.2%	1,458	0.1%
30	mp3	1,327	0.1%	2,200	0.2%	1,353	0.1%
31	xxx	3,010	0.3%	2,274	0.2%	1,335	0.1%
32	cards	1,195	0.1%	2,663	0.3%	1,282	0.1%
33	christmas	3,515	0.3%	6,088	0.6%	1,277	0.1%
34	chat	3,515	0.3%	2,253	0.2%	1,277	0.1%
35	codes	1,222	0.1%	2,247	0.2%	1,185	0.1%
36	naked	1,968	0.2%	1,489	0.1%	1,074	0.1%
37	diana	1,885	0.2%	123	~0.0%	69	~0.0%
		106,538	10.4%	108,960	10.6%	85,414	8.3%

Table 4-12. Frequency of Term Co-Occurrence for the Excite Data Set 1997

	carolina	free	how	north	nude	of	pics	pictures	sex	teen	to	women
carolina	-											
free		-										
how			-									
north	382			-								
nude					-							
of						-						
pics	1098				380		-					
pictures					486	637		-				
sex							295	496	-			
teen	293									-		
to			627								-	
women					382							-

High up in the frequency list of term co-occurrence are several sexual oriented topics (*sex pics, sex pictures, nude pics, nude pictures, nude women*). There are also location pairs (*north carolina*) and question pairs (*how to*). At the time of this data collection, AskJeeves was a referred user of Excite (Spink and Ozmutlu, 2002).

Table 4.13 shows the ten most frequently occurring term co-occurrences pairs for the 1999 data set in a correlation matrix fashion.

Sexual term co-occurrence pairs still occur (*free sex, free porn*) but both pairs contain the term *free*, probably an indication of the searching for an alternative to paid sex sites. The number of location pairs increased (*las vegas, new york*) and question term pair (*how to*) still occurs. Term pairs indicating commerce topics also appear (*real estate, for sale, free sale*).

Table 4.14 displays the ten most frequently occurring term co-occurrences pairs for the 2001 data set in a correlation matrix fashion.

Table 4-13 Frequency of Term Co-Occurrence for the Excite Data Set 1999

	estate	for	free	high	how	las	new	of	pics	pictures	porn	real	sale	school	sex	to
estate	-															
for		-														
free			-													
high				-												
how					-											
las						-										
new							-									
of								-								
pics									-							
pictures								1040		-						
porn			662								-					
real	994											-				
sale		871	975										-			
school				882										-		
sex			1106												-	
to					1231											-
vegas						1390										
york							1590									

Table 4-14. Frequency of Term Co-Occurrence for the Excite Data Set 2001

	britney	cards	free	greeting	how	new	nude	of	pics	pictures	sex	spears	to	university	york
britney	-														
cards		-													
free			-												
greeting		962		-											
how					-										
nude			863			-	-								
of								-							
pics			1336						-						
pictures			839					1052		-					
Sex	954	1606									-				
To					1113								-		
university								1251						-	
york					1816										-

The ever-present sexual term co-occurrence pairs occur (*britney sex, free nude, free sex*), and again the same two pairs containing the term *free*. Location terms pairs also occurred (*new york*) along with the commerce topic (*greetings cards*).

4.3.3   Topic Trends

A random sample of approximately 2,414 queries from the 1997, 2,539 queries from the 1999, and 2,453 queries from the 2001 transaction logs were qualitatively analyzed into 11 non-mutually exclusive, general topic categories developed by Spink, Jansen, Wolfram and Saracevic (2002). Two independent evaluators manually classified each of the queries independently. The evaluators then met and resolved discrepancies.

Table 4.15 displays the evaluation results for these 7,406 manually classified queries.

Table 4-15. Distribution of Excite General Topic Categories

Rank	Categories	1997	1999	2001	% Increase / Decrease from 1997 to 1999
1	Commerce, travel, employment, or economy	13.30%	24.50%	24.70%	86%
2	People, places, or things	6.70%	20.30%	19.70%	194%
3	Non-English or unknown	4.10%	6.80%	11.30%	176%
4	Computers or Internet	12.50%	10.90%	9.60%	–23%
5	Sex and pornography	16.80%	7.50%	8.50%	–49%
6	Health or sciences	9.50%	7.80%	7.50%	–21%
7	Entertainment or recreation	19.90%	7.50%	6.60%	–67%
8	Education or humanities	5.60%	5.30%	4.50%	–20%
9	Society, culture, ethnicity, or religion	5.70%	4.20%	3.90%	–32%
10	Government	3.40%	1.60%	2.00%	–41%
11	Performing or fine arts	5.40%	1.10%	1.10%	–80%

In Table 4.15 the categories are ordered in descending order based on 2001 percentages. Table 4.15 shows an ongoing shift in search topics from 1997 to 2001. *Commerce, travel, employment, or economy* and *People, places, or things* searching increased by 86% and searching for *People, places, or things* increased by 194%. The shift to e-commerce queries coincided with changes in information distribution on the publicly indexed Web. By 1999, some 83 percent of Web servers contained terms indicating a request for commercial content. By 2001, Web searching and Web content continued to evolve from an entertainment to a business medium.

Surprisingly, the *non-English or unknown* topic increased by 176%. *Unknown* are queries for which the evaluators could not determine the topic. *Non-English* queries have nearly tripled since 1997. Many queries are also single terms with little supporting contextual data, such as *naz*; numbers such as *182*; or acronyms, such as *TOF*. Without additional terms, it is difficult for Web search engines (and people!) to interpret such queries.

The biggest declines were in the categories of *Performing or fine arts* (–80%), *Entertainment or recreation* (–67%), and *Sex and pornography* (–49%). In 1997, approximately one in six Web queries was about sex. By 2001, this was down to one in 12, and many of these related to human sexuality, not pornography. This may indicate a declining interest in these topics relative to other uses of the Web. But there are also indications that Web users may no longer require Web search engines to locate pornographic content (Fox, 2002b).

5.   CONCLUSION

This chapter has examined Web query terms in detail from three Web search engines and six data sets. What can we say about term usage on Web search engines? Firstly, AlltheWeb.com users' search topics are diverse but there is a high concentration of technology and entertainment searching. The usage of unique terms on this search engine is a smaller percentage relative to the searching on AltaVista and Excite. With AltaVista, there appears to be broader searching interests than with users of AlltheWeb.com. The frequency of the top occurring terms was much smaller. In other term usage statistics, AltaVista is similar to Excite. The most notable standout for Excite was the rapid increase in searching for information on people and things, along with the increase in commerce-related searching.

Generally, there are some common characteristics of searching on all three Web search engines, with some expected variations based on both particular Web search engine and date. Perhaps the most telling in this regard is the most frequently occurring terms. Of the 105 terms on the most frequently occurring lists from the three Web search engines, 58 terms (55%) appear on at lest two of lists. When combined with other evidence presented, such as term co-occurrence and topical classification, it appears Web searchers have some common topic interests that transcend particular Web search engines.

6. REFERENCES

Budzik, J., Hammond, K. and Birnbaum, L. (2001). Information Access in Context. *Knowledge Based Systems, 14*(1), 37–53.

Cole, J. I., Suman, M., Schramm, P., Lunn, R. and Aquino, J. S. (2003, February). *The UCLA Internet Report Surveying the Digital Future Year Three* [website]. UCLA Center for Communication Policy. Retrieved 1 February, 2003, from the World Wide Web: <http://www.ccp.ucla.edu/pdf/UCLA-Internet-Report-Year-Three.pdf>.

Dennis, S., Bruza, P. and McArthur, R. (2002). Web Searching: A Process-Oriented Experimental Study of Three Interactive Search Paradigms. *Journal of the American Society of Information Science and Technology, 53*(2), 120–133.

Fox, C. (1990). A Stop List for General Text. *ACM SIGIR Forum, 24*(2), 19–21.

Fox, S. (2002a, July). *Search Engines* [website]. The Pew Internet & American Life Project. Retrieved 15 October 2002, 2002, from the World Wide Web: <http://www.pewinternet. org/reports/toc.asp>.

Fox, S. (2002b, July). *Search Engines: A Pew Internet Project Data Memo* [website]. The Pew Internet & American Life Project. Retrieved 15 October, 2002, from the World Wide Web: <http://www.pewinternet.org/reports/toc.asp>.

Hsieh-Yee, I. (1993). Effects of Search Experience and Subject Knowledge on the Search Tactics of Novice and Experienced Searchers. *Journal of the American Society for Information Science and Technology, 44*(4), 161–174.

Iivonen, M. and Sonnenwald, D. H. (1998). From Translation to Navigation of Different Discourses: A Model of Search Term Selection During the Pre-Online Stage of the Search Process. *Journal of the American Society of Information Science and Technology, 49*(4), 312–326.

Jansen, B. J. (2003). Designing Automated Help Using Searcher System Dialogues. In *Proceedings of the 2003 IEEE International Conference on Systems, Man & Cybernetics*, pp. 10–16. Washington, D.C., USA. 5–8 October.

Lawrence, S. and Giles, C. L. (1999). Accessibility of Information on the Web. *Nature, 400*, 107–109.

Leydesdorff, L. (1989). Words and Co-Words as Indicators of Intellectual Organization. *Research Policy, 18*, 209–223.

National Telecommunications and Information Administration. (2002). *A Nation Online: How Americans Are Expanding Their Use of the Internet*. Washington, D.C.: U.S. Department of Commerce.

Ozmutlu, S., Ozmutlu, H. C. and Spink, A. (2004). Are People Asking Questions on General Web Search Engines? *Online Information Review, 6*, 396–406.

Peat, H. J. and Willett, P. (1991). The Limitations of Term Co-Occurrence Data for Query Expansion in Document Retrieval Systems. *Journal of the American Society for Information Science, 42*(5), 378–383.

Pu, H-T., Chuang, S-L., and Yang, C. (2002). Subject categorization of query terms for exploring Web users' search interests. *Journal of the American Society for Information Science and Technology, 53*(8), 617–630.

Schaale, A., Wulf-Mathies, C. and Lieberam-Schmidt, S. (2003). *A New Approach to Relevancy in Internet Searching – the "Vox Populi Algorithm"* (Computing Research Repository (CoRR)): Siegen University, Germany.

Silverstein, C., Henzinger, M., Marais, H. and Moricz, M. (1999). Analysis of a Very Large Web Search Engine Query Log. *SIGIR Forum, 33*(1), 6–12.

Spink, A. (1997). A Study of Interactive Feedback During Mediated Information Retrieval. *Journal of the American Society for Information Science, 48*(5), 382–394.

Spink, A., Jansen, B. J., Wolfram, D. and Saracevic, T. (2002). From E-Sex to E-Commerce: Web Search Changes. *IEEE Computer, 35*(3), 107–111.

Spink, A. and Ozmutlu, H. C. (2002). Characteristics of Question Format Web Queries: An Exploratory Study. *Information Processing and Management, 38*(4), 453–471.

Spink, A., Ozmutlu, S., Ozmutlu, H. C. and Jansen, B. J. (2002). U.S. Versus European Web Searching Trends. *SIGIR Forum, 32*(1), 30–37.

Spink, A. and Saracevic, T. (1997). Interaction in Information Retrieval: Selection and Effectiveness of Search Terms. *Journal of the American Society for Information Science, 48*(5), 382–394.

Spink, A., Wolfram, D., Jansen, B. J. and Saracevic, T. (2001). Searching of the Web: The Public and Their Queries. *Journal of the American Society of Information Science and Technology, 52*(3), 226–234.

WebMasterWorld.com. (2004). *Glossary: Filter Words* [Web site]. WebmasterWorld.com. Retrieved 14 January, 2004, from the World Wide Web: <http://www.webmasterworld.com/glossary/filter_words.htm>.

Wolfram, D. (1999). Term Co-Occurrence in Internet Search Engine Queries: An Analysis of the Excite Data Set. *Canadian Journal of Information and Library Science, 24*(2/3), 12–33.

Chapter 5

SEARCH QUERIES

1. INTRODUCTION

A Web query consists of one or more search terms. Queries are an integral component of Web searching and the expression of a searcher's information problem to the Web search engine. When using a Web search engine, a searcher usually has an information problem that drives their use of a Web search engine. The searcher must express this information problem to the Web search engines through queries. Web search must be entered in a form that is understandable by the Web search engine.

This chapter reports results from studies investigating the queries submitted by users to three major Web search engines – AlltheWeb.com, AltaVista and Excite. Major findings from the studies include: (1) the mean query length is slowly increasing, approaching three terms, (2) the use of query operators is about 10% of all Web queries, with the PHRASE operator being the most prevalent, (3) Web searchers generally view two or three documents per query, (4) the use of Web search engines as navigational short-cuts is increasing, (5) some searchers are conducting successive or longitudinal and multitasking searches over time, (6) users generally submit short queries (i.e., *cnn, yahoo!, or msn*), (7) Web search engines are being used to locate a broadening array of information, (8) there has been little increase in natural language querying, and (9) there are some common patterns of Web querying across Web search engines.

2.   WEB QUERYING

Web queries can take many forms. There are many query formulation techniques, and query structure is an extensively researched IR area. Most Web search engines use Boolean logic (i.e., the use of query operators such as AND, OR, NOT along with associated operators such as MUST APPEAR, MUST NOT APPEAR and PHRASE) in matching the user's query with Web content (Belew, 2001; Korfhage, 1997). Web search engines augmented these techniques with other methods such as anchor text and link analysis.

As with any methodology, these Web search engines do not perfectly match the query with Web documents (Frants, Shapiro, Taksa and Voiskunskii, 1999). The issue of correctly matching the Web query with Web content is one of the key elements in providing quality service for users of Web search engines. The study and analysis of Web queries is a critical issue in the development of better Web search engines and in understanding the people who use these systems.

Boolean logic is certainly not the only technique for matching queries and content. An alternate to Boolean systems is the vector space model. In the vector space model, vectors represent documents and usually queries. These vectors represent concepts such as preference, terms, and term co-occurrence. In response to a query, the system matches the query vector with document vectors, returning a set of documents within some threshold (Lesk, 1997; Salton and McGill, 1983). One can represent a query as a vector similar to a document vector. However in many ways, a query may be distinct from the documents that the user is trying to retrieve (Peter Bollmann-Sdorra, 1993). Some researchers have explored methods of combining Boolean and vectors models in the same system (Croft, 1986).

Some Web search services supplement query matching of the entire content collection with directory-based search (cf., Yahoo <http://www.yahoo.com> or Open Directory <http://dmoz.org/>). Although seemingly helpful, some research has shown that directory-based searching does not improve searching performance and also takes longer (Dennis, Bruza and McArthur, 2002). The idea behind directory services is that they provide some organization to the content. Variations of this idea are the many specialized or niche search engines that provide content within a specific search engines, including computer science literature (cf., CiteSeer <http://www.researchindex.com>), e-commerce (cf., Froogle <http:/froogle. google.com/>), or personal information (cf., <http://www.switchboard. com>). Some search engines providing clustering (cf., Vivisimo <http:// vivisimo.com/>), which one can view as an automated, real time, and virtual directory service.

3. WEB QUERY STRUCTURE

There has been much work on investigating ways of query structuring and some into the effect of various query structures. Lucas and Topi (2002) investigated the premise that queries will yield more relevant results if they contain multiple topic-related terms and use Boolean and phrase operators. In their experiment, the researchers showed that the difference in the number of terms, the percentage of matching terms between those searches, and the erroneous use of non-supported operators explain most of the variation in the relevancy of search results. Eastman and Jansen (2003) submitted over six hundred queries to three major Web search engines and examined nearly six thousand Web documents. The researchers found no significant different between queries with operators and queries without operators in metrics of coverage, relevance and ranking.

With the focus on the important of terms within queries, there has been much work into ways to expand the possible number of terms within the query. Crouch, Crouch, Chen and Holtz (2002) explore an automatic approach designed to improve the retrieval effectiveness of very short queries, and Alemayehu (2003) showed that query expansion improves document ranking. Others have explored ways to increase searcher awareness of how search engine reformulate queries (Muramatsu and Pratt, 2001) in the hopes of inducing the searcher to formulate better queries. In order to improve efficiency, some have explored clustering of query results (Wen, Nie and Zhang, 2001) based on transaction log data.

Given that queries and query formulation are so important in order for Web search engines to address users' information problems, this chapter reports results from major studies investigating how Web queries are structured, with a focus on the complexity of these queries. This important area of research can affect Web search engine design, Web site development, the structure of Web site, and production of online content. The results identify trends across three Web search engines – AlltheWeb.com, AltaVista, and Excite, including query length, query operator usage, and repeat queries.

4. WEB SEARCH ENGINE QUERY TRENDS

Examining query trends includes at least two key areas, use of query operators and query length. Based on use of advanced operators, the complexity of Web interaction appears to be remaining stable.

Figure 5.1 shows the results for query operator usage on the various Web search engines.

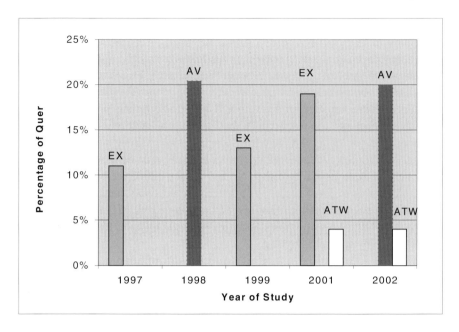

Figure 5-1. Percentage of Operator Usage

The usage of query operators appears to be Web search engine dependent. For the AltaVista Web search engine, the usage of query operators has held steady at approximately 20%. For the Excite Web search engine, the usage increased steadily from 1997 to 2001. The trend for United States based Web search engines appears to be one of increasing or at least stable usage.

For the European-based Web search engine, AlltheWeb.com, the usage has remained stable. However, the most notable feature of operator usage may be the rather large gap between usage on the AltaVista and Excite search engines compared to that of AlltheWeb.com. The usage of query operators on the AltaVista and Excite search engines varied from 11% to 20%. The usage on the AlltheWeb.com search engine held stable at under 5% from 1998 to 2001.

Figure 5.2 displays the results for the analysis of Web query lengths.

For AltaVista and Excite Web search engines, the percentage of one terms queries is holding steady, within a range of 20% to 29% of all queries. Using data from 1999 onward, the trend with these two Web search engines is of one term queries declining as a percentage of all queries, dropping from 30% to 20%. For AlltheWeb.com, there is a spike in 2002 with AlltheWeb.com users of about 9%. Overall, it appears that the complexity of Web searches is increasing slightly as indicated by longer queries.

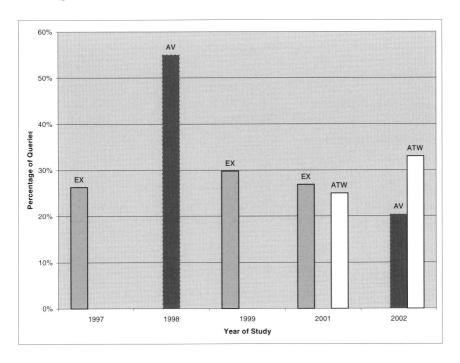

Figure 5-2. Percentage of One Term Queries

5. AGGREGATE DATA BY SEARCH ENGINE

The next section examines the Web queries submitted to each of the three search engines – AlltheWeb.com, AltaVista and Excite.

5.1 AlltheWeb.com

Table 5 presents the aggregate results for the AlltheWeb.com analysis.

The 2001 data set is about half the size of the 2002 data; however, both contain sizable number of queries. Based on mean terms and percentage of queries containing Boolean operators, there are similarities between the two data sets. There does appear to be a higher percentage of shorter queries in the 2002 data set.

Table 5-1. Comparative results for AlltheWeb.com data sets

	AlltheWeb.com 2001		AlltheWeb.com 2002	
Sessions	153,297		345,093	
Queries	451,551		957,303	
Terms	1,350,619		2,225,141	
Mean terms per query	2.4		2.3	
Terms per query				
1 term	113,447	25%	316,514	33%
2 terms	161,541	36%	312,498	33%
3+ terms	176,563	39%	328,291	34%
Boolean Queries	6,780	1.5%	9,461	1%

5.2   AltaVista

Table 5.2 presents the aggregate results for the AltaVista analysis in comparison with the results from an 1998 AltaVista analysis conducted by Silverstein, Henzinger, Marais and Moricz (1999).

Table 5-2. Aggregate Results for Data Analysis of 1998 and 2002 AltaVista Data Sets

	AltaVista 1998		AltaVista 2002	
Sessions	285,474,117		369,350	
Queries	993,208,159		1,073,388	
Terms			3,132,106	
Mean terms per query	2.35 (sd=1.74)		2.92 (sd=1.91)	
Terms per query				
1 term	39,640,423	25.8%	218,628	20.4%
2 terms	39,947,713	26.0%	330,875	30.8%
3+ terms	42,406,034	27.6%	523,885	48.5%
Boolean Queries and Other Operators	202,614,464	20.4%	191,171	27.6%

Notes: For the 1998 study, percentage and figures use the 575,244,993 non-empty queries.
The 1998 data from this and other tables is from or calculated from data reported in
    (Silverstein, Henzinger, Marais, and Moricz, 1999).

Overall, the data analysis shows a move toward greater complexity between the users and the Web search engine. The percentage of three-term queries increased from nearly 28% in 1998 to 49% in 2002. Overall usage of Boolean and other queries operators was similar with both at about 20%. It is difficult to determine the changes for just Boolean usage because the 1998 study combined Boolean and other operators, reporting an overall usage of

20%. In the 2002 study, the use of Boolean was at 6% (61,065 queries), which is comparable to findings reported by Spink, Jansen, Wolfram and Saracevic (2002). These results are higher than findings reported in searching on European Web search engines (Hölscher and Strube, 2000; Jansen and Spink, forthcoming).

5.3   Excite

Table 5.3 presents the aggregate results for the Excite analysis.

Table 5-3. Aggregate Results for Data Analysis of 1997, 1999, and 2001 Excite Data Sets

	Excite 1997		Excite 1999		Excite 2001	
Sessions	210,590		325,711		262,025	
Queries	545,206		1,025,910		1,025,910	
Mean terms per query	2.4 (sd= 1.61)		2.4 (sd= 1.56)		2.6 (sd=1.79)	
Terms per query						
1 term	145,125	26.62%	305,721	29.8%	275,970	26.9%
2 terms	174,248	31.96%	346,758	33.8%	312,903	30.5%
3+ terms	225,833	41.42%	373,431	36.4%	437,038	42.6%
Boolean Queries	51,295	5.0%	51,065	5.0%	72,250	7.0%

The percentage of three-term queries has remainder stable at approximately 40%. Overall usage of Boolean queries operators doubled but remained less than 10%, which is comparable to that of usage on AltaVista (Jansen, Spink and Saracevic, 2000; Silverstein, Henzinger, Marais and Moricz, 1999), substantially more than on AlltheWeb.com, and more than reported in studies of other Web search engines (Cacheda and Viña, 2001; Hölscher and Strube, 2000).

6.   ALLTHEWEB.COM IN-DEPTH ANALYSIS

6.1   Query Length

Table 5.4 shows the results from the query length analysis.

Query lengths of 1 through 3 terms inclusive account for 73% of all queries in 2001 and 84% of all queries in 2002. The percentage of queries with one term has increased by 11%. Beyond three terms, there is a sharp decline in the frequency of occurrences, dropping to almost minimal occurrences after four terms per query. These figures are similar to those reported by other researchers (Cacheda and Viña, 2001; Hölscher and Strube, 2000) analyzing other European Web search engines. However, this tendency with European Web searchers is counter to that reported from analysis of United States search engines (Spink, Jansen, Wolfram and Saracevic, 2002) where the mean query length is edging higher.

Table 5-4. AlltheWeb.com Query Lengths

Query Length	AlltheWeb.com 2001		AlltheWeb.com 2002	
	Occurrences	%	Occurrences	%
0	3,682	0.8%	2,905	0.3%
1	113,447	25.1%	316,514	33.1%
2	161,541	35.8%	312,498	32.6%
3	101,276	22.4%	181,270	18.9%
4	43,473	9.6%	78,162	8.2%
5	16,498	3.7%	32,233	3.4%
6	6,493	1.4%	13,287	1.3%
7	2,619	0.6%	6,286	0.7%
8	1,137	0.3%	8,225	0.9%
9	581	0.1%	1,812	0.2%
≥10	804	0.2%	4,111	0.4%
Total	451,551	100.00%	957,303	100.00%
Mean	2.4		2.3	

The next section examines how AlltheWeb.com searchers utilized advanced Web searching features.

6.2   Use of Advanced Web Search Features

Table 5.5 reports results from the analysis of the AlltheWeb.com 2002 data to determine the use of Web query operators.

Table 5.5 shows that Web query operator usage is low among AlltheWeb.com searchers. In some cases, it is so low to be almost non-existent. The use of the AND and MUST NOT APPEAR operator were the most used. However, many of these queries may actually be the use of *and* as a conjunction and the use of *or* within a phrase rather than as a MUST NOT appear operator. The low usage of Web query operators places even greater emphasis on the proper selection of query terms. The use of operators was also low in the examination of Fireball and BWIE queries (Cacheda and Viña, 2001; Hölscher and Strube, 2000).

Table 5-5. AlltheWeb.com Advanced Web Query Operator Usage

Query Operators	AlltheWeb.com 2001	AlltheWeb.com 2002
AND	6,532 (1.45%)	8,862 (0.93%)
OR	247 (0.05%)	568 (0.06%)
NOT	1 (~ 0%)	31 (~ 0%)
Total Boolean	6,780 (1.5%)	9,461(1.0%)
+	0 (0%)	0 (0%)
-	12,993 (2.9%)	34,485 (3.6%)
"	0 (0%)	0 (0%)
Total Operators	12,992 (2.9%)	34,485 (3.6%)
Total	19,772 (4.3%)	43,946 (4.6%)

In general, we see that that Web queries with operators are occurring infrequently.

Some researchers have focused on repeat queries or queries that occur frequently over multiple searches, primarily in an effort to enhance system performance and topic trends. In the Web system performance area, there has been extensive research into the caching of repeat queries in order to improve Web search engine performance in terms of response time (Lempel and Moran, 2003).

6.3   Repeat Web Queries

Table 5.6 presents the top occurring queries from the 2001 and 2002 AlltheWeb.com data sets.

The top ten queries were selected from the 2001 and 2002 query data sets. The list was then combined to report the number of occurrence for each Web query in each year. Only four Web queries appeared in both lists (*blank query, mp3, sex, and sexe*). What is surprising is the total of all of these Web queries represents less than 1% to 3% of all Web queries in any given year. If one does not include the *[Blank Query]*, the top Web queries account for approximately 1% or less of the total submitted Web queries in each year. These low occurrences raise questions concerning the feasibility of caching to improve Web search engine performance.

The next section examines the language specifications of AlltheWeb.com searchers.

Table 5-6. AlltheWeb.com Top Occurring Queries

	Top Queries	AlltheWeb.com 2001		AlltheWeb.com 2002	
	Total	7,461	1.66%	5,775	0.60%
1	[Blank query]	3,682	0.82%	2,905	0.30%
2	sex	819	0.18%	340	0.04%
3	mp3	405	0.09%	194	0.02%
4	anal sex	341	0.08%	–	0.00%
5	google	362	0.08%	125	0.01%
6	lolita	351	0.08%	104	0.01%
7	porn	290	0.06%	90	0.01%
8	sexe	275	0.06%	251	0.03%
9	warez	280	0.06%	149	0.02%
10	porno	225	0.05%	178	0.02%
11	yahoo	248	0.05%	358	0.04%
12	teen	161	0.04%	249	0.03%
13	hotmail	22	~0.00%	214	0.02%
14	caramail	–	0.00%	227	0.02%
15	dictionary	–	0.00%	168	0.02%
16	lycos	–	0.00%	223	0.02%

Note: – means this query did not occur.

6.4   Language Preference

There has been extensive research into multi-lingual translation of Web documents (Ballesteros and Croft, 1998), cross-lingual retrieval (Maeda, Sadat, Yoshikawa, and Uemura, 2000), and the language of content on the Web (Pastore, 2000). However, there has been limited study of the language preferences of Web searchers.

The AlltheWeb.com search engine has a drop box tool where the searcher can narrow the search to documents of a particular language. The AlltheWeb.com 2002 data was analyzed to determined language preferences of the users for Web documents, with results reported in Table 5.7. The language preferences were not available for the 2001 dataset.

This transaction log captured the language that the searcher requested as the preferred language of the Web content retrieved. Table 5.7 shows that these Web users appear not to be concerned with specifying the language of the Web documents they retrieve, with the vast majority of searchers accepting the AlltheWeb.com default of *ANY*. The use of the particular query terms themselves itself may provide the needed selectivity for most Web users (i.e., the use of a query containing terms in Russian, for example, will retrieve primarily Web documents written in Russian).

Table 5-7. AlltheWeb.com Terms, Queries and Sessions Analysis by Language

Language	Queries	Mean Terms Per Query	Sessions	Mean Queries Per Session	Total Terms
Entire Data Set	957,303	2.3	345,093	2.8	2,225,141
Default [1]	874,168	2.3	313,987	2.8	2,025,072
French	53,047	2.3	33,959	1.6	119,511
Spanish	13,293	2.6	8,455	1.6	34,352
German	8,650	1.9	5,765	1.5	16,721
Italian	4,839	2.3	3,386	1.4	11,310
Russian	1,337	9.5	1,124	1.2	12,671
English	526	5.0	194	2.7	2,620
Japanese	499	3.1	292	1.7	1,523
Portuguese	443	2.3	338	1.3	1,026
Polish	161	1.7	5	32.2	276
Afrikaans	70	1.5	45	1.6	106
Dutch	67	1.7	8	10.2	116
Swedish	40	1.9	6	6.7	77
Danish	24	1.2	6	4.0	28
Turkish	19	1.7	12	1.6	33
Catalan	15	1.7	14	1.1	26
Arabic	7	9.1	7	1.0	64
Norwegian	6	1.5	6	1.0	9
Portugal	4	4.3	1	4.0	17
Hebrew	3	3.0	1	3.0	9
Korean	2	2.5	2	1.0	5
Albanian	2	1.5	1	2.0	3
Ukrainian	1	2.0	1	1.0	2
Greek	1	2.0	1	1.0	2
Latin [2]	1	0.0	1	1.0	–
Basque [2]	1	0.0	1	1.0	–
Other [3]	77	–	–	–	–

1. The default language selection is ANY.
2. The queries were blank.
3. Non-language options such as Domain and All.

The majority of AlltheWeb.com customers are German (Spink, Ozmutlu, Ozmutlu and Jansen, 2002). However, the top non-English language preferences are French, followed by Spanish, with German at a distance third. Italian and Russian also had high rates of occurrences. There was little difference in the mean query length among the languages, with the notable exceptions of Russian and Arabic.

6.5   Web Documents Viewed Per Query

For those who market information, services or products online, Web site traffic is a critical component of the business. The AlltheWeb.com 2001 query data set captures this information, known as click through data.

Table 5.8 shows how many documents that searchers view per Web query.

Table 5-8. Results Viewed per AlltheWeb.com Query

Results Viewed	Occurrences	%
1	274,644	54.3%
2	95,532	18.9%
3	47,770	9.4%
4	27,625	5.5%
5	16,800	3.3%
6	11,024	2.2%
7	7,653	1.5%
8	5,231	1.0%
9	3,802	0.8%
10	2,975	0.6%
> 10	12,498	2.5%
	505,554	100.00%

The 153,297 AlltheWeb.com searchers viewed 505,554 Web documents. The mean documents viewed per query were 2.5, with a standard deviation of 3.9 documents. AlltheWeb.com users viewed five or less Web documents per query over 90% of time. The largest percentage of users by far viewed only one document per query (approximately 55% of queries).

7.   ALTAVISTA IN-DEPTH ANALYSIS

7.1   Web Query Length

Table 5.9 shows that AltaVista queries composed of one to three terms account for 67% of all queries in 1998 (Silverstein, Henzinger, Marais and Moricz, 1999) and 73% of all queries in 2002.

Table 5-9. Query Lengths for AltaVista

Query Length	AltaVista 1998		AltaVista 2002	
	Occurrences	%	Occurrences	%
0	31,650,880	20.6%	301	~0%
1	39,640,423	25.8%	218,628	20.4%
2	39,947,713	26.0%	330,875	30.8%
3	23,046,758	15.0%	244,777	22.8%
4	19,359,276 *	12.6%	128,485	12.0%
5			63,025	5.9%
6			27,125	2.5%
7			12,432	1.2%
8			5,636	0.5%
9			37,487	3.5%
≥10			4,617	0.4%
			1,073,388	100%

Notes: For the 1998 figure, calculated based on 153,645,993 distinct queries only.
Number and percentages are for queries of 4 and more terms.

Table 5.9 shows that the percentage of one-term queries decreased by 5% during the same period. Beyond three terms, there is a sharp decline in the frequency of occurrences, dropping to a minimal percentage after five terms per query. The number of one-term queries is notably lower than has been reported elsewhere (Cacheda and Viña, 2001; Spink, Ozmutlu, Ozmutlu and Jansen, 2002). In other published temporal analyses of United States-based Web search engines (Spink, Jansen, Wolfram and Saracevic, 2002), Web query length is also moving slowly upwards.

7.2   Use of Advanced Web Search Features

Table 5.10 shows the 2002 data to determine the use of Web query operators.

Table 5.10 shows that Boolean Web query operator usage is low among AltaVista searchers when compared to usage among users on traditional IR systems (Siegfried, Bates and Wilde, 1993). However, the use of all Web operators is notable, at over 27%. This percentage is probably a little high, given that all the uses of *and* and the symbol '–' may not be intended as Boolean or Web query operators. The usage is notably higher than that of AlltheWeb.com users. The use of the PHRASE operator is by far the most common, at over 12% of the queries. Again, the low usage of Web query operators places even greater emphasis on the proper selection of Web query terms. The total percentage of Web operators is high, but over 50% of this usage is the PHRASE operator.

Table 5-10. AltaVista Advance Query Operator Usage

Query Operators	AltaVista 2002
AND	29,732 (2.8%)
OR	20,652 (1.9%)
NOT	200 (0.02%)
Total Boolean	50,584 (4.72%)
+	8,221 (0.8%)
-	1,979 (0.2%)
"	130,387 (12.1%)
Total Operators	140,587 (22.54%)
Total	191,171 (27.26%)

7.3   Repeat Web Queries

Table 5.11 displays the top occurring queries in the two AltaVista query data sets.

Table 5.11 shows that only four Web queries in the top twenty-five in both 1998 and 2002 (*yahoo*, *hotmail*, *porn*, and *sex*). The percentages of the top ten Web queries in 2002 were approximately half of the corresponding percentages in 1998. This would be an indication of a broadening of information problems, which confirms findings from previous studies (Jansen and Spink, Forthcoming; Spink, Jansen, Wolfram, and Saracevic, 2002).

The analysis shows a decrease in sexual Web queries from 1998 to 2002 and an increase in general entertainment and alternate information sources during the same period. The decrease in sexual searching parallels the increase of non-sexual content on the Web (Lawrence and Giles, 1999). Of course, other factors may be influencing this trend including other methods of locating online sexual material (Fox, 2002). The trend to locate other information sources may relate to the move to increased e-commerce searching (Jansen and Spink, Forthcoming; Spink, Jansen, Wolfram, and Saracevic, 2002), as searchers locate product and location information.

There also appears to be an increased use of Web search engines not to search for information but instead as a short cut for navigation. Some Web users appear to be submitting the name of a particular Web site to the search engine and just clicking on the uniform resource locator (URL) in the results page rather than type the URL in the address box of the browser or locate a bookmark, favorite, or short cut. If the Web page's URL appears in the search engine's first page of results, this method many times requires less effort than other methods of accessing a particular URL.

Table 5-11. Top 25 Queries with Frequency of Occurrence and Percentage of Queries

AltaVista 1998			AltaVista 2002		
Query	Occurrences	%	Query	Occurrences	%
sex	1,551,477	0.27%	google	837	0.09%
applet	1,169,031	0.20%	yahoo	727	0.08%
porno	712,790	0.12%	ebay	720	0.08%
mp3	613,902	0.11%	sex	412	0.05%
chat	406,014	0.07%	yahoo.com	395	0.04%
warez	398,953	0.07%	dictionary	374	0.04%
yahoo	377,025	0.07%	hotmail	336	0.04%
playboy	356,556	0.06%	translator	324	0.04%
xxx	324,923	0.06%	hotmail.com	308	0.03%
hotmail	321,267	0.05%	thumbzilla	306	0.03%
(non-ASCII query)	263,760	0.05%	www.yahoo.com	305	0.03%
pamela anderson	256,559	0.04%	lyrics	278	0.03%
p****	234,037	0.04%	maps	276	0.03%
sex	226,705	0.04%	babelfish	267	0.03%
porn	212,161	0.04%	mapquest	264	0.03%
nude	190,641	0.03%	porn	260	0.03%
lolita	179,629	0.03%	kazaa	241	0.03%
games	166,781	0.03%	translate	238	0.03%
spice girls	162,272	0.03%	nfl.com	234	0.03%
beastiality	152,143	0.03%	literotica	232	0.03%
animal sex	150,786	0.03%	nfl	226	0.03%
SEX	150,699	0.03%	weather	219	0.02%
gay	142,761	0.02%	search engines	213	0.02%
titanic	140,963	0.02%	www.hotmail.com	211	0.02%
bestiality	136,578	0.02%	google.com	210	0.02%
	8,998,413	1.56%		8,413	0.93%

In the 2002 data set, there are arguably twelve top Web queries (i.e., *google, yahoo, ebay, yahoo.com, hotmail, hotmail.com, www.yahoo.com, babelfish, mapquest, nfl.com, www.hotmail.com, google.com*) that are very likely the result of using the search engine as a navigation tool. This Web search engine usage appears only three times in the 1998 data set (i.e., *warez, yahoo, hotmail*). This interesting change in usage of search engines may skew our comparison of Web search topics.

The queries that appeared to be navigation-related were removed in order to arrive at the twenty-five top Web searching queries. Eleven Web queries identified and removed, and we added the next eleven most frequent Web queries. Of these, five were most likely navigation queries (i.e., *espn, AskJeeves, MSN, richard realms, sublime directory*). The sites *richard realms* and *sublime directory* are popular pornography sites. These queries were removed these from the list, and we added five more Web queries. This process was repeated until twenty Web queries remained that were reasonably not navigation queries. During the process, four more navigation queries were eliminated (i.e., *www.google.com*, *warez*, *babel fish*, *voyeurweb*).

Table 5.12 shows the top 25 Web queries submitted to AltaVista.

Table 5-12. Top 25 Queries from AltaVista Data Sets with Frequency of Occurrence and Percentage of Queries (Navigation Queries Removed from 2002 Data Set)

AltaVista 1998			AltaVista 2002		
Query	Occurrences	%	Query	Occurrences	%
sex	1,551,477	0.27%	sex	412	0.05%
applet	1,169,031	0.20%	dictionary	374	0.04%
porno	712,790	0.12%	thumbzilla	306	0.03%
mp3	613,902	0.11%	lyrics	278	0.03%
chat	406,014	0.07%	maps	276	0.03%
warez	398,953	0.07%	porn	260	0.03%
yahoo	377,025	0.07%	kazaa	241	0.03%
playboy	356,556	0.06%	translate	238	0.03%
xxx	324,923	0.06%	literotica	232	0.03%
hotmail	321,267	0.05%	nfl	226	0.03%
(non-ASCII query)	263,760	0.05%	weather	219	0.02%
pamela anderson	256,559	0.04%	search engines	213	0.02%
p****	234,037	0.04%	florida lottery	195	0.02%
sex	226,705	0.04%	white pages	193	0.02%
porn	212,161	0.04%	free porn	189	0.02%
nude	190,641	0.03%	games	187	0.02%
lolita	179,629	0.03%	music	176	0.02%
games	166,781	0.03%	mp3	175	0.02%
spice girls	162,272	0.03%	Internet Explorer	170	0.02%
beastiality	152,143	0.03%	quotes	151	0.02%
animal sex	150,786	0.03%	home depot	140	0.02%
SEX	150,699	0.03%	sex stories	138	0.02%
gay	142,761	0.02%	wallpaper	137	0.02%
titanic	140,963	0.02%	September 11	135	0.02%
bestiality	136,578	0.02%	erotic stories	135	0.02%
	8,998,413	1.56%		5,396	0.63%

Table 5.12 shows that the broadening of Web search topics is even more apparent with the percentages of the top ten Web queries in 2002 compared with the corresponding percentages in 1998. There are six sexual terms in 2002 (i.e., *sex, porn, literotica, free porn, sex stories, erotic stories*) compared to thirteen in 1998 (i.e., *sex, porno, playboy, xxx, p*****, SEX, porn, nude, lolita, beastiality, SEX, bestiality*). The remaining terms appear to be for a variety of information and commerce content. Certainly, some of the remaining queries, one could argue, may also be navigation queries.

8.   EXCITE IN-DEPTH ANALYSIS

8.1   Web Query Length

Table 5.13 shows the Excite Web query length results.

Table 5-13. Web Query Length for 1997, 1999, and 2001 Excite Data Sets

Query Length	Excite 1997		Excite 1999		Excite 2001	
	Occurrences	%	Occurrences	%	Occurrences	%
0	39,383	7.2%	101	0.01%	93	0.01%
1	145,125	26.6%	291,062	28.37%	256,535	25.01%
2	174,248	32.0%	357,897	34.89%	324,993	31.68%
3	101,755	18.7%	210,723	20.54%	234,034	22.81%
4	44,754	8.2%	84,891	8.27%	90,653	8.84%
5	20,813	3.8%	42,878	4.18%	65,130	6.35%
6	8,771	1.6%	15,248	1.49%	17,262	1.68%
7	4,651	0.9%	10,790	1.05%	19,647	1.92%
8	2,176	0.4%	3,928	0.38%	3,780	0.37%
9	1,355	0.2%	3,522	0.34%	7,069	0.69%
≥10	2,175	0.4%	4,869	0.47%	6,674	0.7%
	545,206	100.00%	1,025,909	100.00%	1,025,870	100.00%

Table 5.13 shows a small increase in Excite Web query length. The percentage of one-term Web queries has dropped approximately 5%. The use of one- or two-term queries is quite high at more than 55% in 2001. After three terms, there is a sharp decline in the frequency of occurrences, dropping to a minimal percentage after five terms per query. The number of one-term Web queries is about 5% higher compared to that of AltaVista and about 5% lower than AlltheWeb.com.

8.2   Use of Advanced Search Features

Table 5.14 presents the results from the analysis of the 2002 data to determine the use of Web query operators.

Table 5.14 shows that less than 7% of all queries used any Boolean operators; however, the usage of Boolean operators is trending up. Of these, AND was used most, although some or all of these may be the use of *and* as a conjunction rather than as a Boolean operator. A much smaller percentage of Web queries used OR and a minuscule percentage AND NOT. The MUST APPEAR and MUST NOT APPEAR operators were used less than 5%.

The use of the PHRASE operator remained consistent over the three data collection periods. Many Web queries incorporated query operators that Excite does not support. These failures may be carry-over from experiences with other Web search engines, on-line public access catalogs, and IR systems. For example, there were 914 occurrences of the operator SEARCH and 1,459 uses of the symbol ":" (colon) as a separator for terms. The symbol "." (period) was used 51,804 times, either as a separator or as a part of URL and email addresses. Web searchers used the symbol "&" in lieu of the Boolean AND 3,342 times. These symbols are common to some other IR systems.

Table 5-14. Advanced Query Operator Usage for 1997, 1999, and 2001 Excite Data Sets

Query Operators	Excite 1997	Excite 1999	Excite 2001
AND	29,146 (2.8%)	48,413 (4.7%)	71,056 (6.9%)
OR	1,149 (0.1%)	2,550 (0.2%)	1,096 (0.1%)
NOT	307 (~ 0%)	102 (~ 0%)	98 (~ 0%)
Total Boolean	30,602 (2.90%)	51,065 (4.90%)	72,250 (7.00%)
+	44,320 (4.3%)	39,178 (3.8%)	29,945 (2.9%)
-	21,951 (2.1%)	23,008 (2.2%)	14,433 (1.4%)
"	52,354 (5.1%)	74,047 (5.9%)	60,659 (5.9%)
Total Operators	66,271 (6.40%)	62,186 (6.00%)	44,378 (4.30%)
Total	96,873 (9.30%)	113,251 (10.90%)	116,628 (11.30%)

8.3   Repeat Web Queries

Table 5.15 displays the top occurring queries in the three Excite query data sets.

The top ten Web queries from the 1997, 1997, and 2001 data sets were identified. The combined list shows the number of occurrences for each Web query in each year. The twenty-three resulting Web queries represent approximately 1% or less of the total Web queries from each, a very small percentage. The trend of broadening information topics appears with a steady decline in the representation of the top Web query as a total percentage of all Web queries. By 2001, the top Web query represents approximately 0.14% of the total Web queries, down from 0.45% in 1998. There are six Web queries that appear in at least two of the years (*chat, games, horoscopes, hotmail, maps, porn*) and two Web queries that appear in all three years (*sex, yahoo*).

The top queries were classified into categories – locations (*las vegas, miami*), celebrities (*britney spears, princess diana*), sex (*sex, porn, xxx,* p****, *porno, playboys, beastiality*), Web sites (*yahoo, hotmail, ebay*), information sources (*maps, games, horoscopes, weather*), popular items (*pokemon, casino*) and Web tools (*chat, chat rooms*). The results do not show much use of the Excite Web search engine as a navigation aid, relative to the AltaVista analysis. It is interesting, even with these snap shots, to plot the rise of (e.g., *britney spears*), fall of (e.g., *playboy*), and, in some cases, the rise and fall of (e.g., *pokemon*) interest in certain Web searching topics.

Table 5-15. Top Web Queries for 1997, 1999, and 2001 Excite Data Sets

	Query	Excite 1997		Excite 1999		Excite 2001	
1	yahoo	1,137	0.11%	1,892	0.18%	1,401	0.14%
2	sex	**4,632**	**0.45%**	**2,636**	**0.26%**	1,118	0.11%
3	las vegas	159	0.02%	152	0.01%	1,003	0.10%
4	hotmail	477	0.05%	724	0.07%	922	0.09%
5	ebay	18	~ 0.0%	552	0.05%	665	0.06%
6	maps	376	0.04%	735	0.07%	656	0.06%
7	games	440	0.04%	684	0.07%	618	0.06%
8	horoscopes	343	0.03%	974	0.09%	609	0.06%
9	miami	10	~ 0.0%	36	~ 0.0%	594	0.06%
10	casino	63	0.01%	40	~ 0.0%	586	0.06%
11	porn	999	0.10%	771	0.08%	514	0.05%
12	weather	333	0.03%	740	0.07%	455	0.04%
13	chat	1,099	0.11%	814	0.08%	349	0.03%
14	xxx	844	0.08%	485	0.05%	342	0.03%
15	britney spears	–		692	0.07%	307	0.03%
16	p****	681	0.07%	443	0.04%	295	0.03%
18	porno	862	0.08%	388	0.04%	287	0.03%
19	playboy	1,083	0.11%	358	0.03%	252	0.02%
20	beastiality	759	0.07%	203	0.02%	147	0.01%
21	chat rooms	645	0.06%	235	0.02%	105	0.01%
22	pokemon	–		767	0.07%	61	0.01%
23	princess diana	694	0.07%	11	~ 0.0%	59	0.01%
	Total	17,665	0.79%	16,345	0.57%	13,360	1.10%

(1) – means this query did not occur.
(2) p**** – expletive.
(3) The number one occurring query is in bold in the 1997 and 1999 columns.

9.   NATURAL LANGUAGE WEB QUERIES

Large-scale studies of Web searching show that most Web users enter few queries consisting of few search terms, conduct little query reformulation and have difficulty developing effective keyword or Boolean queries (Silverstein, Henzinger, Marais and Moricz, 1999; Spink, Jansen, Wolfram and Saracevic, 2002). Web search services such as AskJeeves – publicly accessible question and answer (Q&A) search engines – encourage queries in question or request format. A growing body of studies is investigating queries in question and request format.

Jansen, Spink, Pfaff and Goodrum (2000) conducted a linguistic analysis of Excite users' queries contained in a 1997 data set and identified less than 1% of queries in elicitation format or requests for information. However, with the emergence of a more question and answer (Q&A) approach to Web querying, the nature of users' queries in question format are becoming important and significant to the development of more effective Web IR systems.

Spink, Milchak, Sollenberger and Hurson (2000) found a low use of elicitation queries by Excite users. Spink and Ozmutlu (2002) compared Excite and AskJeeves Web question queries in 1999. They found that Web search engine users generally enter four types of queries: keyword, Boolean, question, and request. Most Web question format queries are about 7 terms in length, and non-question/request queries are less that 5 terms long, and contain few Boolean operators or modifiers. When users expressed themselves in the form of questions they generally asked either "where", "what", or "how" questions. The most common form of question format query begins with the words "Where can I find ..." for general information on a topic.

Less frequently do users ask "which", "when", or "does" questions. Users are sometimes likely to ask for subjective opinion and more likely to request directions to information. The most common form of request format query was "Find me information on ...". There was little query reformulation by Excite during question query sessions. Most users entered only one question format query and then examined the results.

Ozmutlu, Ozmutlu and Spink (2004) studied queries to the Excite and AlltheWeb.com Web search engines and show that few users submit more complex queries in question or request format to general Web search engines. Results also suggest that: (1) Excite users formed longer question and request format queries than AlltheWeb.com users, (2) request and question format queries occurred in shorter sessions than general query sessions, (3) a range of question formats is occurring, and (4) there is a shift from "where" to "what" questions.

Overall, various studies show little movement to more natural language querying by general Web search engine users. However, there seem to be some common patterns of Web question and request format query structure, although a small proportion of Web search engine users still prefers to use question or request format. Further research is needed to relate question and request Web query construction to users' gender, communication style, or interaction style, and to examine why some users generate natural language queries.

10.   CONCLUSION

The results reported in this chapter show certain similarities among the users of all three Web search engines. However, there are also some Web search engine dependences. Generally, Web query complexity, as measured by query length and use of query operators, appears to be increasing. At the very least, it is holding steady and not decreasing.

Mean query length on the AlltheWeb.com search engine is about 2.4 terms per query. For the AltaVista search engine, the mean query length increases about 0.5 terms from 1998 to 2002 (i.e., from 2.3 to 2.9 terms). Mean query length also increased on Excite to over 2.5 terms per query. Generally, from this data, one could say the average query length appears to be increasing, albeit slowly.

Query operator usage was almost non-existent on AlltheWeb.com, with usage well under 5%. For the AltaVista Web search engine, the usage of query operators has held steady at approximately 20%. However, the use of the PHRASE operator accounts for over 50% of query operator usage, with the AND operator coming in a distant second. For the Excite Web search engine, the usage increased steadily from 1997 to 2001, at about 11% for both Boolean and other operators. Similar to AltaVista, the PHRASE and the AND operators accounted for most of the total query operator usage.

From analysis of AlltheWeb.com data, users are usually unconcerned about specifying the language of the Web document. This is not to say they are unconcerned about the language, but, rather, they may have other means of addressing this concern than specifying it to the Web search engine. We also know from the analysis of AlltheWeb.com data that users view about 2 to 3 documents per query. This information, combined with the information on query lengths and query operator usage, indicates that the interactions between searcher and search engine are still simple relative to searching more traditional IR systems. However, these interactions are trending toward more complexity.

11. REFERENCES

Alemayehu, N. (2003). Analysis of Performance Variation Using Query Expansion. *Journal of the American Society for Information Science and Technology, 54*(5), 379–391.

Ballesteros, L. and Croft, W. B. (1998). Resolving Ambiguity for Cross-Language Retrieval. In *Proceedings of the 21st Annual International ACM SIGIR Conference on Research and Development in Information Retrieval,* pp. 64–71. Melbourne, Australia. 24–28 August.

Belew, R. K. (2001). *Finding Out About: A Cognitive Perspective on Search Engine Technology and the Www.* New York: Cambridge University Press.

Cacheda, F. and Viña, Á. (2001). Experiences Retrieving Information in the World Wide Web. In *Proceedings of the 6th IEEE Symposium on Computers and Communications,* pp. 72–79. Hammamet, Tunisia. July.

Croft, W. B. (1986). Boolean Queries and Term Dependencies in Probabilistic Retrieval Models. *Journal of the American Society for Information Science, 37*(2), 71–77.

Crouch, C. J., Crouch, D. B., Chen, Q. and Holtz, S. J. (2002). Improving the Retrieval Effectiveness of Very Short Queries. *Information Processing & Management, 38*(1), 1–36.

Dennis, S., Bruza, P. and McArthur, R. (2002). Web Searching: A Process-Oriented Experimental Study of Three Interactive Search Paradigms. *Journal of the American Society for Information Science and Technology, 53*(2), 120–133.

Eastman, C. M. and Jansen, B. J. (2003). Coverage, Ranking, and Relevance: A Study of the Impact of Query Operators on Search Engine Results. *ACM Transactions on Information Systems, 21*(4), 383–411.

Fox, S. (2002, July). *Search Engines: A Pew Internet Project Data Memo* [website]. The Pew Internet & American Life Project. Retrieved 15 October, 2002, from the World Wide Web: http://www.pewinternet.org/reports/toc.asp.

Frants, V. I., Shapiro, J., Taksa, I. and Voiskunskii, V. G. (1999). Boolean Search: Current State and Perspectives. *Journal of the American Society for Information Science, 50*(1), 86–95.

Hölscher, C. and Strube, G. (2000). Web Search Behavior of Internet Experts and Newbies. *International Journal of Computer and Telecommunications Networking, 33*(1–6), 337–346.

Jansen, B. J. and Spink, A. (Forthcoming). An Analysis of Web Searching by European Alltheweb.Com Users. *Information Processing and Management.*

Jansen, B. J., Spink, A., Pfaff, A. and Goodrum, A. (2000). Web Query Structure: Implications for IR System Design. In *Proceedings of the 4th World Multi-Conference on Systematics, Cybernetics and Informatics (SCI'2000),* pp. 169–176. Orlando, FL. July 23–26.

Jansen, B. J., Spink, A. and Saracevic, T. (2000). Real Life, Real Users, and Real Needs: A Study and Analysis of User Queries on the Web. *Information Processing and Management, 36*(2), 207–227.

Korfhage, R. (1997). *Information Storage and Retrieval.* New York, NY: Wiley.

Lawrence, S. and Giles, C. L. (1999). Accessibility of Information on the Web. *Nature, 400,* 107–109.

Lempel, R. and Moran, S. (2003). Predictive Caching and Prefetching of Query Results in Search Engines. In *Proceedings of the 11th World Wide Web Conference,* pp. 19–28. Budapest, Hungary. 20–24 May.

Lesk, M. (1997). *Practical Digital Libraries: Books, Bytes, and Bucks.* San Francisco, CA, USA: Morgan Kaufmann.

Lucas, W. and Topi, H. (2002). Form and Function: The Impact of Query Term and Operator Usage on Web Search Results. *Journal of the American Society for Information Science and Technology, 53*(2), 95–108.

Maeda, A., Sadat, F., Yoshikawa, M. and Uemura, S. (2000). Query Term Disambiguation for Web Cross-Language Information Retrieval Using a Search Engine. In *Proceedings of the 5th International Workshop on Information Retrieval with Asian Languages*, (pp. 25–32). Hong Kong, China. 30 September–01 October.

Muramatsu, J. and Pratt, W. (2001). Transparent Queries: Investigation Users' Mental Models of Search Engines. In *Proceedings of the 24th Annual International ACM SIGIR Conference on Research and Development in Information Retrieval*, pp. 217–224. New Orleans, Louisiana, United States.

Ozmutlu, S., Ozmutlu, H. C. and Spink, A. (2004). Are People Asking Questions on General Web Search Engines? *Online Information Review, 6*, 396–406.

Pastore, M. (2000, 5 July). *Web Pages by Language* [Wen site]. CyberAtlas. Retrieved 26 November, 2003, from the World Wide Web: <http://cyberatlas.internet.com/big_picture/demographics/article/0,1323,5901_408521,00.html>

Peter Bollmann-Sdorra, V. V. R. (1993). On the Delusiveness of Adopting a Common Space for Modeling IR Objects: Are Queries Documents? *Journal of the American Society for Information Science, 44*(10), 579–587.

Salton, G., and McGill, M. J. (1983). *Introduction to Modern Information Retrieval*. New York: McGraw-Hill.

Siegfried, S., Bates, M. and Wilde, D. (1993). A Profile of End-User Searching Behavior by Humanities Scholars: The Getty Online Searching Project Report No. 2. *Journal of the American Society for Information Science, 44*(5), 273–291.

Silverstein, C., Henzinger, M., Marais, H. and Moricz, M. (1999). Analysis of a Very Large Web Search Engine Query Log. *SIGIR Forum, 33*(1), 6–12.

Spink, A., Jansen, B. J., Wolfram, D. and Saracevic, T. (2002). From E-Sex to E-Commerce: Web Search Changes. *IEEE Computer, 35*(3), 107–111.

Spink, A., Milchak, S., Sollenberger, M. and Hurson, A. R. (2000). Elicitations Queries to the Excite Web Search Engine. In *Proceedings of the 2000 ACM CIKM International Conference on Information and Knowledge Management*, pp. 134–140. McLean, VA, USA. 6–11 November.

Spink, A. and Ozmutlu, H. C. (2002). Characteristics of Question Format Web Queries: An Exploratory Study. *Information Processing and Management, 38*(4), 453–471.

Spink, A., Ozmutlu, S., Ozmutlu, H. C. .and Jansen, B. J. (2002). U.S. Versus European Web Searching Trends. *SIGIR Forum, 32*(1), 30–37.

Wen, J.-R., Nie, J.-Y. and Zhang, H.-J. (2001). Clustering User Queries of a Search Engine. In *Proceedings of the 10th International Conference on World Wide Web table of contents*, pp. 162–168. Hong Kong.

Chapter 6

SEARCH SESSIONS

1.   INTRODUCTION

Terms are the building blocks of Web queries and queries are the building blocks of Web search sessions. One can view a user session on a Web search engine as the series of interactions between a searcher and a Web system within a specific period (Wong, 2002). During a Web search session, the user may submit a query, view result pages, click on URLs, view Web documents, and return to the Web search engine for query reformulation. With traditional information retrieval (IR) systems, one could usually distinguish one user from another on the basis of a logon. Although much research has been at the term and query level, one can view success or failure at the session level as the critical determinant in the user's perception of the Web search engine.

This chapter presents results from a transaction log analysis of large-scale query data from AlltheWeb.com, AltaVista, AskJeeves, and Excite. Major findings include: (1) the number of queries per Web search session is increasing, (2) Web search engine users are viewing fewer results pages per sessions, (3) the majority of Web sessions are less than 15 minutes in duration, (4) average searchers view about five documents per session spending four minutes or less per document, (5) most question answering sessions contain queries of the form "where", (6) agent sessions contain very simple queries and multiple interactions per second, and (7) longer and more complex multitasking sessions often include three or more topics per session.

2.   WEB SEARCH SESSIONS

On the Web, there are questions about how to exactly to define a search session given the stateless nature of the client–server relationship. With referral sites, Internet service providers (ISP), dynamic Internet Protocol (IP) addressing, and common user terminals it is not always easy to identify a single user session on a Web search engine. Most Web search engines servers have used the IP address of the client machine using a temporal cut to identify unique visitors. A single IP address does not always correspond to a single user, naturally. In response to the move to dynamically allocated IPs, Web search engines have moved to cookies for user identification. This minimizes the problem somewhat, but with common access computers (i.e., computers at libraries, schools, labs, office shops, manufacturing floors which many people share), one computer still does not correspond to one searcher.

Web search engines use a more mechanical definition of a session rather than a conceptual definition that defines a searching session with an information seeking task. He, Göker and Harper (2002) used contextual information from transaction logs and a version of the Dempster–Shafer theory to identify search engine sessions. Using transaction log IP codes and query context, the researchers determined that the average Web user session duration was about 12 minutes. However, within a single Web session, the searcher may be engaged in multitasking searching tasks (Spink, Ozmutlu and Ozmutlu, 2002) or multiple (successive) sessions over time related to the same topic (Spink, Bateman and Jansen, 1998; Spink, Wilson, Ford, Foster and Ellis, 2002).

Regardless of the method that one arrives at a definition, the goal for the user during a Web session is to locate relevant information. Many researchers have studied Web searching sessions hoping to use information about users' searching and navigation activities to improve the performance of Web search engines. Shneiderman, Byrd and Croft (1998) present recommendations for designing interfaces to Web search engines that support the searching session strategies of searchers. Hansen and Shriver (2001) used this approach to cluster search sessions and identify highly relevant Web documents for each query cluster.

Attempts at designing such personalized Web systems have taken a variety of approaches. Using the agent paradigm, researchers have developed browsing systems for Web searching, including Alexa (Kahle, 1999) and Letizia (Lieberman, 1995). There are commercial client-side applications in the searching assistance area that offer a range of searching assistance, such as Copernic (2003) and Bullseye (2000).

Other attempts use a server-side approach. ResearchIndex (Lawrence, Giles and Bollacker, 1999) utilizes an agent paradigm to recommend computer science and computer science-related articles based on a user profile. Anick (2003) examined the interactive query reformulation support of the AltaVista search engine for searchers using transactions logs. The researcher used a baseline group of AltaVista searchers given no terminological feedback and a feedback group offered twelve refinement terms along with the search results. Analysis of the precision of the sessions showed no difference between the two groups, however.

Jansen and Pooch (forthcoming) designed a client-side application for Web search engines that provided targeted searching assistance based on the normal interactions during a session (Jansen, 2003). The researchers noted an improvement in performance within the confines of a very short (i.e., 5 minute) Web session. The researchers also noted that there are predictable patterns of when the user seeks and implements assistance from the system (Jansen, Forthcoming; Jansen and Kroner, 2003). These patterns may indicate when the searcher is open to assistance from the system.

Given that sessions and searching interactions during sessions are so important, perhaps the key, for Web search engines to address the searchers' information needs, we investigate how Web searchers interact with Web search engines during sessions. This important area of research can affect Web search engine design, Web site development, and production of online content.

This chapter identifies trends across three major commercial Web search engines – AlltheWeb.com, AltaVista and Excite, including session length, session duration, result pages viewed, documents viewed, and success of the sessions.

3. WEB SEARCH ENGINE SESSIONS TRENDS

This section analyzes the number of single Web query sessions in order to determine the interaction among searchers and Web search engines. Figure 6.1 displays the results of this session analysis.

Figure 6.1 shows that for United States-based Web search engines, the percentage of single Web query sessions is trending down, indicating that session lengths are increasing. In 2002, approximately 47% of searchers on AltaVista submitted only one query, down from 77% in 1998. In the 1998 study, however, a session was artificially limited to five minutes. Subsequent research has shown that the typical Web session is about fifteen minutes.

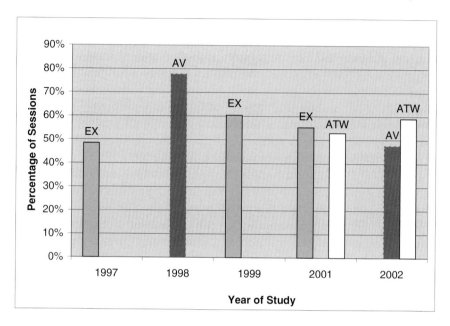

Figure 6-1. Percentage of Single Query Sessions
Note: ATW – AlltheWeb.com, AV – AltaVista, BWIE – BWIE, EX – Excite, FB – Fireball).

Therefore, the 1998 AltaVista study probably over-estimates the number of single Web query sessions. However, the downward trend also appears with Excite users from 1999 to 2002, dropping from 60% to 55%. There was an increase in one-term Web sessions from 1997 to 1999, however. The data analysis methods were similar for all Excite studies and did not impose a session time limit. With AlltheWeb.com there was an increase in one-query Web sessions, from 53% to 59%, in 2002.

4.   AGGREGATE DATA BY WEB SEARCH ENGINE

This section provides overall data from each of the three Web search engines – AlltheWeb.com, AltaVista and Excite.

4.1   AlltheWeb.com

Table 6.1 shows the aggregate results for the analysis of AlltheWeb.com sessions from 2001 and 2002.

Table 6-1. Comparative Results Statistics for AlltheWeb.com Data Sets

	AlltheWeb.com 2001		AlltheWeb.com 2002	
Sessions	153,297		345,093	
Queries	451,551		957,303	
Mean queries per user	3.0		2.8	
Users modifying queries	72,261	47%	142,649	41%
Session size				
1 query	81,036	53%	202,444	59%
2 queries	28,117	18%	55,664	16%
3+ queries	44,144	29%	86,985	25%
Results Pages Viewed				
1 page	373,559	84%	730,363	76%
2 pages	42,957	10%	125,420	13%
3+ pages	30,839	6%	101,520	11%

Table 6.1 shows a trend toward greater simplicity in Web search sessions. The number of users modifying Web queries decreased approximately 6%, from 47% of all users in 2001 to 41% in 2002. Concerning overall Web session length, the percentage of shorter sessions trended higher, with 53% of users with a one-query session in 2001 to 59% in 2002. There was an increase in the percentage of users viewing more than the first Web results page, although this may be a result of the more naïve searching rather than an increased persistence in locating relevant results.

4.2   AltaVista

Table 6.2 shows the aggregate results for the AltaVista analysis, including a comparison with results from an 1998 AltaVista analysis conducted by Silverstein, Henzinger, Marais and Moricz (1999).

Table 6.2 shows a move toward greater interactivity between the user and the AltaVista Web search engine. The number of AltaVista users modifying Web queries has increased approximately 32%, from 20% of all users in 1998 to 52% in 2002. Examining session length, the percentage of longer sessions is trending higher, with 32% of users with three or more queries (i.e., Table 6.2, *3+ queries*) per session in 2002 compared to 7% in 1998. There has been an increase in the percentage of users viewing more than the first results page, which, when combined with other increased interactions, may indicate an increased persistence in locating relevant results.

Table 6-2. Aggregate Results for Data Analysis of 1998 and 2002 AltaVista Data Sets

	AltaVista 1998		AltaVista 2002	
Sessions	285,474,117		369,350	
Queries	993,208,159		1,073,388	
Terms			3,132,106	
Mean queries per user	2.02 (sd =123.4)		2.91 (sd=4.77)	
Users modifying queries	34,416,491	20.4%	193,468	52.4%
Session Length				
1 query	119,228,559	77.6%	175,882	47.6%
2 queries	20,742,082	13.5%	75,343	20.4%
3+ queries	13,674,409	6.9%	118,125	32.0%
Results Pages Viewed				
1 page	718,615,763	85.2%	781,483	72.8%
2 pages	63,258,430	7.5%	139,088	13.0%
3+ pages	13,674,409	7.3%	150,904	14.1%

Notes: For the 1998 study, percentage and figures use the 575,244,993 non-empty queries.
The 1998 data from this and other tables is from or calculated from data reported in (Silverstein, Henzinger, Marais, and Moricz, 1999).

4.3 Excite

Table 6.3 shows the aggregate results for the Excite analysis of the 1997, 1999 and 2001 transaction logs.

Table 6.3 shows little change over the four-year period as measured by Web queries per user or pages per query – although queries per user took a dip in 1999. More than 50% of 2001 users submitted a single short query, about 20% submitted two queries, and another 29% entered three or more unique queries. Users typically do not add or delete many terms in their subsequent Web queries.

A fluctuating percentage of users modify Web queries, with 52% modifying Web queries in 1997, declining to 39.6% in 1999, and increasing to 44.6% in 2001. Users tend to move from broad to narrow terms when modifying their Web queries by changing some individual terms. However, the total number of terms often remains the same.

The trend since 1997 shows users viewing fewer pages of results per query. An Excite results page contains 10 ranked Web sites, and the percentage of Excite users who examined only one page of results per query increased from 1997 to 2001. By 2001, more than 80% of Excite users looked at only one results pages.

Table 6-3. Aggregate Results for Data Analysis of 1997, 1999, and 2001 Excite Data Sets

	Excite 1997		Excite 1999		Excite 2001	
Sessions	210,590		325,711		262,025	
Queries	545,206		1,025,910		1,025,910	
Terms	1,224,245		1,500,500		1,538,120	
Mean queries per user	2.5	sd=2.99	1.9	sd=1.94	2.3	sd=2.43
Users modifying queries	109,753	52.00%	128,982	39.60%	116,863	44.60%
Session size						
1 query	94,224	44.74%	196,729	60.40%	145,162	55.40%
2 queries	48,324	22.95%	64,556	19.82%	50,571	19.30%
3+ queries	68,042	32.23%	64,426	19.78%	66,292	25.30%
Results pages viewed						
1 page	335,661	66.3%	717,397	69.9%	868,160	84.60%
2 pages	91,121	18.0%	126,121	12.3%	79,576	7.80%
3+ pages	79,115	15.7%	182,291	17.8%	78,174	6.90%

The next section provides results from all three search engines related to session length, session duration, result pages viewed, Web pages viewed, and the topical relevance of documents viewed.

5. ALLTHEWEB.COM IN-DEPTH ANALYSIS

5.1 Web Session Length

Table 6.4 shows the Web session length analysis of the AlltheWeb.com transaction logs.

Table 6.4 shows an increase in single Web query sessions resulted in shorter sessions for all except a small (about 4%) group of very persistent users. This trend parallels what is reported from analyses of United States-based Web search engines, namely a move toward great simplicity in Web searching (Spink, Jansen, Wolfram and Saracevic, 2002), but differs from the longer sessions lengths found by Spink, Ozmutlu, Ozmutlu and Jansen (2002). The longer Web search sessions reported by Spink, Ozmutlu, Ozmutlu and Jansen (2002) was due to the inclusion of result page request in the session count.

Table 6-4. Occurrences and Percentages of Session Length for AlltheWeb.com 2001 and 2002

	AlltheWeb.com 2001		AlltheWeb.com 2002	
Session Length	Occurrences	%	Occurrences	%
1	81,036	52.9%	202,444	58.7%
2	28,117	18.3%	55,664	16.1%
3	14,445	9.4%	27,307	7.9%
4	8,335	5.4%	17,440	5.1%
5	5,100	3.3%	10,046	2.9%
6	3,534	2.3%	7,059	2.0%
7	2,431	1.6%	4,461	1.3%
8	1,833	1.2%	3,476	1.0%
9	1,290	0.8%	2,532	0.7%
≥ 10	7,176	4.7%	14,664	4.2%
	153,297	100%	345,093	100%
Average Session Length (number of queries)	3.0		2.8	

5.2   Web Session Duration

Table 6.5 presents the session duration, as measured from the time the first query is submitted until the user departs the search engine for the last time (i.e., does not return) for the 2001 data set. Unfortunately, the server did not properly report the login times for the 2002 data set.

Table 6-5. Occurrences and Percentage of AlltheWeb.com Session Duration

	AlltheWeb.com 2001	
Session Duration	Occurrences	%
< 5 minutes	55,966	26.2%
5 to 10 minutes	13,275	6.2%
10 to 15 minutes	41,987	19.7%
15 to 30 minutes	19,314	9.1%
30 to 60 minutes	30,955	14.5%
1 to 2 hours	8,691	4.1%
2 to 3 hours	21,901	10.3%
3 to 4 hours	2,635	1.2%
> 4 hours	18,605	8.7%
Mean	2 hours and 22 minutes	
Standard Deviation	4 hours and 37 minutes	

With this definition of search duration, we can measure the total user time on the search engine and the time spent viewing the first and subsequent Web documents, except the final document. This final viewing time is not available since the Web search engine server records the time stamp. Naturally, the time between visits from the Web document to the search engine may have not been entirely spent viewing the Web document.

However, this may not be a significant issue as shown from the data in Table 6.5. The mean session duration was 2 hours, 21 minutes and 55 seconds, with a standard deviation of 4 hours, 45 minutes, and 36 seconds. However, that analysis shows that the longer session durations skewed our result for the mean, masking significant details. Fully 52% of the Web search sessions were less than 15 minutes. This is in line with earlier reported research on Web session length (He, Göker and Harper, 2002). Perhaps even more surprisingly, over 25% of the sessions were less than 5 minutes (Jansen and Spink, 2003).

5.3   Results Pages Viewed

Table 6.6 presents a more in-depth analysis of the number of pages viewed per Web query submitted.

Table 6-6. AlltheWeb.com Results Pages Viewed

Results Pages Viewed	AlltheWeb.com 2001		AlltheWeb.com 2002	
	Occurrences	%	Occurrences	%
1	373,559	83.5%	730,363	76.3%
2	42,957	9.6%	125,420	13.1%
3	13,602	3.0%	37,270	3.9%
4	6,027	1.3%	21,375	2.2%
5	3,481	0.8%	13,510	1.4%
6	1,955	0.4%	8,488	0.9%
7	1,339	0.3%	5,464	0.6%
8	912	0.2%	3,512	0.4%
9	639	0.1%	2,277	0.2%
10	542	0.1%	1,615	0.2%
>10	2,342	0.5%	1,170	0.8%
	447,355	99.80%	950,464	100.00%

There was a sharp decrease in the number of viewings between the first and second, and the second and third pages of results, with very few users viewing more than four or five pages of results. The percentage of AlltheWeb.com searchers viewing only one page of results is significantly higher (5% to 25%) than reported in previous research (Jansen, Spink and

Saracevic, 2000; Silverstein, Henzinger, Marais and Moricz, 1999). AlltheWeb.com searchers appear to have a low tolerance for wading through large numbers of results.

5.4   Click Through Analysis

Although most searchers viewed only the first one or two pages of results, this does not tell us the number of Web documents they actually visited. They may have viewed all documents presented or they may have viewed none.

Table 6.7 shows the Web documents viewed per session (Jansen and Spink, 2003).

Table 6-7. Pages Viewed Per AlltheWeb.com Session from 2001 Transaction Log

Documents Viewed	Occurrences	%
1	42,499	27.6%
2	22,997	14.9%
3	15,740	10.2%
4	11,763	7.6%
5	9,032	5.8%
6	7,157	4.6%
7	5,746	3.7%
8	4,563	2.9%
9	3,869	2.5%
10	3,308	2.1%
>10	26,062	16.9%
Total	152,736	98.80%

Note: 561 sessions – no documents viewed

Table 6.7 shows that the mean Web documents viewed were 8.2, with a standard deviation of 26.9. Previous studies report that most Web searchers rarely few more than the first result page, which is usually 10 results (Spink, Jansen, Wolfram and Saracevic, 2002). While 10 documents is in line with the average, our analysis shows that over 66% of searchers examine fewer than 5 documents in a typical session and almost 30% view only one document in a given session.

Table 6.8 reports the duration of viewing of Web documents by Web search engine users.

Table 6-8. Duration of Web Document Viewing

Page View Duration	Occurrences	%
<30 seconds	46,303	13.9%
30 to 60 seconds	16,754	5.0%
1 to 2 minutes	48,059	14.5%
2 to 3 minutes	16,237	4.9%
3 to 4 minutes	47,254	14.2%
4 to 5 minutes	15,203	4.6%
5 to 10 minutes	47,254	14.3%
10 to 15 minutes	14,047	4.2%
15 to 30 minutes	41,215	12.4%
30 to 60 minutes	9,054	2.7%
>60 minutes	30,592	9.3%
Total	331,972	100.00%

Table 6.8 shows that the mean time spent viewing a particular Web document was 16 minutes and 2 seconds, with a standard deviation of 43 minutes and 1 second. However, some lengthy document views skewed our mean. Over 75% of the users viewed the retrieved Web documents for less than 15 minutes.

More surprisingly, perhaps, nearly 40% of the users viewed the retrieved Web document for less than 3 minutes. Fewer than 14% of the users viewed the Web document for less than 30 seconds.

These results for Web document viewing time are substantially less than has been previously reported using survey data (Cyber Atlas, 2002). These results suggest the need for Web site designers to place more emphasis on the presentation of Web documents given the short assessment time by searchers. Again, the time between visits from the Web document to the search engine may have not been entirely spent viewing the Web document.

5.5   Topical Relevance of Documents Viewed

For this portion of the study, we used a random subset of records from the 2001 transaction log that included the Web site the searcher actually visited. Three independent raters visited the sites and evaluated the Web document to determine topical relevance. Topical relevance is a relevance metric using a direct topic matching between the search terms used and the terms in the retrieved document, not necessarily related to the user's information seeking stage or information problem (Spink and Greisdorf, 2001).

Table 6.9 addresses the question of whether Web search sessions are short because the searchers are potentially finding topically relevant information.

Table 6-9. Topical Relevance Results for Pages Viewed by AlltheWeb.com Users from 2001 Transaction Log

Topical Relevance Score	Number of Documents	%
3	199	37.5%
2	74	14.0%
1	103	19.4%
0	154	29.1%
Total web documents reviewed	530	

Three independent raters assessed 530 uniform resource locators (URLs) and evaluate these Web documents for topical relevance based on their interpretation of the query submitted. Each rater assigned a topical relevance Web document a rating of 1 if the document was relevant. A non-relevant page received a rating of zero. Therefore, the maximum topical relevance score a Web page could receive was three, meaning that all three reviewers rated the document as topically relevant.

Approximately 52% of the time, two or more raters evaluated a page to be topically relevant. Approximately 48% of the time, two or more raters evaluated a page to be not topically relevant. These percentages, taking in total, represent precision for this set of results retrieved by this search engine. In our study, about 50% of the Web documents viewed by AlltheWeb.com searchers will be topically relevant. Note that this percentage is of the documents viewed by the searchers, not the documents retrieved by the Web search engines.

The next section provides an analysis of the AltaVista Web search engine.

6.   ALTAVISTA IN-DEPTH ANALYSIS

6.1   Session Length

Table 6.10 shows a sharp decrease in the percentage of one-query sessions and a corresponding increase in percentages of longer Web search sessions.

Table 6-10. Occurrences and Percentages of Session Length for AltaVista 1998 Study and 2002 Transaction Log

Session Length	AltaVista 1998		AltaVista 2002	
	Occurrences	%	Occurrences	%
1	119,228,559	77.6%	175,882	47.62%
2	20,742,082	13.5%	75,343	20.40%
3	6,760,382	4.4%	40,445	10.95%
4	6,914,027 *	4.5%	23,463	6.35%
5			14,719	3.99%
6			9,726	2.63%
7			6,664	1.80%
8			4,731	1.28%
9			3,481	0.94%
≥10			14,896	4.03%
	153,645,050	100.00%	369,350	100.00%

Notes: For the 1998 study, percentage and figures use the 575,244,993 non-empty queries.
* Number and percentages are for sessions of four and more queries.

Table 6.10 shows that the AltaVista findings were counter to previous studies of Web search engines trends. Spink, Jansen, Wolfram and Saracevic (2002) reported a move toward great simplicity in searching with shorter sessions on the Excite Web search engine from 1997. Jansen and Spink (forthcoming), in their analysis of European searching, noted a similar inclination. Perhaps AltaVista users are most sophisticated in their searching characteristics.

However, the number of one-query Web sessions from 1998 is much higher than that reported in similar Web studies from that time period (Hölscher, 1998; Jansen, Spink, Bateman and Saracevic, 1998). The number of one-query Web sessions from the 2002 study is more in-line with results from other studies within this time period (Cacheda and Viña, 2001; Spink, Jansen, Wolfram and Saracevic, 2002). This discrepancy when compared to other Web studies may indicate that the temporal cut-off (Silverstein, Henzinger, Marais and Moricz, 1999) used may have been too low. He, Göker and Harper (2002) report that the average Web session is approximately 15 minutes.

6.2   Web Session Duration

Table 6.11 presents the Web session durations results for the AltaVista 2002 data.

Table 6-11. Occurrences and Percentage of AltaVista Session Duration for 2002

Session Duration	Occurrences	%
Less than 5 minutes	264,494	71.6%
5 to 10 minutes	22,374	6.1%
10 to 15 minutes	12,573	3.4%
15 to 30 minutes	18,794	5.1%
30 to 60 minutes	13,259	3.6%
1 to 2 hours	8,952	2.4%
2 to 3 hours	4,317	1.2%
3 to 4 hours	2,671	0.7%
More than 4 hours	21,916	5.9%
	369,350	100.00%

Note: For the 1998 study, all sessions were 5 minutes or less by definition.

Silverstein, Henzinger, Marais and Moricz (1999) assigned a temporal cut-off of 5 minutes as the maximum Web session duration. For the analysis of the 2002 data set, we measured the Web session duration from the time the first query was submitted until the user departed the search engine for the last time (i.e., does not return).

With this definition of Web search duration, we can measure the total user time on the Web search engine and the time spent viewing the first and subsequent Web documents, except the final document. This final viewing time is not available since the Web search engine server records the time stamp. Naturally, the time between visits from the Web document to the search engine may not have been entirely spent viewing the Web document.

However, this may not be a significant issue as shown from the results in Table 6.11 that show a large percentage of very short session durations. The mean session duration was 58 minutes and 10 seconds, with a standard deviation of 3 hours, 34 minutes, and 12 seconds. However, we see that the longer session durations skewed our result for the mean, masking significant details. Fully 81% of the sessions were less than 15 minutes.

Perhaps even more surprisingly, nearly 72% of the sessions were less than 5 minutes. This is substantially shorter than earlier reported research on Web session length (Cyber Atlas, 2002; He, Göker and Harper, 2002), although He, Göker and Harper (2002) predicted that the average Web session is approximately 15 minutes based on analysis of Excite and Reuter transaction logs. The percentage of sessions of 5 minutes or less (approximately 72%) is nearly three times that of AlltheWeb.com searchers (26%). In the query level analysis of the 2002 AltaVista transaction log, researchers noted a high percentage of navigational queries (i.e., queries that appeared to be short cuts for navigation). This phenomenon may, in part, explain the high percentage of very short session durations.

During these sessions, searchers not only submitted queries but also examining result pages, an interaction that we examine in the next section.

6.3   Results Pages Viewed

Table 6.12 presents the results pages viewed by AltaVista searchers from the 1998 and 2002 transaction logs.

Table 6-12. Results Pages Viewed by AltaVista Searchers from 1998 Study and 2002 Transaction Log

Number of Results Pages Viewed	AltaVista 1998		AltaVista 2002	
	Occurrences	%	Occurrences	%
1	846,213,351	85.2%	781,483	72.8%
2	74,490,612	7.5%	139,088	13.0%
3	29,796,245	3.0%	60,334	5.6%
4	42,707,951*	4.3%	27,196	2.5%
5			16,898	1.6%
6			11,646	1.1%
7			6,678	0.6%
8			4,939	0.5%
9			3,683	0.3%
10			4,074	0.4%
>10			17,324	1.6%
Total	993,208,159	100.00%	1,073,343	100.00%

Notes: For the 1998 figure, calculated based on 153,645,993 distinct queries only.
Number and percentages are for results pages of 4 and more.

Table 6.12 shows there is a decrease in the number of viewings between the first and second and the second and the third pages of results, with very few users viewing more than four or five pages of results.

The percentage of AltaVista searchers viewing only one page of results is heading lower (85% to 72%) from 1998 to 2002 and there is a corresponding increase in searchers viewing more results pages. The overall number of results pages viewed is still quite low, with approximately 85% to 92% of users viewing no more than the first two results pages. As with searchers of other Web search engines (Cacheda and Viña, 2001; Hölscher and Strube, 2000; Jansen and Spink, Forthcoming; Spink, Jansen, Wolfram and Saracevic, 2002), AltaVista users appear to have a low tolerance for reviewing large numbers of results.

The next section examines session level interactions with the Excite Web search engine.

7.   EXCITE IN-DEPTH ANALYSIS

7.1   Session Length

Table 6.13 shows a decrease in the percentage of one-query sessions and a corresponding increase in percentages of longer sessions.

Table 6-13. Occurrences and Percentages of Session Length for Excite 1997, 1999, and 2001

Session Length	Excite 1997		Excite 1999		Excite 2001	
	Occurrences	%	Occurrences	%	Occurrences	%
1	102,154	48.51%	138,949	42.7%	107,994	40.5%
2	43,901	20.85%	69,052	21.2%	51,063	19.1%
3	23,850	11.33%	36,817	11.3%	28,816	10.8%
4	13,930	6.61%	22,668	7.0%	18,479	6.9%
5	8,654	4.11%	14,655	4.5%	12,815	4.8%
6	5,699	2.71%	10,022	3.1%	8,999	3.4%
7	3,799	1.80%	7,100	2.2%	6,786	2.5%
8	2,322	1.10%	5,252	1.6%	5,189	1.9%
9	1,689	0.80%	3,940	1.2%	4,234	1.6%
≥10	4,592	2.18%	17,307	5.3%	11,237	4.2%
Total	210,590	100.0%	325,762	100.0%	266,680	100.0%

Some 48.4% of users submitted a single query, 20.8% two queries, and about 31% of users entered three or more unique queries. About 1.9% of users entered nothing but a zero term query. However, the distribution is skewed toward the lower end of the number of queries submitted, with a long tail of very few users submitting a large number of unique queries. In general, users did not enter many queries in a session, and close to half entered only one query, although the trend is to enter more queries.

7.2   Results Pages Viewed

Table 6.14 displays the results pages analysis from the 1997, 1999, and 2001 Excite transaction logs.

Table 6.14 shows that users are viewing fewer results pages in 2001 relative to 1997. Over 84% of the users by 2001 viewed no more than only one results page.

Table 6-14. Comparative Statistics for Excite Web Query Data Sets

Result pages viewed per query	Excite 1997		Excite 1999		Excite 2001	
	Occurrences	%	Occurrences	%	Occurrences	%
1	335,661	66.3%	717,397	69.9%	868,160	84.6%
2	91,121	18.0%	126,121	12.3%	79,576	7.8%
3	34,232	6.8%	56,079	5.5%	32,082	3.1%
4	16,565	3.3%	33,150	3.2%	15,434	1.5%
5	9,019	1.8%	21,408	2.1%	9,239	0.9%
6	5,383	1.1%	15,016	1.5%	5,480	0.5%
7	3,471	0.7%	10,725	1.0%	3,527	0.3%
8	2,485	0.5%	8,162	0.8%	2,490	0.2%
9	1,725	0.3%	6,157	0.6%	2,096	0.2%
10	1,217	0.2%	5,008	0.5%	1,622	0.2%
>10	5,092	1.0%	26,586	2.6%	6,204	0.6%
	505,971	100.00%	1,022,044	100.00	1,025,910	100.00%

Note: Does not include the 39,309 blank queries for 1997 or 101 blank queries for 1999.

8. AGENT SESSIONS

Many Web users employ automated agents to gather information for them. It is often assumed that this approach represents a more sophisticated method of searching. However, there is little research investigating how Web agents search for online information. We examine how agents search for information on Web search engines, including the session, query, term, duration and frequency of interactions.

We analyzed queries submitted by 2,717 agents to the AltaVista Web search engine on 8 September 2002. Findings include: (1) agents interacting with Web search engines use queries comparable to human searchers, (2) Web agents are searching for a relatively limited variety of information, with only 18% of the terms used being unique, and (3) agent–Web search engine interaction typically spans several hours with multiple instances of interaction per second.

Table 6.15 presents general searching information of the agent–Web search engine interactions. Table 6.15 shows that at the Web query level, Web agent queries are comparable to queries submitted by human Web searchers. About 46% of agent queries contained more than 3 terms compared to 45% for human searchers (Spink, Jansen, Wolfram and Saracevic, 2002). The standard deviation (2.8) (Jansen and Pooch, 2001) is about twice that of human searchers The use of Boolean operators by agents is about double that of human searchers, but still represents a minimal usage at 20%.

Table 6-15. Aggregate Results for General Search Trends

Sessions	2,717	
Queries	896,387	
Terms		
Unique	570,214	17.7%
Total	3,224,840	
Terms per query	mean 3.6	sd 2.8
Terms per query		
1 term	216,105	24%
2 terms	268,076	30%
3+ terms	411,988	46%
Queries per Agent	mean 329.9	sd 1383.9
Agents modifying queries	2,386	88%
Session size		
1 query	331	12%
2 queries	109	4%
3+ queries	2,277	84%
Results Pages Viewed		
1 page	760,071	85%
2 pages	67,755	8%
3+ pages	68,561	8%
Boolean Queries	177,182	20%
Terms not repeated in data set	411,577	13%
Use of 100 most frequently occurring terms	834,251	26%

In terms of results pages, over 86% of the Web agents accessed only the first page of results, which is higher than in research on human Web searches (approximately 40%) (Cacheda and Viña, 2001; Hölscher and Strube, 2000; Jansen, Spink and Saracevic, 2000). There are major differences between agent and human searchers at the term and session level of analysis. The percentage of agent sessions with more than three queries (84%), after duplicate queries were removed, was significantly higher than that of human searchers (25%) (Spink, Jansen, Wolfram and Saracevic, 2002).

The number of unique terms (18%) was very low compared to human searchers (61%) (Spink, Jansen, Wolfram and Saracevic, 2002) indicating a tight jargon used by Web agents and a limited subject matter. The use of the 100 most frequently occurring terms (26%) submitted by agents was also high compared to human searchers (usually under 20%) (Spink, Jansen, Wolfram and Saracevic, 2002).

Table 6.16 shows the duration and frequency of the agent interactions with the AltaVista Web search engines.

Table 6-16. Time, Queries, and Queries Per Second

	Duration of Interaction Hours: Minutes: Seconds	Queries	Queries Per Second
Average	9:27:30	615	0.43
St Dev	8:05:49	2,609	4.17
Max	23:59:57	99,595	137
Min	0:00:02	101	< 0.00

Table 6.16 shows that the duration and frequency of agent–Web search engine interaction is substantially different than that of human searchers. The mean agent session (approximately 9 1/2 hours) is 38 times the mean human session of 15 minutes (Jansen and Spink, 2003). However, the standard deviation was relatively high at just over 8 hours. The maximum sessions duration was the full temporal span of the data sampling period. The minimum duration was 2 seconds.

The mean queries per session (615) is 300 times that of human searchers (just over 2) (Jansen, Spink, Bateman and Saracevic, 1998). The average agent submits a query about every 2 seconds, with a standard deviation of approximately 4 queries. The maximum session frequency was just less than 100,000 queries in the 24-hour span, and the maximum queries per second were 137.

9.   SUCCESSIVE SEARCH SESSIONS

Recent research in the Web context shows that users with a broader problem at hand often seek information in stages over extended periods and use a variety of information resources (Spink, Bateman and Jansen, 1998). As time progresses, users tend to search the same or possibly different interactive systems (digital libraries, IR systems, Web services) for answers to the same or evolving problem-at-hand. The process of repeated, successive searching over time in relation to a given, possibly evolving information problem (including changes or shifts in beliefs, and cognitive, affective, and situational states), is called *a successive search phenomenon* (Spink, Ozmutlu and Ozmutlu., 2002).

Spink, Bateman and Jansen (1999) found, as Table 6.17 shows, one third of respondents to a survey on the Excite Web search engine homepage were first time users, conducting their first search of Excite on their current topic; two-thirds reported a pattern of successive searches of between 1 and 5 Excite searches on their current topic; 30% reported more than 5 Excite searches on their topic; and 13% reported conducting more than 20 searches on their topic.

Table 6-17. Number of Excite Searches on Current Topic

Excite Searches	Number of Users	% of Users
First Search	112	39%
2–5 Searches	88	31%
6–10 Searches	32	11%
11–15 Searches	10	3%
16–20 Searches	9	3%
20+ Searches	37	13%
Total	288	100%

Table 6.17 shows that by self-reported user estimates, most users are repeatedly searching Excite for information on the same or evolving topic. The phenomenon shows *successive Web search episodes* and is an important user behavior when interacting with Web search engines. The further modeling of users in successive searches is then *successive user modeling*.

A key dimension is time, and the key variable is changes or shifts in successive search episodes over time. The key constant is the same or evolving information problem. The evolution, if any, of a problem and other cognitive, affective and situational variables can be mapped, and the history of successive search episodes can be recorded and analyzed, i.e., the phenomenon can be a subject of research. The successive search phenomenon is just beginning to be investigated to any extent by Web researchers.

10. MULTITASKING SEARCH SESSIONS

Recent studies suggest that users' searches may have multiple goals or topics and occur within the broader context of their information-seeking behaviors (Spink, Ozmutlu and Ozmutlu, 2002). A user's single session with a Web search engine may consist of seeking information on single or multiple topics (Spink, forthcoming). Spink and Park (forthcoming) provide a model of multitasking, task switching and dual tasking during human information behavior.

Spink, Ozmutlu and Ozmutlu (2002) show that IR searches often include multiple topics, during a single search session or *multitasking search*. Recent studies have also examined multitasking searching on the Excite and AlltheWeb.com Web search engines. Spink, Batemen and Jansen (1999) found that eleven (3.8%) of the 287 Excite users responding to a Web-based survey reported multitasking searches. Ozmutlu, Ozmutlu and Spink (2003) found that: (1) almost one third of AlltheWeb.com users perform multitasking Web searching; (2) multitasking sessions often included more than three topics per session; (3) multitasking sessions are longer in duration than regular searching sessions; and (4) most of the topic in multitasking searches were on general information, computers and entertainment.

Ozmutlu, Ozmutlu and Spink (2003) found that: (1) multitasking Web searches are a noticeable user behavior, one tenth of Excite users and one third of AlltheWeb.com users conducted multitasking searches; (2) multitasking search sessions are longer than regular search sessions in terms of queries per session and duration; (3) both Excite and AlltheWeb.com users search for about three topics per multitasking session and submit about 4–5 queries per topic; and (4) there is a broad variety of search topics in multitasking search sessions.

Most Web search sessions consist of two queries of two words (Spink, Jansen, Wolfram and Saracevic, 2002). Spink, Park, Jansen and Pedersen (2002) found that: (1) 81% of two-query Excite and AltaVista Web search sessions were multitasking searches, and (2) there are a broad variety of search topics in multitasking search sessions. Typical Web search sessions of two queries often include more than one topic concurrently due to the complex nature of work or living tasks. Spink, Park and Jansen (2004) found that (1) 91.3% of three or more query sessions contained multiple topics, (2) multitasking sessions contained frequent topic changes, and (3) there are a broad variety of search topics in multitasking search sessions. Multitasking is a key element within overall Web search.

11. CONCLUSION

Our in-depth analysis of Web search sessions on three major commercial Web search engines shows that Web searchers' sessions are dynamic and evolving. Overall, at the session level, the percentage of sessions with only one query (i.e., a searcher submits one query then departs) has declined on each Web search engine.

It appears that Web search session length is increasing, although slightly, with more searchers submitting more queries on the Excite and AltaVista Web search engines during the periods of data collection. The indications on AlltheWeb.com are counter to this, however, with more searchers with one session queries. Web search session durations for the vast majority of Web search engine users is 15 minutes or less, although the average is a couple of hours. A substantial percentage of Web sessions are less than 5 minutes. We also see that some sessions include two or more topics.

Searchers do not appear willing to go to the second or three results pages. A near majority still look no further than the first results page. Based on data from AlltheWeb.com, the typical user views an average of 8 Web documents per session. A significant percentage of Web search engine users, however, view no more than 5 Web documents per session. The mean viewing time for a Web document is 16 minutes, but the longer viewing sessions skew the mean. Typically, a Web searcher will spend about 5 minutes or less evaluating a Web document, with almost 15% spending less than 30 seconds.

Alternatively, our studies show that some users engage in successive or repeated Web search sessions on the same topic over time. Some users are also engaging in longer and more complex multitasking Web search sessions that include queries related to diverse topics. The dichotomy between the shorter and longer search sessions is a major area for further research and trend analysis.

12.   REFERENCES

Anick, P. (2003). Using Terminological Feedback for Web Search Refinement – a Log-Based Study. In *Proceedings of the 26th Annual International ACM SIGIR Conference on RE search and Everyone in Information Retrieval*, pp. 88–95. Toronto, Canada. 28 July – 1 August.

Bullseye. (2000). *Intelliseek Releases Updated Version of Its Popular Search Software* [Web site]. Intelliseek. Retrieved 1 November, 2003, from the World Wide Web: <http://www.intelliseek.com/releases2.asp?id=54>.

Cacheda, F. and Viña, Á. (2001). Experiences Retrieving Information in the World Wide Web. In *Proceedings of the 6th IEEE Symposium on Computers and Communications*, pp. 72–79. Hammamet, Tunisia. July.

Copernic. (2003). *Copernic: Software to Search, Find, and Manage Information* [Website]. Copernic. Retrieved 1 November, 2003, from the World Wide Web: <www.copernic.com/>.

Cyber Atlas. (2002). *November 2002 Internet Usage Stats* [website]. Nielsen//NetRatings Inc. Retrieved 1 January, 2003, from the World Wide Web: <http://cyberatlas.internet.com/big_picture/traffic_patterns/article/0,,5931_1560881,00.html>.

Hansen, M. H. and Shriver, E. (2001). Using Navigation Data to Improve Ir Functions in the Context of Web Search. In *Proceedings of the 10th International Conference on Information and Knowledge Management*, pp. 135–142. Atlanta, Georgia, USA. October.

He, D., Göker, A. and Harper, D. J. (2002). Combining Evidence for Automatic Web Session Identification. *Information Processing & Management, 38*(5), 727–742.

Hölscher, C. (1998). How Internet Experts Search for Information on the Web. In *Proceedings of the World Conference of the World Wide Web, Internet, and Intranet*, pp. 1–6. Orlando, FL. July 1998.

Hölscher, C. and Strube, G. (2000). Web Search Behavior of Internet Experts and Newbies. *International Journal of Computer and Telecommunications Networking, 33*(1–6), 337–346.

Jansen, B. J. (2003). Designing Automated Help Using Searcher System Dialogues. In *Proceedings of the 2003 IEEE International Conference on Systems, Man & Cybernetics*, pp. 10–16. Washington, D.C., USA. 5–8 October.

Jansen, B. J. (Forthcoming). *Seeking and Implementing Automated Assistance During the Search Process.*

Jansen, B. J. and Kroner, G. (2003). The Impact of Automated Assistance on the Information Retrieval Process. In *Proceedings of The ACM CHI 2003 Conference on Human Factors in Computing Systems*, pp. 1004–1006. Fort Lauderdale, Florida. 5–10 April.

Jansen, B. J. and Pooch, U. (2001). Web User Studies: A Review and Framework for Future Work. *Journal of the American Society of Information Science and Technology, 52*(3), 235–246.

Jansen, B. J. and Pooch, U. (Forthcoming). Assisting the Searcher: Utilizing Software Agents for Web Search Systems. *Internet Research – Electronic Networking Applications and Policy.*

Jansen, B. J. and Spink, A. (2003). An Analysis of Web Information Seeking and Use: Documents Retrieved Versus Documents Viewed. In *Proceedings of the 4th International Conference on Internet Computing*, pp. 65–69. Las Vegas, Nevada. 23–26 June.

Jansen, B. J. and Spink, A. (Forthcoming). An Analysis of Web Searching by European Alltheweb.Com Users. *Information Processing and Management.*

Jansen, B. J., Spink, A., Bateman, J. and Saracevic, T. (1998). Real Life Information Retrieval: A Study of User Queries on the Web. *SIGIR Forum, 32*(1), 5–17.

Jansen, B. J., Spink, A. and Saracevic, T. (2000). Real Life, Real Users, and Real Needs: A Study and Analysis of User Queries on the Web. *Information Processing and Management, 36*(2), 207–227.

Kahle, B. (1999). *Alexa Internet Press Releases* [Web site]. Alexa Internet. Retrieved 12 February, 2000, from the World Wide Web: <http://www.alexa.com/company/recent_articles.html>.

Lawrence, S., Giles, C. L. and Bollacker, K. (1999). Digital Libraries and Autonomous Citation Indexing. *IEEE Computer, 32*(6), 67–71.

Lieberman, H. (1995). Letizia: An Agent That Assists Web Browsing. In *Proceedings of the 14th International Joint Conference on Artificial Intelligence*, pp. 924–929. Montreal, Quebec, Canada. August.

Ozmutlu, S., Ozmutlu, H. C. and Spink, A. (2003). A Study of Multitasking Web Searching. In *Proceedings of the IEEE ITCC'03: International Conference on Information Technology: Coding and Computing.*, pp. 145–150. Las Vegas, Nevada. 23–26 June.

Shneiderman, B., Byrd, D. and Croft, W. B. (1998). Sorting out Searching: A User-Interface Framework for Text Searches. *Communications of the ACM, 41*(4), 95–98.

Silverstein, C., Henzinger, M., Marais, H. and Moricz, M. (1999). Analysis of a Very Large Web Search Engine Query Log. *SIGIR Forum, 33*(1), 6–12.

Spink, A. (Forthcoming). Multitasking Information Behavior and Information Task Switching: An Exploratory Study. *Journal of Documentation.*

Spink, A., Bateman, J. and Jansen, B. J. (1998). Searching Heterogeneous Collections on the Web: Behavior of Excite Users. *Information Research, 4*(2), 317–328.

Spink, A., Bateman, J. and Jansen, B. J. (1999). Searching the Web: A Survey of Excite Users. *Journal of Internet Research: Electronic Networking Applications and Policy, 9*(2), 117–128.

Spink, A. and Greisdorf, H. (2001). Regions and Levels: Mapping and Measuring Users' Relevance Judgments. *Journal of the American Society for Information Science, 52*(2), 161–173.

Spink, A., Jansen, B. J., Park, M. and Pedersen, J. (2002). Multitasking on AltaVista.. In *Proceedings of the IEEE ITCC'04: International Conference on Coding and Computing*, pp. Las Vegas, NV. April 2004.

Spink, A., Jansen, B. J., Wolfram, D. and Saracevic, T. (2002). From E-Sex to E-Commerce: Web Search Changes. *IEEE Computer, 35*(3), 107–111.

Spink, A., Ozmutlu, H. C. and Ozmutlu, S. (2002). Multitasking Information Seeking and Searching Processes. *Journal of the American Society for Information Science and Technology, 53*(8), 639–652.

Spink, A., Ozmutlu, S., Ozmutlu, H. C. and Jansen, B. J. (2002). U.S. Versus European Web Searching Trends. *SIGIR Forum, 32*(1), 30–37.

Spink, A. and Park, M. (Forthcoming). *Multitasking and Information Task Switching During Human Information Behavior.*

Spink, A., Park, M. and Jansen, B. J. (Forthcoming). *Multitasking on Web Search Engines.*

Spink, A., Wilson, T. D., Ford, N., Foster, A. and Ellis, D. (2002). Information Seeking and Mediated Searching. Part 1. Theoretical Framework and Research Design. *Journal of the American Society for Information Science and Technology, 53*(9), 695–703.

Wong, M. (2002). *Ecommerce Dictionary* [Web site]. AMGY.com Network. Retrieved 19 January, 2004, from the World Wide Web: <http://www.ecommerce-dictionary.com/>.

Section III

SUBJECTS OF WEB SEARCH

Chapter 7

E-COMMERCE WEB SEARCHING

1. INTRODUCTION

Accessing e-commerce information on the Web is becoming a key aspect of consumerism in the digital age. Web queries are a primary means for translating people's need for business product and service information for effective e-commerce. Few studies have examined large-scale e-commerce-related queries from various Web search engines. This chapter reports form a study of e-commerce queries submitted to Web search engines from 1997 to 2002. The study provides insights into the trends in e-commerce-related Web searching.

Findings include: (1) business queries often include more search terms, are less modified, lead to fewer Web pages viewed, and include less advanced search features than non-business queries; (2) a small number of terms are used with very high frequency and tend to be more generic, such as "shopping" and "pizza"; and (3) company or product name queries were the most common form of business query. By 1999, e-commerce queries were the largest group of Web queries, forming some 25% of Web queries. Many people are searching for company Web sites. A need exists for new search tools that more easily facilitate company and product searches. Despite the growing business nature of the Web, many users' access to business information is limited due to poor searching tools, and a lack of a standardized approach to search engine functionality and terminology. Our ongoing research is further investigating the trends in e-commerce-related Web searching.

2.   WEB E-COMMERCE

Web traffic has increased exponentially as people use Web search engines as a major tool to dig their way through Web-based information. The Web has become a major outlet for all kinds of e-commerce transactions. Since the inception of major businesses on the Web, and easy and relatively less costly access to Web services, customers are using the Web as a transaction medium e-commerce and business information (DeCovny, 1998; Keeney, 1999; Chun, Lee and Lee, 1999-2000). Buying and selling products and services over the Web is becoming a part of everyday life for many people who search via many different Web search engines (Leonard, 2003). People and organization are spending increasing amounts of time working with electronic information and engaging in e-commerce (Bellman, Lohse and Johnson, 1999; Hoffman, Novak and Chatterjee, 2000; Koufaris, Kambil and La Barbera, 2001-2002; Steinfield, Kraut and Plummer, 1995). Web searching services are now everyday tools for information seeking and e-commerce. However, many users Web search engine interactions are often frustrating and constrained.

Buying and selling products and services over the Web is becoming a part of everyday life for many people who search via many different Web search engines. Spiteri (2000) compared the effectiveness of six Internet search engines. She found ambiguous and sometimes misleading categories in e-commerce sites, moderate consistency in e-commerce Web site organization, and few opportunities for comparison-shopping. Spiteri (2000) identified two types of consumer Web behavior: (1) *goal-directed* – to find a product or information, and (2) *experiential* – non-directed exploratory browsing or surfing.

E-commerce is a growing force in the world economy and the Web is becoming a major source of business products, services and information for many people worldwide (Zwass, 2000). Web search tools are important for the development of e-commerce, as people use search engines to find business-related information on the Web. Many shopping and business Web sites have search capabilities on their Web sites. Apart from entering a business-related URL, most users have little choice but to interact with a Web search engine, such as MSN or Google.

Large-scale, quantitative or qualitative studies have explored how users' search the Web (Silverstein, Henzinger, Marais and Moricz, 1999; Spink, Wolfram, Jansen and Saracevic, 2000; Spink, Jansen, Wolfram and Saracevic, 2002). To support human information behaviors we are seeing the development of a new generation of Web tools, such as Web meta-search engines and portals, that help users persist in electronic information.

Studies show that, in general, most Web queries are short, without much modification, and are simple in structure (Spink, Wolfram, Jansen and Saracevic, 2000; Spink, Jansen, Wolfram and Saracevic, 2002). Few queries incorporate advanced search techniques, and when such techniques are used many mistakes result.

However, relevance feedback and some advanced search features are growing in use. Frequently, people retrieve a large number of Web sites, but view few results pages and tend not to browse beyond the first or second results page (Spiteri, 2000). Overall, a small number of terms are used with high frequency and many terms are used once. Web queries are very rich in subject diversity and some unique. The subject distribution of Web queries does not seem to map to the distribution of Web sites subject content. However, limited studies have specifically examined large-scale e-commerce-related Web queries.

3. E-COMMERCE WEB SEARCH

Using Web search engines to find information and conduct e-commerce transactions is challenging for many users (Jansen, Spink and Saracevic, 2000; Wolfram, Spink, Jansen and Saracevic, 2001). Many Web users find it difficult to conduct e-business via an information system more akin to an automated library catalog than an effective sales transaction system. Studies of e-commerce-related Web queries are important for understanding Web usage and for the development of Web tools and systems to facilitate more effective e-commerce.

Spink and Guner (2001) sampled 10,000 Excite queries and 10,000 AskJeeves question-format queries for e-commerce-related queries. Findings include: (1) business queries often include more search terms, are less modified, lead to fewer Web pages viewed, and include less advanced search features, than non-business queries, (2) company or product name queries were the most common form of business, and (3) AskJeeves business queries in question form were largely limited to the format "Where can I buy …?" or the request "I want to buy ...".

Spink and Ozmutlu (2003) also showed that many AskJeeves e-commerce queries were in request not question format. The most common format for e-commerce request queries were "I want to buy …" and "Get me …" Spink, Wolfram, Jansen and Saracevic (2002) found that in 2001 e-commerce queries formed about 25% of Web queries.

The large-scale study of users' e-commerce-related queries to Web search engines is important for understanding information access on the Web. This research can also help design company Web sites and develop better e-commerce search engines. In this chapter we explore the extent and nature of business-related searching on the Web.

This chapter presents results from a longitudinal meta-analysis of six major Web studies, of two European and four U.S.-based Web search engines, over a seven year period. We provide a comparison of differences in Web searching between U.S. and European-based Web searches. We further present results related to the structure and types and subjects of search terms in e-commerce queries.

Our objectives were to investigate trends in e-commerce-related Web queries, including the proportion of Web queries that are e-commerce-related, and the structure and types of e-commerce-related information requested. The study of users' e-commerce-related queries to Web search engines is important for understanding information access on the Web. This research can also help understand trends in e-commerce-related Web searching, the design of company Web sites and develop better e-commerce search engines. In this paper we explore the extent and nature of business-related searching on the Web.

4.   TRENDS ANALYSIS

The six studies of e-commerce-related Web queries that we compare in this paper are shown chronologically in Table 7.1.

Table 7-1. Aggregate Data from Web Search Engine Studies from 1997 through 2002

	1 Excite	2 Excite	3 AlltheWeb.com
Region	U.S.	U.S.	Europe
Data	Tuesday	Wednesday	Tuesday
Collection	16 Sep. 1997	1 Dec. 1999	6 Feb. 2001
Sessions	210,590	325,711	153,297
Queries	545,206	1,025,910	451,551
Terms	1,224,245	1,500,500	1,350,619

	4 Excite	5 AlltheWeb.com	6 AltaVista
Region	U.S.	Europe	U.S.
Data	Monday	Tuesday	Sunday
Collection	30 Apr. 2001	28 May 02	8 Sep. 2002
Sessions	262,025	345,093	369,350
Queries	1,025,910	957,303	1,073,388
Terms	1,538,120	2,225,141	3,132,106

The six studies include: (1) a 1997 study of the Excite Web search engine, (2) a 1999 study of Excite Web search engine, (3) a 2001 study of the AlltheWeb.com Web search engine, (4) a 2001 study of Excite Web search engine, (5) a study of 2001 and 2002 AlltheWeb.com Web query data sets. Collectively, the nine studies represent over 1.5 million Web searching sessions and over 5.5 million queries submitted to the various Web search engines.

5. E-COMMERCE WEB QUERY TRENDS

Table 7.2 shows the proportion of e-commerce-related Web queries in each Web query sample from 1997 to 2002.

Table 7-2. Proportion of E-Commerce-related Web Queries in Each Sample from 1997 to 2002

	1	2	3
	Excite	Excite	AlltheWeb.com
Region	U.S.	U.S.	European
Data	Tuesday	Wednesday	Tuesday
Collection	16 Sep. 1997	1 Dec. 1999	6 Feb. 2001
Sample Size	2414 queries	2539 queries	2503 queries
E-Commerce Queries	13.3%	24.5%	12.3%

	4	5	6
	Excite	AlltheWeb.com	AltaVista
Region	U.S.	European	U.S.
Data	Monday	Tuesday	Sunday
Collection	30 Apr. 2001	28 May 02	8 Sep. 2002
Sample Size	2453 queries	2525 queries	2603 queries
E-Commerce Queries	24.7%	12.7%	12.5%

Results are provided from the longitudinal meta-analysis of results from six major studies of queries from three major Web search engines. For the U.S.-based Excite Web search engines, in 1999 and 2001, e-commerce-related queries were the top ranked category with a large percentage increase from 1997 to 1999.

By 1999, e-commerce queries accounted for approximately 25% of the Excite queries. Noticeably percentage decreases occurred in 2002. Alternatively, e-commerce-related queries held steady at around 12.5% for the European AlltheWeb.com users. Jansen and Spink (2004a, b) and Spink, Ozmutlu, Ozmutlu and Jansen (2002) had also found differences in the subjects of U.S. versus European based Web searchers.

Studies showed that business-related queries were increasing as a proportion of all Web queries. Jansen, Spink and Saracevic (2000) found that in 1997 business-related terms constituted 8.3% of the 63 top terms and 13.5% of queries entered into the Excite search engine. Wolfram, Spink, Jansen and Saracevic (2001) found an increase to 24.4% for business-related queries in 1999. Spink and Ozmutlu (2003) found that business-related question queries were the second largest category of question queries behind people and places.

6.   EXCITE 2001 E-COMMERCE SESSIONS

6.1   E-Commerce Query Structure

We identified characteristics of Excite user's e-commerce queries and sessions (Table 7.3).

Table 7-3. Excite 2001 E-Commerce Sessions

Number of e-commerce sessions	388
Maximum queries per e-commerce session	7
Minimum queries per e-commerce session	1
Mean queries per e-commerce session	1.2
Maximum e-commerce query length	11
Minimum e-commerce query length	1
Mean e-commerce query length	2.3
Maximum topics per e-commerce session	5
Minimum topics per e-commerce session	1
Mean topics per e-commerce session	1.1

- We qualitatively identified 388 e-commerce-related sessions.
- The maximum queries users searched in a single e-commerce session were 7, the minimum queries per session was 1, and the mean queries per e-commerce session was 1.2.
- E-commerce queries often included more search terms, are less modified, lead to fewer Web pages viewed, and include less advanced search features than non-e-commerce queries.
- The great majority of Web e-commerce queries posed by the public were short, not much modified, and very simple in structure.
- Few queries incorporate advance search features and when they do many contained spelling mistakes.

Web users searching for e-commerce information viewed few result pages, and tended not to browse beyond the first or second page of results and do not use relevance feedback.

6.2 Excite E-Commerce Query Subjects

Table 7.4 shows the subjects of the Excite e-commerce-related queries.

Table 7-4. Excite 2001 E-Commerce Subject Categories

Subject Categories	%
Company URL	27%
Industry or Association Name	23.5%
Trade and Commerce	16.3%
Tourism, Travel & Places	9%
Finance	7.5%
Products	6.5%
Real Estate	5%
Employment	2.5%
Business Education	2%
Legal Issues	0.6%
Total	100%

- Few queries incorporate advance search features and when they do many contained spelling mistakes.
- Web users for e-commerce information viewed few result pages, and tended not to browse beyond the first or second page of results and did not use relevance feedback.
- Company or product name queries were the most common form of e-commerce query.
- Company (and industry) related queries account for more than half the e-commerce-related Web searches. Many people are searching for company web sites, despite getting, as a rule, a large number of Web sites as answers to their queries,
- A small number of terms are used with very high frequency and tend to be more generic, such as "shopping" and "pizza".
- Alternatively, a great many terms are used only once as the language of Web queries is very rich and varied, with many unique company and product names appearing as queries.

7. E-COMMERCE WEB SEARCH TRENDS

From our analysis of e-commerce-related queries from 1997 to 2002, we found that most e-commerce Web queries posed by the public are short, not much modified, and very simple in structure. Few queries incorporate advance search features and when they do many contain mistakes. Despite getting, as a rule, a large number of Web sites as answers to their queries,

Web users for e-commerce information view few result pages, tend not to browse beyond the first or second page of results and do not use relevance feedback.

A small number of terms are used with very high frequency tend to be more generic, such as "shopping" and "pizza". Alternatively, a great many terms are used only once as the language of Web queries is very rich and varied, with many unique company and product names appearing as queries. Company or product name queries were the most common form of business query. Company (and industry) related queries account for more than half the e-commerce-related Web searches. In general, Web search engines are currently trying to cater to the broad rather than specialized nature of human information needs.

People are increasingly searching for e-commerce-related information using Web search engines. The nature of their e-commerce-related information needs are broad and relate to all aspects of e-commerce. Company (and industry) related queries account for more than half the e-commerce-related Web searches. Many people are searching for company Web sites. A need exists for new search tools that more easily facilitate company and product searches. Excite allows industry search, but it would be easier for people to use it if Excite brought this feature to the main page.

Many people appeared to be searching for shopping sites via the search engine, as the number of e-commerce-related queries appeared to be directly shopping-related. They are searching under brand names as well as generic types of products, such as "cars" or "golf clubs". Many people were seeking advice or product comparisons or they are just not sure what they want or how to find it on the Web. Web services such as "Ask Simon" are attempting to cater to this need. Many users need a conversation with an "expert' to guide them to expressing and finding their real information need. Many Web search engines and e-commerce sites are beginning to provide some forms of interaction for customers to help them sort through the plethora of Web sites, services, and products that confront them. Some search engines, such as AltaVista, are providing some form of comparison-shopping.

There is a great market for niche Web services and search engines that facilitate more effective and targeted access to e-commerce sites. Our study with search log data as the only available data cannot answer other questions about the results of these queries or the performance of different search engines. However, they do provide a snapshot for comparison of public behavior while searching, a behavior that can also serve as a clue for improvement of Web services.

Despite the growing e-commerce nature of the Web, many users' access to e-commerce information is limited due to poor searching tools, and a lack of a standardized approach to search engine functionality and terminology.

The e-commerce terminology on the Web is also incredibly various and difficult for the average user to predict with total accuracy.

In general, Web search engines are currently trying to cater to the broad rather than specialized nature of human information needs. People are increasingly searching for e-commerce-related information using Web search engines. The nature of their e-commerce-related information needs are broad and relate to all aspects of e-commerce.

8. CONCLUSION

As the Web continues to become a key centerpiece for e-commerce, new tools and new ways of searching for e-commerce information on the Web are needed (Wigand and Benjamin, 1995). Searching the Web today is somewhat akin to searching a library catalog and equally as frustrating. The Web also lacks a standardized approach to search engine functionality and terminology.

The e-commerce terminology on the Web is also incredibly various and difficult for the average user to predict with total accuracy. As more Web users begin to ask questions rather than producing Boolean queries, methods and approaches are needed to analyze and process question queries in a "question and answer" format to diagnose the users' real information requirements, to complete the cycle of e-commerce and facilitate the effective sale of goods and services over the Web.

9. REFERENCES

Bellman, S., Lohse, G.I. and Johnson, E.J. (1999).Predictors of Online Buying Behavior. *Communications of the ACM*, 42(12), 32–38.

Chun, I-S., Lee, J-G. and Lee, E-S. (1999–2000). I-SEE: An Intelligent Agent for Electronic Commerce. *International Journal of Electronic Commerce*, 4(2), 83.

DeCovny, S. 1998. Electronic commerce comes of age. *Journal of Business Strategy*, 19, 6.

Hoffman, D. L., Novak, T. P. and Chatterjee, P. (2000). Commercial Scenarios for the Web: Opportunities and Challenges. *Journal of Computer Mediated Communication*, 1(3).

Jansen, B. J. and Spink, A. (2004a). An Analysis of Web Searching by European AlltheWeb.com Users. *Information Processing and Management* (in press).

Jansen, B. J. and Spink, A. (2004b). Searching the World Wide Web: Comparing the Usage of European and United States Search Engines. *Journal of the American Society for Information Science and Technology.* (in press).

Jansen, B. J., Spink, A. and Saracevic, T. (2000). Real Life, Real Users and Real Needs: A Study and Analysis of Users' Queries on the Web. *Information Processing and Management,* 36(2), 207–227.

Keeney, R. L. (1999). The Value of Internet Commerce to the Customer. *Management Science*, 45(4), 533–542.

Koufaris, M., Kambil, A. and LaBarbera, P.A. (2001–2002). Consumer Behavior in Web-Based Commerce: An Empirical Study. *International Journal of Electronic Commerce,* 9(2), 115.

Leonard, N. K. (2003). Acquiring Goods and Services Via the Internet: Consumer Shopping Perceptions. *First Monday,* 8(11).

Silverstein, C., Henzinger, M., Marais, H. and Moricz, M. (1999). Analysis of a Very Large Web Search Engine Query Log. *Association for Computing Machinery, Special Interest Group on Information Retrieval (ACM SIGIR) Forum,* 33, 3.

Spink, A. and Guner, O. (2001). E-Commerce Web Queries: Excite and Ask Jeeves Study. *First Monday,* 6(7).

Spink, A., Jansen, B. J., Wolfram, D. and Saracevic, T. (2002). From E-Sex to E-Commerce: Web Search Changes. *IEEE Computer,* 35(3), 133–135.

Spink, A. and Ozmutlu, H. C. (2003). Characteristics of Question Format Web Queries: An Exploratory Study. *Information Processing and Management,* 38(4), 453–471.

Spink, A., Ozmutlu, S., Ozmutlu, H. C. and Jansen, B. J. (2002). US Versus European Web Searching Trends. *ACM SIGIR Forum, 36,* 2.

Spink, A., Wolfram, D., Jansen, B. J. and Saracevic. T. (2000). Searching the Web: The Public and Their Queries. *Journal of the American Society for Information Science,* 53(2), 226–234.

Spiteri, L. F. (2000). Access to Electronic Commerce Sites on the World Wide Web: An Analysis of the Effectiveness of Six Internet Search Engines. *Journal of Information Science,* 26(3), 173–183.

Steinfield, C., Kraut, R. and Plummer, A. (1995). The Impact of Inter- Organizational Networks on Buyer–Seller Relationships. *Journal of Computer-Mediated Communication,* 1, 3.

Wigand, R. T. and Benjamin, R. L. (1995). Electronic Commerce: Effects of Electronic Markets. *Journal of Computer Mediated Communication,* 1, 3.

Wolfram, D., Spink, A. Jansen, B. J. and Saracevic, T. (2001). Vox Populi: The Public Searching of the Web. *Journal of the American Society for Information Science and Technology,* 52(12), 1073–1074.

Zwass, V. (2000). Structure and Macro-Level Impacts of Electronic Commerce: From Technological Infrastructure to Electronic Marketplaces. *Foundations of Information Systems – E-Commerce Paper,* 2000 <http://www.mhhe.com/business/mis/zwass/ecpaper. html>.

Chapter 8

MEDICAL AND HEALTH WEB SEARCHING

1. INTRODUCTION

In this chapter, we report findings from an analysis of medical or health queries submitted to different Web search engines. We report results: (1) comparing samples of 10,000 Web queries taken randomly from 1.2 million query logs from the AlltheWeb.com and Excite.com commercial Web search engines in 2001 for medical or health queries, (2) comparing the 2001 findings from Excite and AlltheWeb.com users with results from a previous analysis of medical and health-related queries from the Excite Web search engine for 1997 and 1999, and (3) medical or health advice-seeking queries beginning with the word "should".

Findings suggest: (1) a small percentage of Web queries are medical or health-related; (2) the top five categories of medical or health queries were: general health, weight issues, reproductive health and puberty, pregnancy/obstetrics, and human relationships; and (3) over time, the medical and health queries may have decreased as a proportion of all Web queries, as the use of specialized medical/health Websites and e-commerce related queries has increased. Findings provide insights into medical and health-related Web querying and suggests some implications for the use of the general Web search engines when seeking medical/health information.

2.   RELATED STUDIES

Medical and health information is proliferating on the Web. A recent study by the American Medical Association (2002) reported an increase in the use of the Internet by physicians. Consumers also search the Web for information related to medical and health issues. This information may become the basis for shared patient and provider communication and decision-making. In addition to seeking factual or general information on medical and health issues, people may use Web search engines to seek advice on personal problems, where related queries may be very detailed and solicit specific medical or health information.

In this growing shared decision-making medical environment, the quality of Web-based information retrieved by the patient becomes of growing importance to the provider (Impicciatore, Pandolfini, Casella and Bonati, 1997). Many studies have examined aspects of consumer-health-related Web use, including Web sites and electronic lists (Jones, Balfour, Gillies, Stobo, Cawsey and Donaldson, 2001; McCray, Dorfman, Ripple, Ide, Jha, Katz, Loane and Tse, 2000; Rozic-Hristovski, Hristovski and Todorovski, 2000).

Studies have evaluated the accuracy, quality and reliability of medical information on the Web (European Commission Information Society, 2001; Fallis and Fricke, 2002; McLeod, 1998; Pandolfini, 2002). McCray, Loane, Browne and Bangalore (1998) studied users' queries on the National Library of Medicine Web site. Some 94% of terms submitted were medical terms covering a broad range of medical topics. Many medical terms were misspelled and short (less than 4 words). Many users also asked specific questions that went beyond the National Library of Medicine (NLM) Website.

Medical Website quality is being tested through the URAC <http://webapps.urac.org/websiteaccreditation/default.htm> accreditation process, 'health on the Net' logo program, and the HI Ethics project. As part of the European Union's eEurope: Health Online actions, Member State representatives and experts have agreed to establish a set of guidelines for quality criteria for health-related Websites. Such criteria are designed to increase user confidence in use of such sites and foster best practices in the development of sites.

In addition, Barnas and Kahn (1999) surveyed users of the Medical College of Wisconsin HealthLink Web site. The study revealed a broad range of users' medical topic interests, including women's health, weight control, allergies, and back problems. In a related study, Eysenbach, Yihune, Lampe, Cross and Brickley (2000) discussed MedCERTAIN, a project attempting to label the quality of Internet health information.

Current research suggests that medical and health information seeking constitutes an important use of the Web. The Pew Internet & American Life (2002a, b) study, one of the largest national surveys accomplished to date, estimate that 62% of Internet users (some 73 million people living in the United States) search the Web for health information. Results from the Pew study indicated that 93% of health information seekers surveyed looked for information about a specific illness or condition, 65% sought information on exercise, nutrition or weight control, 64% for prescription drugs, and 33% for sensitive health information. More than half the respondents reported using the Web for health information every few months or less frequently.

Clearly, many American are using the Web for medical and health information, often as a supplement to seeking help from medical providers. Recently, the Pew Internet & American Life (2003) study found that half of American adults surveyed have searched online for health information. Some 80% of adult Internet users (93 million people) have searched for at least one of 16 major health topics online. The Pew (2003) study suggests that the act of looking for health or medical information is a popular online activity. It did not compare the frequency of health searching with other topics.

3.   MEDICAL WEB SEARCHING

Many researchers have studied users' medical searching and information retrieval within complex abstracting systems, such as MEDLINE (Hersh and Hickam, 1998). Eysenbach and Kohler (2002) found that for 21 consumer Web users, searching for health information is suboptimal, but users nevertheless found health information successfully. Atlas (2001) found that first-year medical students reported that general Web search engines produced better results than meta-medical Web sites and medicine-specific search engines. Duran, Eastman, and Jansen (2003) arrived at a similar finding with nutritional Web sites. Many researchers have called for a new generation of Web-based medical retrieval tools (Bin and Li, 2001; Rogers, 2001; Suarez, Hao, Chang and Masys, 1997).

Recent studies by Spink, Jansen, Wolfram and Saracevic (2002) show that users' general Web search engine sessions are usually short and contain few search terms or queries. Medical and health-related topics generated approximately 9.5% of Excite Web searches in 1997, 7.8% in 1999 and 7.5% in 2001. Spink and Ozmutlu (2002) found that 11.5% of AskJeeves question queries were medical or health-related.

Studies of health information seeking on the Web also indicate that lay terminology is only partly successful at locating useful health information and search effectiveness (Bin and Li, 2001), where Web searching often yields misleading or unrelated information for the lay health consumer. Berland, Elliot, Morales, Algazy, Kravitz and Broder (2002) likewise concluded that accessing health information using search engines and simple search terms was not efficient, since high reading levels are required to comprehend Web-based health information.

Patients further seek medical advice from physicians via email (Borowitz and Wyatt, 1998; Spielberg, 1998) and from the Web (Ferguson, 1998; O'Connor and Johanson, 2000). Macleod (McLeod, 1998) summarized the limitations of the Web as an electronic consumer resource: "while immediate access to such information has been of great benefit to health care professionals and patients, there is growing concern that a substantial proportion of clinical information on the Web might be inaccurate, erroneous, misleading, or fraudulent, and thereby pose a threat to public health ..."

Often, then, the Web-enabled health information seeker must know, within the realm of language, the near-specific location of the knowledge they seek. When an exact clinical term is not known, most laypersons will resort to their only available resource, the popular/lay terminology for the concept, illness, or subject of interest. While the capacity of the patient to gather and collect such information remains a matter for the clinician to assess, it is undeniable that Internet-derived information can serve as a powerful catalyst for seeking health services (Faxon and Lenfant, 2001; Muhlhauser and Berger, 2000; Rivera, Kim, Garone, Morgenstern and Mohsenifar, 2001).

4.   MEDICAL/HEALTH QUERIES

Table 8.1 compares results from previous Web query studies with results from the analysis of the 2001 Excite and Alltheweb.com data sets for medical or health queries.

Medical or health issues were a declining proportion of the queries submitted to the Excite Web search engines. The decline has progressed from a high of 9.5% in 1997 to 7.5% in 2001. The proportion of medical or health-related queries submitted to the European AlltheWeb.com Web search engine was also lower at 3.2% (Spink, Ozmutlu, Ozmutlu and Jansen, 2002).

For both the Excite and AlltheWeb.com data sets, the mean terms per query was 2.3, the mean queries per user session was 2.2, and the mean pages of results viewed per user session was 1.6. We had no click-through data for these sessions. These figures are fairly equivalent to statistics for general Web searching (Spink, Jansen, Wolfram and Saracevic, 2002). In other words, medical or health-related Web searches were equivalent in length, complexity and lack of query reformulation to non-medical or health searches (Spink, Yang, Jansen, Nyganen, Lorence, Ozmutlu, and Ozmutlu, 2004).

Table 8-1. Trends in Prevalence of Medical and Health-related Web Queries

1997 Excite Queries (2414 Queries) *	1999 Excite Web Queries (2539 Queries)*	2001 Excite Web Queries (10,000 Queries)*	2001 AlltheWeb.com Web Queries (10,257 Queries)
9.5% medical or health queries	7.8% medical or health queries	7.5% medical or health queries	3.2% medical or health queries
Mean of 2.3 terms per medical or health query	Mean of 2.3 terms per medical or health query	Mean of 2.3 terms per medical or health query	Mean of 2.3 terms per medical or health query
Mean of 2.2 queries per medical or health session	Mean of 2.2 queries per medical or health session	Mean of 2.2 queries per medical or health session	Mean of 2.2 queries per medical or health session

*Spink et al. (2002).

5. MEDICAL ADVICE-SEEKING

Table 8.2 shows the percentage of medical or health-related queries in the 2001 Excite searches and AskJeeves advice-seeking question-answering data.

Table 8-2. Excite and AskJeeves Medical and Health Advice Seeking Topic Categories

Topic Categories	% of 2001 Excite Medical or Health-related Queries (4.5% of 2500 queries = 112)		% of AskJeeves Advice-Seeking Medical or Health-related Queries (24% of 1792 queries = 332)	
	Number	%	Number	%
General Medical /Health	23	21.3%	118	35.6%
Human Relationships	40	35.2%	70	21.3%
Weight	17	15.3%	69	20.8%
Reproductive Health/Puberty	21	18%	45	13.8%
Pregnancy/Baby	11	10.2%	28	8.5%
Total	112	100%	332	100%

Some 332 (24%) of the 1,792 advice-seeking question-answering AskJeeves queries were medical or health-related.

5.1   General Medical/Health

Many queries were related to general medical or health issues. A query was considered to be searching for general medical/health information if it named a medical term, such as a disease, a pharmaceutical drug, or a symptom or general health issue. Example of such terms would be "AIDS," "dizziness," and "flu."

5.2   Human Relationships

A query was regarded as falling into the human relationship category if it was seeking information about psychological health issues (for example, dating, marriage, psychological disorders, known psychologists, or psychological tests). Examples of these queries would be "How I do I get a mental health doctor?" This type of question required a complex and more psychologically based response.

5.3   Weight

Many queries in this category requested information on the appropriate weight for a given height or age. For example, "What should be my weight if my height is 4' 10"? Many users just asked "How much should I weigh?".

5.4   Reproductive Health

Reproductive health queries often related to sexual issues and infertility or sexual health issues. For example, one user asked, "How often should men ejaculate?" or "Is my vagina normal?"

5.5   Pregnancy/Baby

Many queries related to health issues during pregnancy or the health of a baby. For example, "When should I take a pregnancy test?" and "Should pregnant women fly in an airplane?"

6.   MEDICAL AND HEALTH ADVICE-SEEKING

Table 8.3 provides the number of advice-seeking queries using various starting terms including the term "should".

Table 8-3. AskJeeves Advice-Seeking Medical or Health-related Query – Starting Terms (Total = 332 queries)

Should Query Starting Terms	Number of Queries	%
What should I	82	24.7%
How should	48	14.4%
What should you	46	13.8%
Should	35	10.6%
Should I	30	9.2%
Should we	27	7.8%
Where should	22	6.8%
How should	16	4.8%
Why should	12	3.7%
When should	10	3%
Which should	4	1.2%
Total	332	100%

Most people who used the AskJeeves question-answering Web search engine asked for medical or health advice within a limited question structure. Of interest, most users *seeking advice* about medical or health asked "What should" or "How should" questions, rather then "Where should I" questions. In general, most non-medical or health Web users ask more location-related questions, such as "Where can I find" questions or "What is" questions.

6.1   Personified and Opinion Queries

Medical or health-related queries were also often advice seeking and personalized, e.g. "Hey Jeeves, what should I take for the flu?" Medical/health users also sought more human-like answers. A few users actually addressed AskJeeves as a human being by saying: "Hey Jeeves" or "Jeeves…." or ask for opinion. Some users requested help by saying: "Help me Jeeves". Some users were polite and phrased their query as "May I…." or "Please…" However, most users were not that polite, particularly those who entered a request as opposed to a question format query, discussed later in this paper.

While not readily seen in individual search observations, it becomes apparent from a large log of AskJeeves question queries that many medical and health information seeking searchers do not clearly understand the Web search process. They ascribe human abilities to AskJeeves that go way beyond its current capabilities. Many users do not understand how a Web search engine works in conjunction with their own knowledge base or how it affects information seeking and searching processes. Users are often frustrated and emotional during their Web search engine interactions.

7.   DISCUSSION

Findings from our analysis suggest that a small proportion of searches on commercial Web search engines, in the United States and Europe, are medical or health-related. Despite the large percentage of Internet users who conduct medical or health searchers reported by The Pew Internet Project (2002a, b) survey, examination of large-scale commercial Web query logs suggests that medical or health Web searching may be a small proportion of Web searches. As stated previously, Pew (2003) does not compare health searching with other topics.

Our findings also suggest an on-going shift in Web users' search topics. From 1997 to 2001, queries related to entertainment or recreation and medical or health, have declined proportionally as the queries related to e-commerce, travel, employment or economy and people, places or things have increased (Spink, Jansen, Wolfram and Saracevic, 2002). This proportional shift may also reflect a shift by Web users to more specialized medical or health Web sites, such as WebMD (http://www.webmd.com/), and a shift towards more e-commerce Websites and Web searching.

Medical or health Web queries and sessions are short and equivalent in length to non-medical or health querying. Users also do not reformulate their medical or health searches to a great extent. Thus, they express medical and health issues succinctly. Few people create long medical or health queries that include synonyms or alternate terms. Few users look beyond the first or second page of Web sites retrieved in response to their queries. Users may be finding the information they seek in the first ten to twenty Websites.

The analysis of advice seeking and personified Web queries suggests that when seeking medical and health information, most consumers fail to understand the limitations of the Web search process. Many also ascribe human and advice-seeking abilities to Web search engines, such as AskJeeves, that go beyond the system's current capabilities. Many users do not really understand how a Web search engine works in conjunction with their own information seeking and searching processes. Users are often frustrated and emotional during their Web search engine interactions. They wish to engage in an advice-seeking interaction, but they may be frustrated by the inability of the search engine to respond to their personal medical and health needs and concerns.

Commercial Web search engines were designed to help people use natural language expressions and formulate searches as readable and understandable queries. When seeking medical information, such technologies have the potential to make medical language, terms, and expressions understandable in searching for help and asking opinions from the search engine. This technology could offer more human-like communication, and it is often marketed and promoted as a health information service. Such context, however, is problematic when the use of precise clinical terms, descriptions, or concepts is called for.

Current search technologies are becoming more akin to natural language communication, and are being used more frequently by users for health information retrieval, health services, or the sharing of health experiences. Most users may still lack the specialized vocabulary needed to effectively retrieve the information relevant to their condition.

Most studies to date have presupposed that people are able to reach (arguably) credible clinical or health information through commercial Web search engines. However, for many people, the operation and outcomes of the commercial Web search engine still pose a significant barrier to usable health information. Research is needed to explore the limitations of Web search engines and Websites for medical or health information seeking.

Large-scale studies of Web queries, as outlined in this paper, have strengths and weaknesses. Such studies using real data from Web search engines can show large-scale patterns and trends. Frequently, however, they lack demographic data on individual users and their Web search effectiveness.

In an era of health consumerism, evidence-based medicine, and growing shared decision-making between patients and providers, it becomes imperative to provide consistent, reliable, health information via the Web. People expect and require information they can trust, delivered in a format that is understandable and usable. Further research is underway that examines the characteristics of medical or health-related queries and sessions using query data from other Web search engines.

8.   REFERENCES

American Medical Association. (2002). *Study on Physicians' Use of the World Wide Web*. Chicago: AMA Press.

Atlas, M. C. (2001). First-Year Students' Impressions of the Internet. *Medical Reference Services Quarterly, 20*, 11–25.

Barnas, G. P. and Kahn, C. E. (1999). Assessing Consumers' Interest in Internet-Based Health Information. *AMIA '99: Proceedings of the American Medical Informatics Association*.

Berland, G. K., Elliot, M. N, Morales, L. S. Algazy, J. I, Kravitz, R. L, and Broder, M. S. (2002). Health Information on the Internet: Accessibility, Quality, and Readability in English and Spanish. *Journal of the American Medical Association, 285*, 2612–2621.

Bin, L. and Li, K. C. (2001). The Retrieval Effectiveness of Medical Information on the Web. *International Journal of Medical Information, 62*, 155–163.

Borowitz, S. M. and Wyatt, J. C. (1998). The Origin, Content, and Workload of E-mail Consultations. *Journal of the American Medical Association, 280*, 1321–1324.

Duran, S., Eastman, C., and Jansen, B.J. (2003). Nutritional Information on the Web. An Analysis of Information Sought and Information Provided. *Information Resource Management Association Conference, Philadelphia, PA, 18–21 May 2003*. pp. 106–108.

European Commission Information Society. (2001). *Guidelines for Quality Criteria. Workshop on Quality Criteria for Health-related Websites* (Workshop Report). Sept 2001.

Eysenbach, G. and Kohler, C. (2002). How Do Consumers Search For and Appraise Health Information on the World Wide Web? Qualitative Study Using Focus Groups, Usability Tests, and In-Depth Interviews. *British Medical Journal, 24*, 573–577.

Eysenbach, G., Yihune, G., Lampe, K., Cross, P. and Brickley, D. (2000). Quality Management, Certification and Rating of Health Information on the Net with MedCERTAIN: Using a MedPICS/RDF/XML Metadata Structure for Implementing eHealth Ethics and Creating Trust Globally. *Journal of Medical Internet Research, Apr–Jun 2* (2 Suppl.), 2E1.

Fallis, D. and Fricke, M. (2002). Indicators of Accuracy of Consumer Health Information on the Internet: A Study of Indicators Relating to Information for Managing Fever in Children in the Home. *Journal of the American Medical Informatics Association, 9*, 73–79.

Faxon, D. and Lenfant, C. (2001). Timing is Everything: Motivating Patients to Call 9-1-1 at Onset of Acute Myocardial Infarction. *Circulation, 104*, 1210–1211.

Ferguson, T. (1998). Digital Doctoring: Opportunities and Challenges in Electronic Patient–Physician Communication. *Journal of the American Medical Association, 280*(15), 1361–1362.

Hersh, W. R. and Hickam, D. H. (1999). How Well Do Physicians Use Electronic Information Retrieval Systems? A Framework for Investigation and Systematic Review. *Journal of the American Medical Association, 280*, 1347.

Impicciatore, P., Pandolfini, C., Casella, N. and Bonati, M. (1997). Reliability of health Information for the Public on the World Wide Web: A Systematic Survey of Advice and Managing Fever in Children at Home. *British Medical Journal, 314*, 1875–1881.

Jones, R. B., Balfour, F., Gillies, M., Stobo, D., Cawsey, A. J. and Donaldson, K. (2001). The Accessibility of Computer-Based Health Information for Patients: Kiosks and the Web. *Med Info, 10*, 1469–1473.

McCray, A. T., Dorfman, E., Ripple, A., Ide, N. C., Jha, M., Katz, D. G., Loane, R. F. and Tse T. (2000). Usability Issues in Developing a Web-Based Consumer Health Site. *AMIA'00: Proceedings of the Annual Fall Symposium of the American Medical Informatics Association*, 556–561.

McCray, A. T., Loane, R. F., Browne, A. C. and Bangalore, A. K. (1998). Terminology Issues in User Access to Web-Based Medical Information. *AMIA'98: Proceedings of the American Medical Informatics Association*.

McLeod, S. D. (1998). The Quality of Medical Information on the Internet: A New Public Health Concern. *Archives of Ophthalmology, 116*, 1663.

Muhlhauser, I. and Berger M. (2000). Evidence-Based Patient Information in Diabetes. *Diabetic Medicine, 17*, 823–829.

O'Connor, J. B. and Johanson, J. F. (2000). Use of the Web for Medical Information by a Gastroentology Clinic Population. *Journal of the American Medical Association, 284*, 1902–1904.

Pandolfini, C. (2002). Follow Up of Quality of Public Oriented Health Information on the World Wide Web: Systematic Re-evaluation. *British Medical Journal, 324*, 582–583.

Pew Internet & American Life. (2002a). *Search Engines: A Pew Internet Project* . Data Memo. June, 2002.

Pew Internet & American Life. (2002b). *Vital Decisions: How Internet Users Decide What Information to Trust When They or Their Loved Ones Are Sick.* Pew Internet & American Life Project Report, 2002.

Pew Internet & American Life. (2003). *Internet Health Resources: Health Searches and Email Have Become More Commonplace, But There is Room for Improvement in Searches and Overall Internet Access.* Pew Internet & American Life Project Report, 2003.

Rivera, S., Kim, D., Garone, S., Morgenstern, L. and Mohsenifar Z. (2001). Motivating Factors in Futile Clinical Interventions. *Chest, 119*, 1944–1947.

Rozic-Hristovski, A., Hristovski, D. and Todorovski, L. (2000). Users' Information Seeking Behavior on a Medical Library Website. *Journal of the Medical Library Association, 90*, 210–217.

Rogers, R. P. (2001). Searching for Biomedical Information on the World Wide Web. *Journal of Medical Practice Management, 15*, 306–313.

Spielberg, A. R. (1998). Sociohistorical, Legal and Ethical Implications of E-mail for Patient–Physician Relationship. *Journal of the American Medical Association, 280*, 1353–1359.

Spink, A., Jansen B. J. and Wolfram D. Saracevic, T. (2002). From E-Sex to E-Commerce: Web Searching Changes. *IEEE Computer, 35*, 107–109.

Spink, A. and Ozmutlu, H. C. (2002). Characteristics of Question Format Web Queries: An Exploratory Study. *Information Processing and Management, 38*, 453–471.

Spink, A., Ozmutlu, S., Ozmutlu, H. C. and Jansen, B. J. (2002). United States Versus European Web Searching Trends. *ACM SIGIR, 36*(2).

Spink, A., Yang, Y., Jansen, B, J., Nyganen, P., Lorence, D. P., Ozmutlu, S. and Ozmutlu, H. C. (2004). A Study of Medical and Health Queries to Web Search Engines. *Health Information and Libraries Journal.*

Suarez, H. H., Hao, X., Chang, I. F. and Masys, D. R. (1997). Searching for Information on the Internet Using IMLS and Medical World Search. *AMIA'97: Proceedings of the Annual Fall Symposium of the American Medical Informatics Association, Philadelphia, PA,* 824–828, Hanley & Belfus, 1997.

Chapter 9

SEXUALLY-RELATED WEB SEARCHING

1. INTRODUCTION

Sexual information seeking is an important element within human information behavior. Sexually-related information seeking on the Internet takes many forms and channels, including chat room discussions, accessing Websites or searching Web search engines for sexual materials. The study of sexual Web queries provides insight into sexually-related information-seeking behavior, of value to Web users and providers alike. We qualitatively analyzed queries from logs of 1,025,910 AltaVista and AlltheWeb.com Web user queries from 2001. We compared the differences in sexually-related Web searching between AltaVista and AlltheWeb.com users. Differences were found in session duration, query outcomes, and search term choices. Implications of the findings for sexual information seeking are discussed.

2. HUMAN INTERNET SEXUALITY

Human Internet sexuality is a growing area of research in the social sciences (Cooper, 2002), highlighting, for example, gender differences in Internet sexuality (Cooper, Morahan-Martin, Mathy and Maheu, 2002). Sexual information seeking falls within the realm of human information behavior theory and models. Sexual information seeking is not considered to be task- or occupation-oriented. Sexual information seeking, with its connection to reproduction, mate seeking, etc., is related to the wider concerns of everyday life, social adaptation, and survival in the information age. In particular, seeking sexual information on the Internet forms a subset of human information behavior (HIB) research that attempts to explore all aspects of information-connected human behaviors (Spink and Ozmutlu, 2001; Spink, Ozmutlu and Lorence, 2003; Spink, Ozmutlu, Ozmutlu and Cole, 2004).

Spink and Cole (forthcoming) integrate the diverse information behaviors using principles from evolutionary psychology. From the evolutionary psychology perspective, human information foraging is fundamental to human adaptation and survival. Driven by this need, humans engage in a constant foraging of their environment for data/information that will facilitate their adaptation and survival. Such information behavior can occur without human attention, and may occur and be attached to information the user finds while seeking information for the satisfaction of other physiological, affective or cognitive needs (Spink and Cole, 2001).

Sexual information behavior can be included as part of human adaptation and survival. Seen in this light, the seeking of sexual information on the Internet and elsewhere in the environment may occur not only for the fundamental human purpose of mating and the propagation of the species, but also for the diverse information behavior mechanisms concerned with adaptation and survival. These mechanisms may perhaps be discerned via an examination of sexual information seeking.

Here we start at the beginning, analyzing sexual information seeking behavior on the Internet. The base-line elements in Internet sexual information seeking are the searching characteristics of the online user. One such search characteristic is the query the user selects to access sexual information on the Web. Query-oriented studies are just beginning, and there is a need for studies examining sexually-related queries to further identify the characteristics of sexual Web searching. The study reported in this paper explores sexually-related human information searching on the Web via a statistical examination of Web queries containing sexual terms.

3.   SEXUALITY AND WEB SEARCHING

Pornography or sexually-related materials are available widely on the Web, including online sex shops (Fisher and Bakar, 2000). Rimm (1995) found that pornographic images were widely available on the Web, particularly on bulletin boards and USENET. A 1998 study estimated the existence of 22,000 pornographic Web sites (Willems, 1998). These studies are part of an ongoing debate regarding the accessibility of sexually-related material on the Web (Quayle, 2002). Li (2000) discusses this debate, including the issues of obscenity, child pornography and filtering, and the studies conducted particularly in relation to libraries.

A growing body of studies is strongly contributing to our understanding of human sexuality in the new frontier of the Internet. Human Internet sexuality is a growing area of research in the social sciences (Cooper, 1998; Cooper, 2002; Cooper, Putnam, Planchon and Boies, 1999, Cooper, Delmonico and Burg, 2000). Cooper, Scherer, Boies and Gordon (1999) and Goodson, McCormick and Evan (2000, 2001) highlight the divergent views of Internet sexuality or "cybersex".

The *pathological perspective* focuses on Internet sexuality as deviant, addictive or criminal behavior (Bingham and Piotrowski, 1996; Durkin and Bryant, 1995; King, 1999; Van Gelder, 1985; Young and Rogers, 1998). The *adaptive-perspective – sexual expression* is a more adaptive view that places Internet sexuality within the context of sexual human development and exploration, and love and romance (Cooper and Sportolari, 1997; Leiblum, 1997; Newman, 1997).

Studies also show gender differences in Internet sexuality (Cooper, Morahan-Martin, Mathy and Maheu, 2002; Cooper, Scherer, Boies and Gordon, 1999). Cooper, Boies, Maheu and Greenfield (2000) found that men are more dominant in online sexual activities, such as sexually-related chat rooms and pornographic Website use, Internet abuse and sexual problems. The researchers also found that heavy Internet users, or about 8% of users, who spend the most time online for sex, also reported significant problems associated with compulsive disorders and addiction. The goal of their research is to recommend treatments for outreach prevention programs. Cooper, Scherer, Boies and Gordon (1999) also identify "paraphilics" as dependent on cybersex as a source of stimulation and satisfaction for often unconventional sexual desires.

4.   SEXUALLY-RELATED WEB SEARCHING

Recent studies have also begun to examine the nature of sexually-related information seeking on Web search engines. Goodrum and Spink (2001) found that 25 of the most frequently occurring terms in multimedia-related queries submitted to the Excite commercial Web search engine were clearly sexually-related. Spink, Wolfram, Jansen and Saracevic (2001) found that although sexually-related searching by users of the Excite Web search engine represented only a small proportion of all queries and terms (>5%), about one in every four terms in the list of 63 highest used terms can be classified as sexual in nature.

Spink and Ozmutlu (2002) also found that terms such as "sex", "nude" and "naked" were high frequency terms submitted to the AskJeeves commercial Web search engine. Spink, Jansen, Wolfram and Saracevic (2002) examined large-scale Excite Web query data sets from 1997, 1999 and 2001. They found that sexually-related queries decreased as a proportion of all Web queries from the second largest category (16.8%) in 1997 to fourth largest category (7.5%) in 1999 and the fifth largest category (8.5%) in 2001. Web queries related to business, computers and people increased as a proportion of all Web queries.

Spink, Ozmutlu, Ozmutlu and Jansen (2002) compared the topics of United States Excite search engine users versus European AlltheWeb.com search engine searches in 2001. They found that sexually-related queries were the fifth largest Excite topic category (8.5%) and the fourth largest category (10.8%) on AlltheWeb.com. Spink, Ozmutlu, Ozmutlu and Jansen (2002) compared the topics of United States Excite search engine users versus European Fast search engine searches in 2001. They found that that sexually-related queries was the fifth largest Excite topic category (8.5%) and the fourth largest AlltheWeb.com topic category (10.8%).

Spink and Ozmutlu (2002) and Spink, Ozmutlu and Lorence (2004) found that sexual and non-sexual-related queries by Excite users exhibited differences in session duration, query outcomes, and search term choices. They also identified a more limited vocabulary used in sexual queries when compared to non-sexual queries. Sexual queries involved fewer unique terms. Many sexually-related terms were repeated frequently in queries, e.g., *nude, sex, naked*, etc. They found that sexually-related Web search sessions and queries were longer than non-sexual search sessions, and contained more queries.

Sexual queries were generally longer than most non-sexual queries and there was a high probability that a sexual session could be longer than 20+ queries. People seeking sexual information were willing to expend the time and effort to create longer queries and to use more queries. Sexual searchers viewed more pages than non-sexual searchers. Most non-sexual searchers do not view much beyond the first or second page of ten Web sites. For example, a typical sexual information seeker was seeking images of nude women and may view more than 20 pages of Web sites.

Sexual sessions may also longer because images often take quite some time to download. This length duration may also reflect the seeker's willingness to submit more queries. The findings may also relate to the Cooper, Putnam, Planchon and Boies (1999) identification of heavy Web users who exhibit "paraphilic" behaviors and are dependent on cybersex as a source of stimulation and satisfaction.

In the current study, we further investigate the nature and characteristics of sexually-related Web searching.

5. TRENDS IN SEXUAL WEB SEARCHING

Table 9.1 shows the proportion of sexually-related Web queries in each Web query sample from 1997 to 2002.

Table 9-1. Proportion of Sexually-related Web Queries in Each Sample From 1997 to 2002

	1	2	3
	Excite	Excite	AlltheWeb.com
Region	U.S.	U.S.	European
Data	Tuesday	Wednesday	Tuesday
Collection	16 Sep. 1997	1 Dec. 1999	6 Feb. 2001
Sample Size	2414 queries	2539 queries	2503 queries
Sexually-related Queries	16.8%	7.5%	10.8%

	4	5	6
	Excite	AlltheWeb.com	AltaVista
Region	U.S.	European	U.S.
Data	Monday	Tuesday	Sunday
Collection	30 Apr. 2001	28 May 02	8 Sep. 2002
Sample Size	2453 queries	2525 queries	2603 queries
Sexually-related Queries	8.5%	9.5%	3.3%

The six studies include: (1) a 1997 study of the Excite Web search engine, (2) a 1999 study of Excite Web search engine, (3) a 2001 study of the AlltheWeb.com Web search engine, (4) a 2001 study of the Excite Web search engine, (5) a study of 2001 and 2002 AlltheWeb.com Web query data sets. Collectively, the nine studies represent samples from over 1.5 million Web searching sessions and over 5.5 million queries submitted to the various Web search engines.

For the U.S.-based Excite Web search engines, in 1999 and 2001, sexually-related queries declined from 1997 to 2001. By 1999, e-commerce queries accounted for approximately 25% of the Excite queries. Noticeably percentage decreases in sexually-related queries occurred in 1999 as the Web moved from largely an entertainment medium to an e-commerce medium. Alternatively, sexually-related queries held steady at around 10% for the European AlltheWeb.com users. Jansen and Spink (in press) and Spink, Ozmutlu, Ozmutlu and Jansen (2002) had also found differences in the subjects of U.S. versus European-based Web searchers.

6. ALLTHEWEB.COM QUERIES

Table 9.2 shows the most frequently used terms in AlltheWeb.com sexually-related queries.

Table 9-2. Most Frequent Terms in AlltheWeb.com Sexually-Related Queries

Sexually-Related Term	% of All Terms	Sexually-Related Term	% of All Terms
Sex	9.4%	Animal	1.03%
Nude	6.6%	Ass	1.03%
Porn	2.8%	Babes	1.03%
Free	2.6%	Black	1.03%
Teens	2.6%	Boobs	1.03%
Amateur	2.06%	Boy	1.03%
Girl	2.06%	Jobs	1.03%
XXX	2.06%	Lesbians	1.03%
Anal	1.8%	Pornstar	1.03%
Naked	1.8%	Stories	1.03%
Tits	1.8%	Asian	0.8%
Big	1.6%	Gallery	0.8%
Nudist	1.4%	Videos	0.8%
Pics	1.2%	With	0.8%
Pictures	1.2%	Beastiality	0.6%
Shemale	1.2%	Women	0.6%

Table 9.3 shows the percentage of query length in the AlltheWeb.com sexually-related dataset.

Table 9-3. Terms per AlltheWeb.com Sexually-Related Query

Number of Terms	%
1	24.5%
2	48.7%
3	20.5%
4	4.03%
5	1.1%
6	0.0%
7	0.37%
8	0.0%
9	0.0%
10+	0.0%

Table 9.4 shows the queries per AlltheWeb.com sexually-related session.

Table 9-4. Queries Per Alltheweb.com Sexually-Related Session

Queries Per Sexually-Related Session	%
1	67.1%
2	12.6%
3	4.9%
4	6.2%
5	4.2%
6	2.1%
7	0.7%
8	0.0%
9	0.7%
10+	1.4%

Our analysis of the AlltheWeb.com query data showed:
- 273 queries in 143 AlltheWeb.com sessions contained searches for sexual material.
- Sex was the most frequently occurring term in the AlltheWeb.com sessions.
- 273/6000 = 4.5% of AlltheWeb.com queries were identified as sexually-related.
- Mean of 1.7 terms per sexually-related query.
- Mean of 1.9 queries per sexually-related session.
- 19/143 = 13.3% of the sessions included reformulated queries.
- 68/143 = 47.6% of the sessions showed the user searching also for non-sexual material.
- 9/273 = 3.3% of the sexually-related queries were for child pornography. This only included searches that explicitly stated terms for child pornography. Because of the vague nature, queries including the word "teen" were excluded from this number.

7.   ALTAVISTA QUERIES

Table 9.5 shows the most frequent terms in AltaVista sexually-related queries.

Table 9.6 shows the percentage of terms per AltaVista sexual query.

Table 9.7 shows the sexually-related queries per AltaVista session.

Table 9.8 shows the distribution of AltaVista sexually-related queries throughout the day.

Table 9-5. Most Frequent Terms in AltaVista Sexually-Related Queries

Term	%	Term	%
Sex	6.4%	Amateur	1.1%
Free	6.08%	Teen	1.1%
Nude	4.2%	Agony	0.8%
And	3.9%	Erotica	0.8%
Stories	2.9%	Naked	0.8%
Pics	2.7%	Tits	0.8%
Gay	2.4%	Back	0.6%
Her	1.8%	Movie	0.6%
Lolita	1.8%	Of	0.6%
Porn	1.8%	Penis	0.6%
Lesbian	1.6%	Porno	0.6%
Pictures	1.6%	Preteen	0.6%
Gallery	1.4%	Thumbnails	0.6%
Girls	1.4%	Video	0.6%
In	1.4%	Wet	0.6%
Erotic	1.3%	Whore	0.6%
Adult	1.1%	Women	0.6%

Table 9-6. Terms Per AltaVista Sexual Query

Number of Terms	%
1	7.3%
2	27%
3	35.4%
4	14.6%
5	7.3%
6	2.8%
7	1.6%
8	0.5%
9	0.0%
10+	3.3%

Table 9-7. Sexually-related Queries Per AltaVista Session

Number of Queries	%
1	91.3%
2	6.8%
3	1.2%
4	0.6%
5	0.0%
6	0.0%
7	0.0%
8	0.0%
9	0.0%
10+	0.0%

Table 9-8. Distribution of AltaVista Sexually-Related Queries Throughout the Day

Time Frame	%
6:00am–2:00pm	30.3%
2:00pm–10:00pm	30.9%
10:00pm–6:00am	38.8%

Our analysis of the AltaVista query data (Jansen, Spink and Pedersen, in press) showed:

- Sex was the most frequently occurring term.
- 178 queries in 160 sessions were for sexual material.
- 178/5000 = 3.5% of the sampled queries were for sexual material.
- 3.4 mean terms per sexually-related query.
- 1.1 mean queries per sexually-related session.
- 6/160 = 3.7% of the sessions included reformulated queries.
- 24/160 = 15% of sexual sessions showed the user searching also for non-sexual material.
- 10/178 = 5.6% of sexual queries searched for child pornography. This only included searches that explicitly stated terms for child pornography. Because of the vague nature, queries including the word "teen" were excluded from this number.

8.   DISCUSSION

Our data showed a slightly higher percentage of searches for sexual material by the European AlltheWeb.com users. AltaVista users submitted more terms per sexually-related query, but submitted fewer queries per session than the AlltheWeb.com users. In both AlltheWeb.com and AltaVista sexually-related queries, the term "sex" was the most frequently occurring term, and shared many of the most frequently used terms, but with a different percentage of use.

We also found differences in the distribution of terms per sexually-related query. AltaVista users entered a greater number of terms, whereas AlltheWeb.com users had the majority of their term distribution as five or less terms per query. The exact opposite is true when looking at the distribution of queries per sexually-related session. The AlltheWeb.com data was more widely distributed, while AltaVista's distribution was from four or less queries per session.

It was also interesting to look at the percentage of sexually-related sessions that contained reformulated queries. Only 3.7% of AltaVista data sexually-related sessions contained any query reformulation. Alternatively, some 13.3% of AlltheWeb.com sexually-related sessions contained reformulated queries. One reason could be that the AltaVista queries contained better search terms that found what users were looking for sooner. The exact opposite could be the case as well. Perhaps AltaVista users were simply too impatient and gave up when they did not find the desired information.

Another interesting difference between AltaVista and AlltheWeb.com users is the fact that nearly half the AlltheWeb.com users searched for non-sexual material in the same session as sexual material. In the AltaVista data only 14.8% of the sessions searched for non-sexual material in addition to the sexual material. The AltaVista data also showed a slightly higher percentage of queries that were searching for child pornography. However, the difference between AltaVista and AlltheWeb.com was only about 2%. The numbers also do not explicitly show the use of Boolean connectors. None of the AlltheWeb.com queries for sexual information contained Boolean connectors of any sort. AltaVista on the other hand, had several queries. In fact the word "and" was the fourth most frequent term in sexual queries.

This study contributes to the empirical knowledge base research is building on the nature of user queries to Internet search engines generally, and for sexual information specifically. Overall, we know that a user queries a search engine in a session, which can be made up of various iterations of the same query, called reformulation, or entirely different queries from the initial query. These modified queries can be on an entirely different topic than the initial query.

For sexual information seeking, an initial query, which is sexual in nature, can be followed by subsequent queries that are non-sexual in nature. There are other elements of sexual information seeking that we also know due to other query studies. Sexual information seeking is declining as a percentage of total information seeking on the Internet (Spink, Jansen, Wolfram and Saracevic, 2002). There appears to be differences in quantity of sexual information seeking from search engine to search engine, and from one geographical region to another. Further studies focusing on these aspects of sexual information seeking would be of interest for various reasons.

9.   CONCLUSION

The analysis reported here gives a broad overview of sexual information seeking on Web search engines and by the geographical location of their primary user groups (North American for AltaVista and Norway and Germany for AlltheWeb.com). We are currently conducting further studies of the nature and trends in sexually-related information behavior and Web searching.

10.   REFERENCES

Bingham, J. E. and Piotrowski, C. (1996). Online Sexual Addiction: A Contemporary Enigma. *Psychological Reports*, 79, 257–258.

Cooper, A. (1998). Sexuality and the Internet: Surfing into the New Millennium. *CyberPsychology & Behavior, 1*(2), 181–187.

Cooper, A. (2002) (Ed.). *Sex and the Internet: A Guidebook for Clinicians.* New York: Brunner–Routledge.

Cooper, A., Boies, S., Maheu, M. and Greenfield, D. (2000). Sexuality and the Internet: The Next Sexual Revolution. In F. Muscarella & L. Szuchman (Eds.). *The Psychological Science of Sexuality: A Research Based Approach* (pp. 519–545). New York: Wiley Press.

Cooper, A., Delmonico, D. and Burg, R. (2000). Cybersex Users, Abusers, and Compulsives: New Findings and Implications. Sexual Addiction & Compulsivity: *The Journal of Treatment and Prevention, 6*(2), 79–104.

Cooper, A., Morahan-Martin, J., Mathy, R. M. and Maheu, M. (2002). Toward An Increased Understanding of User Demographics in Online Sexual Activities. *Journal of Sex and Marital Therapy, 28*, 105–129.

Cooper, A., Putnam, D., Planchon, L. and Boies, S. (1999). Online Sexual Compulsivity: Getting Tangles in the Net. *Sexual Addiction and Compulsivity: Journal of Treatment and Prevention, 6*(2), 70–104.

Cooper, A., Scherer, C. R., Boies, S. C. and Gordon, B. L. (1999). Sexuality on the Internet: From Sexual Exploration to Pathological Expression. *Professional Psychology: Research and Practice, 30*(2), 154–164.

Cooper, A. and Sportolari, L. (1997). Romance in Cyberspace: Understanding Online Attraction. *Journal of Sex Education and Therapy, 22*(1), 7–14.

Durkin, K. F. and Bryant, C. D. (1995). Log on to Sex: Some Notes on Carnal Computer and Erotic Cyberspace as an Emerging Research Frontier. *Deviant Behavior: An International Journal, 16,* 179–200.

Fisher, W. A. and Barak, A. (2000). Online Sex Shops: Phenomenological, Psychological, and Ideological Perspectives on internet Sexuality. *Cyberpsychology & Behavior, 3*(4), 575–589.

Goodrum, A. and Spink, A. (2001). Image Searching on the Excite Web Search Engine. *Information Processing and Management, 37*(2), 295–312.

Goodson, P., McCormick, D. and Evans, A. (2000). Sex on the Internet: A Survey instrument to Assess College Students' Behavior and Attitudes. *Cyberpsychology & Behavior, 3*(2), 129–149.

Goodson, P., McCormick, D. and Evans, A. (2001). Sex on the Internet: College Students' Emotional Arousal When Viewing Sexually Explicit Materials Online. *Journal of Sex Education and Therapy, 25*(4), 252–260.

Jansen, B. J. and Spink, A. (in press). An Analysis of Web Searching by European AlltheWeb.com Users. *Information Processing and Management.*

Jansen, B. J., Spink, A. and Pedersen, J. (in press). A Temporal Comparison of AltaVista Web Searching. *Journal of the American Society for Information Science and Technology.*

King, S. (1999). Internet Gambling and Pornography. *Cyberpsychology & Behavior, 2*, 175–193.

Leiblum, S. R. (1997). Sex and the Net: Clinical Implications. *Journal of Sex Education and Therapy, 22*(1), 21–28.

Li, J. H-S. (2000). Cyberporn: The Controversy. *First Monday, 5*(8) (August 2000).

Newman, B. (1997). The Use of Online Services to Encourage Exploration of Egodystonic Sexual Interests. *Journal of Sex Education and Therapy, 22*(1), 45–48.

Quayle, E. (2002). Model of Problematic Internet Use in People with a Sexual Interest in Children. *Cyberpsychology & Behavior, 6*(1), 93–106.

Rimm, M. (1995). Marketing Pornography on the Information Superhighway: A Survey of 917,410 Images, Descriptions, Short Stories, and Animations Downloaded 8.5 Million Times By Consumers in Over 2000 Cities in Forty Counties, Provinces and Territories. (11 July 1995). <http://trfn.pgh.pa..us/guest/mrtext.html>.

Spink, A. and Cole, C. (Forthcoming). Human Information Behavior: Integrating Information Use and Diverse Approaches.

Spink, A. and Cole, C. (2001). Everyday Life Information Seeking Research. *Library and Information Science Research, 23*(1), 301–304.

Spink A, Jansen, B. J, Wolfram, D. and Saracevic, T. (2002). From E-Sex to E-Commerce: Web Searching Changes. *IEEE Computer, 35*, 107–109.

Spink A. and Ozmutlu, H. C. (2002). Characteristics of Question Format Web Queries: An Exploratory Study. *Information Processing and Management, 38*, 453–471.

Spink, A. and Ozmutlu, H. C. (2001). Sexually-Related Information Seeking on the Web. *Proceedings of ASIST 2002: American Society for Information Science and Technology, Washington, D.C., November 2001* (pp. 545–554).

Spink, A., Ozmutlu, H. C. and Lorence, D. P. (2004). Web Searching for Sexual Information: An Exploratory Study. *Information Processing and Management, 40*(1), 113–124.

Spink, A., Ozmutlu, S., Ozmutlu, H. C. and Cole, C. (2004). Sexual Searching on Web Search Engines. *Cyberpsychology & Behavior, 7*, 1.

Spink, A., Ozmutlu, S., Ozmutlu, H. C. and Jansen, B. J. (2002). United States Versus European Web Searching Trends. *ACM SIGIR Forum, 36*(2).

Spink, A., Wolfram, D., Jansen, B. J. and Saracevic, T. (2001). Searching the Web: The Public and Their Queries. *Journal of the American Society for Information Science and Technology, 53*(2), 226–234.

Van Gelder, L. (1985). The Strange Case of the Electronic Lover. *Ms.* (October), pp. 94–124.

Willems, H. (1998). Filtering the Net in Libraries: The Case (Mostly) Against. *Computers in Libraries, 18*, 55–58.

Young, K. S. and Rogers, R. C. (1998). The Relationship Between Depression and Internet Addiction. *Cyberpsychology & Behavior, 1*(1), 25–28.

Chapter 10

MULTIMEDIA SEARCHING

1.   INTRODUCTION

The estimated number of images on the publicly indexed Web is several hundred million (Lawrence and Giles, 1999) with millions of digital images added daily. When one includes video and audio files, which comprise songs, movies, and animated computer files (e.g., Flash, Shockwave), it is clear the Web is a vast multimedia repository. As more and more people and organizations load images onto the Web, the searching and retrieval of images has become a major challenge for researchers, commercial practitioners, and recreational users alike.

This chapter provides an extensive review of trends in multimedia Web searching, including an in-depth analysis of multimedia searching using radio buttons to identify specific multimedia content collections. Major findings include: (1) queries per Web multimedia session have decreased since 1997 as a proportion of general queries due to the introduction of multimedia radio buttons, (2) Web multimedia searching is more interactive and more complex than general Web searching, (3) Web multimedia searchers exhibit a broad range of information needs, but sexually-related topics are still dominant, and (4) image searching is more multifaceted than audio or video searching, with a high Boolean operator usage (28% of image queries).

Figure 10.1 shows the difference in mean session length among general, audio, image, and video Web searching.

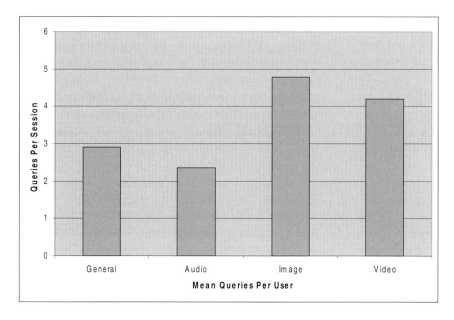

Figure 10-1. Mean Session Length for General, Audio, Image, and Video Web Searching

Figure 10.1 shows that the average number of queries for image searching (4.78 queries), is about twice that of general Web searching (2.91 queries). Average audio sessions (2.36 queries) are similar to general searching sessions, while average video searching sessions (4.19 queries) are more similar to image searching.

The tremendous growth in the quantity of digital images is driving the need for more effective methods of storing, searching, and retrieving image data. How users search for multimedia, and especially image content on the Web, and the design of more effective Web image retrieval systems, is a growing area of research. Most major Web search engines support some type of multimedia searching, and there are several image and multimedia specific search engines, including ImageScape (Lew, 2000) and Webseek (Smith, 2003). With the development of such technologies, image indexing and retrieval have received increasing attention. However, there has been little research into how users search for images in the Web environment.

2.   IMAGE RETRIEVAL

One can classify current image retrieval approaches, whether on traditional information retrieval (IR) systems or on Web search engines, as either concept- or content-based (Rasmussen, 1997). In the concept-based approach, image retrieval research has focused on the retrieval of images utilizing indexed image collections (Goodrum and Kim, 1998). Researchers and practitioners have created thesauri for visual information, such as the Library of Congress Thesaurus for Graphics Materials, Metadata (Greenberg, 1993).

These thesauri are then used to index images within a collection. Many Web search engines use textual clues to automate this concept-based approach, using text surrounding the image and other clues such as file names. This approach is based on the assumption that textual clues, such filenames, relate to the image. This assumption does not always hold, as when software programs for desktop computers and digital cameras automatically generate file names for images. However, it has proven to relatively effective.

In the content-based approach, the focus has been on indexing images at the pixel level and the implementation of search features using pixel comparison (Wang, 2000). Content-based image IR systems allow users to search image collections using color, texture, shape, and spatial similarity. These systems often also provide text-based search functions for notations and text descriptions embedded within images. New technologies have placed the emphasis on content-based retrieval, with commercial systems such as the MediaSite.com <http://www.mediasite.com> system.

However, it is not clear how the retrieval functionality of either of these approaches systems correlates with the image needs of real users. Concerning the context approach, it has been pointed out that experts are not a good source of terms that are preferred by real users. Concerning the content approach, users seldom search using content characteristics (Chen, 2001). Although user studies within specific domains have been conducted, research has shown (Jansen and Pooch, 2001) that Web users differ in their interaction with IR systems relative to users in other environments.

In this respect, studies of the image needs of Web users are especially needed for effective and efficient design of Web-based image IR systems. Examining Web multimedia searching is an important area of research with the potential to increase our understanding of multimedia Web searching, advance our knowledge of user information needs, and positively impact the design of online multimedia systems. This understanding will also assist in addressing many of the challenges of Web multimedia retrieval (Lew, Sebe and Eakins, 2002).

3.   MULTIMEDIA SEARCHING

There has been limited large-scale research examining Web multimedia searching (Goodrum and Spink, 2001; Jansen, Goodrum and Spink, 2000). Although the limited studies conducted provide important insights into multimedia Web searching, we need further research to validate these results across search engines and time. This is especially important as Web information systems are continually undergoing incremental changes. New research can evaluate the effect of these changes on system performance and user searching behaviors over time.

This chapter addresses some these needs by examining Web searchers using the AltaVista Web search engine, including the effect of multimedia radio buttons; an innovation in multimedia searching that received limited study. The chapter also analyzes multimedia searching characteristics, including session duration, query length, results pages viewed and term usage. The research design and a discussion of the key findings and the implications of our research results for online multimedia system users and system designers are also provided.

4.   MULTIMEDIA WEB SEARCHING TRENDS

Jorgensen (2003) and Smeaton (2004) review a number of unique systems for image classification. However, little research has examined the relative effectiveness of these various approaches to image indexing or retrieval using Web search engines. Automatic assignment of textual attributes has been conducted using captions from still images, transcripts, closed captioning, and verbal description for the blind accompanying videos (Turner, 1998). Swain (1999) views text cues extracted from HTML pages and multimedia document headers, supplemented by off-line analysis, to be the primary sources of information for indexing multimedia Web documents. However, Lawrence and Giles (1999) show that the use of Web metadata tags is still not widespread.

Problems with text-based access to images have prompted increasing interest in the development of image-based solutions. This approach relies on the characterization of primitive features such as color, shape, and texture that a system automatically extracts from the images themselves. Research shows that some users may need access to images based on such primitive features such as color, texture or shape, or access to images based on abstract concepts and symbolic imagery (Fidel, 1997). Wang's (2000) SIMPLIcity system (http://wang.ist.psu.edu) uses this approach. Similarly, others have investigated image searching using query by example (Porkaew, Ortega and Mehrotra, 1999).

Figure 10.2 shows the SIMPLIcity interface. SIMPLIcity allows multiple entry points into the system, including both context- and content-based.

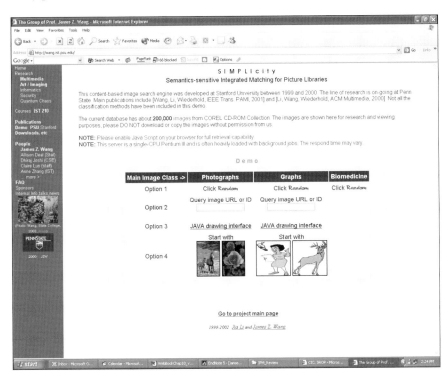

Figure 10-2. SIMPLIcity's Web Interface

A third approach is a combination or blending of the context- and content-based retrieval approaches. This hybrid approach generally uses a machine-learning method to teach computers to annotate images based on pixel-level information and to use the computer-annotated words for retrieval. This potentially allows users to type in keywords for retrieval of un-annotated images in a manner very similar to the way users search for text. This third approach has the advantage of reducing the cognitive load of learning additional searching methods or jargon. Researchers are investigating the feasibility of this approach (Barnard, Duygulu, Freitas, Forsyth, Blei and Jordan, 2003; Li and Wang, 2003).

Most of the major Web search engines have some provision for searching for images. Google <http://www.google.com> provides federated databases for image searching. Metacrawler <http://www.metacrawler.com> provides access to image, audio, and video content collections. Lycos

<http://www.lycos.com> searchers can narrow a query to specifically search for an image. ClipArt Searcher <http://www.Webplaces.com/search/> and the Yahoo Picture Gallery <http://gallery.yahoo.com> provide targeted multimedia collections to searchers. One can see IR-Ware <http://www.ir-ware.biz/aud0en.html> for a comprehensive list of audio, image, and video search engines.

Most of the general Web search engines now use some sort of radio boxes for aspects of multimedia searching. The use of radio boxes attempts to address the semantic gap (Gudivada and Raghavan, 1995) that occurs between the textual expression of a multimedia information and the actual multimedia content. The presentation of retrieved items as text-only lists rather than as thumbnail images, or video key frames exacerbates the problem. On the Web, content image retrieval systems such as WebSEEK (Smith, 2003) and SingingFish <http://www.singingfish.com/> provide a variety of multimedia files to Web searches.

Figure 10.3 shows the AltaVista interface with multimedia tabs for audio, image and video searching. The results page is displaying image thumbnails in response to the query *Cobra*. Notice the variety of domain results for this query term, including snake, car, and cartoon character.

Multimedia research has not only focused on the indexing side; others have examined multimedia searching. Keister (1994) analyzed transaction logs at the National Library of Medicine and showed that most image queries were structured using both abstract concepts as well as concrete image elements. The researcher concluded that the information needs of the user are highly subjective and do not lend themselves to indexing.

In the area of Web multimedia searching, there have been few published research studies (Goodrum and Spink, 2001; Jansen, Goodrum, and Spink, 2000). Goodrum and Spink (2001) analyzed image queries, and Jansen, Goodrum and Spink (2000) analyzed audio, image, and video sessions and queries from the Excite Web search engine from multiple years. On average, there were 3.36 image queries per user containing an average of 3.74 terms per query. Image queries contained a large number of unique terms. The most frequently occurring image-related terms appeared less than 10% of the time, with most terms occurring only once (Goodrum and Spink, 2001).

The researchers noted that multimedia sessions and queries are generally longer than general Web queries indicating an increased cognitive load for multimedia searching. The number of multimedia sessions originating from the general search box decreased since 1997 as a proportion of general queries due to the introduction of multimedia buttons near the query box. Generally, multimedia queries are longer than non-multimedia queries, and audio queries occur more frequently than image or video queries. Overall, we see multimedia Web searching undergoing major changes as Web content and searching evolves (Ozmutlu, Spink, and Ozmutlu, 2003). All three studies (Goodrum and Spink, 2001; Jansen, Goodrum and Spink, 2000; Ozmutlu, Spink and Ozmutlu, 2003) were on the general database and did not examine the effect of separate multimedia collections on Web searching.

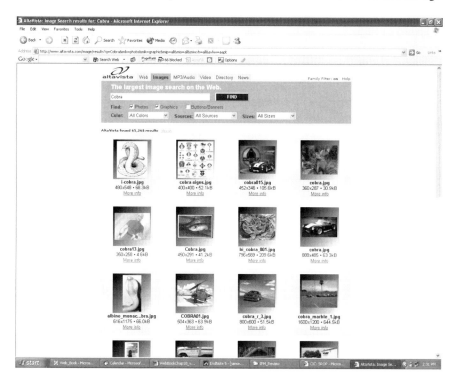

Figure 10-3. AltaVista Interface with Multimedia Tabs for Audio, Image and Video Searching

Table 10.1 compares audio, video and image queries for the 1997, 1999 and 2001 Excite data sets (Ozmutlu, Spink and Ozmutlu, 2003).

Table 10.1 shows that by 2001, audio queries dominated identified video and image queries, with 52.7% of multimedia queries being audio queries, 21.9% were video queries and 25.4% were image queries. This may be due to the development of mp3 technology and the "Napster" software that allowed the free exchange of audio files. It should be noted that the audio queries were not included in the 1999 dataset analysis.

Fidel, Davies, Douglass, Holder, Hopkins and Kushner (1999) studied high school students as the students performed focused searching. The students used Web landmarks, were satisfied with their searches and the results, and impatient with slow response. The students enjoyed searching the Web because it had a variety of formats, especially pictures.

Table 10-1. Comparison of Audio and Video Queries from 1997, 1999 and 2001 Excite Datasets

	Audio Queries			Video Queries			Image Queries		
	1997	1999	2001	1997	1999	2001	1997	1999	2001
Number	3810		9655	7630	17148	4011	27144	22190	4651
Percentage of Data Set	0.37%	–	0.9%	0.7%	1.6%	0.3%	2.6%	2.1%	0.4%
Percentage of Multimedia Queries	9.8%	–	52.7%	19.8%	43.5%	21.9%	70.4%	56.4%	25.4%
Mean Queries Per Session	2.4	–	2.6	2.9	3	2.6	3.2	3.4	2.8
Median Queries Per Session	2	–	1	2	–	1	2	–	1
Maximum Queries Per Session	51	–	119	70	–	59	267	–	102
Standard Deviation for Queries Per Session	2.9	–	4.8	3.8	–	3.8	5.4	–	5

The next section discusses our research into multimedia Web search that examines the multimedia Web searching patterns of AltaVista users. We present results from analysis of both general searching and three multimedia content collections (i.e., audio, image, and video). The broader goal of the study is to gauge the effect of separate multimedia collections on Web searching characteristics and thereby affect the design of multimedia retrieval systems.

5.   DATA COLLECTION

Many Web searchers are interested in multimedia content, such as audio, images, and video files, although the interest is predominantly in images. The AltaVista Web search engine uses a straightforward ontology designed to assist users in searching for multimedia, namely radio buttons that target searches for specific audio, image or video content collections. AltaVista resolves these multimedia searches against separate content collections. Each collection (i.e., audio, image, and video) has different indexing features and relevance ranking functions based on textual attributes of the particular multimedia file. Many have proposed content-based indexing (Djeraba, 2000; Wang, 2000); however, the context-based indexing methods such as used by AltaVista have proven quite effective within the Web searching environment.

6. MULTIMEDIA WEB SEARCH USING DISTINCT CONTENT COLLECTIONS

Table 10.2 presents the aggregate results for the analysis. For comparison, the results from analysis of a general (i.e., textual searching) transaction log recorded on the same day are included.

Table 10-2. Comparison of General, Audio, Image, and Video Searching in 2002

	General	Audio	Image	Video
Sessions	369,350	3,181	26,720	5,789
Queries	1,073,388	7,513	127,614	24,265
Terms				
Unique	297,528 (9.5%)	6,199 (33.4%)	71,873 (14.1%)	8,914 (19.1%)
Total	3,132,106	18,544	510,807	46,708
Mean terms per query	2.91 (sd=4.77)	2.47 (sd=1.62)	4.00 (sd=3.21)	1.92 (sd=1.09)
Terms per query				
1 term	218,628 (20%)	2,128 (28%)	27,808 (22%)	9,465 (39%)
2 terms	330,875 (31%)	2,652 (35%)	40,472 (32%)	9,979 (41%)
3+ terms	523,885 (49%)	2,733 (36%)	59,334 (46%)	4,814 (20%)
Mean queries per user	2.91 (sd=4.77)	2.36 (sd=3.85)	4.78 (sd=10.44)	4.19 (sd=6.1)
Users modifying queries	193,468 (52%)	1,496 (47%)	14,838 (56%)	3,350 (58%)
Session size				
1 query	175,882 (48%)	1,685 (53%)	11,882 (44%)	2,439 (42%)
2 queries	75,343 (20%)	657 (21%)	4,759 (18%)	1,016 (18%)
3+ queries	118,125 (32%)	839 (26%)	10,079 (38%)	2,334 (40%)
Results Pages Viewed				
1 page	781,483 (72.8%)	5,551 (73.9%)	80,455 (63.0%)	13,357 (55.0%)
2 pages	139,088 (13.0%)	1,070 (14.2%)	14,498 (11.1%)	3,905 (16.1%)
3+ pages	150,904 (14.1%)	892 (11.9%)	32,661 (25.65)	1,949 (28.9%)
Boolean Queries	61,065 (6%)	210 (3%)	35,955 (28%)	299 (1%)
Terms not repeated in data set	176,196 (6%)	3,720 (20%)	35,955 (7%)	5,292 (11%)
Use of 100 most frequently occurring terms	592,699 (19%)	4,889 (26%)	26,621 (5%)	17,745 (38%)

Table 10.2 shows that the comparison of the four types of searching (general, audio, image, and video) highlights that the use of unique terms in

audio searching (33%) is substantially higher than the other types of Web searching (10% to 19%), indicating that searching for audio medium utilizes a broader jargon. The mean terms per query for image searching was notably larger (4 terms per query) than the other categories of searching, which were all less than 3 terms. Video searchers also viewed more pages of results than other searchers, with 45% of video searchers viewing more than one results page.

The session lengths for image searchers were longer than any other type of searching, although video sessions were also relatively lengthy. The session lengths of image searches when combined with the longer queries may indicate the image searching is a more difficult cognitive task than other types of searching. Another indicator of the complexity of image searching is Boolean usage, which was 28%. This is more than four times the next highest category of general Web searching. Audio searching had, by far, the highest percentage of terms not repeated in the data set (20%) and the highest percentage usage of most utilized terms (26%).

The next section examines the session lengths for the audio, image, and video Web searching.

7.   MULTIMEDIA SESSIONS

Table 10.3 presents the results of an analysis of session length from the three AltaVista multimedia Web transaction logs.

Table 10-3. Comparison of Session Length for Audio, Image, and Video Searching on AltaVista 2002

Session Length	Audio AltaVista		Image AltaVista		Video AltaVista	
	Freq.	%	Freq.	%	Freq.	%
1	1,685	53.0%	11,882	44.5%	2,439	42.1%
2	657	20.7%	4,759	17.8%	1,016	17.6%
3	347	10.9%	2,551	9.5%	530	9.2%
4	204	6.4%	1,656	6.2%	342	5.9%
5	105	3.3%	1,135	4.2%	248	4.3%
6	52	1.6%	830	3.1%	182	3.1%
7	39	1.2%	595	2.2%	158	2.7%
8	13	0.4%	433	1.6%	105	1.8%
9	26	0.8%	375	1.4%	102	1.8%
10	10	0.3%	291	1.1%	72	1.2%
>10	43	1.4%	2,213	8.3%	595	10.3%
	3,181	100.00%	26,720	99.90%	5,789	100.00%

Table 10.3 shows that in all cases of multimedia searching, the predominant session length was one query, with single query audio searching sessions being about 10% higher than image or video. Given the fairly easy indexing methods of audio files, especially music files, this is reasonable. Single session audio searching sessions are also about 5% higher than general Web searching on AltaVista. The session lengths for image and video are comparable to that of AltaVista general Web searching.

8. MULTIMEDIA QUERIES

Table 10.4 presents the query length percentages for each data set.

Table 10.4 shows that generally the percentages are similar at each length, although with some variation. A notable exception is image queries with length of 9 terms at 27%. Naturally this skewed the average. We cannot account for this clustering at this query length. We examined this query length in more detail. There were several individual images sessions, not a single user. We hypothesize that this is an anomaly of the data collection. Over a longer collection period, the percentage would be more evenly spread at the longer query lengths for image searchers.

Table 10-4. Query Lengths in Each Data Set

Query Length	Percentage of All Queries			
	General	Audio	Image	Video
0	0.03%	0.1%	0.04%	0.03%
1	20.4%	28.3%	21.8%	39.0%
2	30.8%	35.3%	31.7%	41.1%
3	22.8%	17.5%	11.9%	13.2%
4	12.0%	9.5%	3.9%	4.1%
5	5.9%	4.7%	2.7%	1.6%
6	2.5%	2.2%	0.5%	0.5%
7	1.2%	1.0%	0.2%	0.2%
8	0.5%	0.5%	0.1%	0.1%
9	3.5%	0.5%	27.0%	0.1%
≥ 10	0.4%	0.4%	0.2%	0.1%

Table 10.5 presents a comparison of the means and standard deviation using data from Jansen, Goodrum and Spink (2000).

Table 10.5 shows that if we view increased query length and increased session length as indicators of searching complexity, then the use of a relative simple interface (i.e., radio buttons for specific multimedia type) has reduced the complexity of audio and video Web searching. This has not had the same effect on image searching.

Table 10-5. Comparison of Audio, Image, and Video Searching With and Without Multimedia Interface

	Audio		Image		Video	
	With	Without *	With	Without *	With	Without *
Mean Terms Per Query	2.47 (sd=1.62)	4.11 (sd=2.67)	4.00 (sd=3.21)	3.46 (sd=2.20)	1.92 (sd=1.09)	3.32 (sd=1.96)
Mean Queries Per User	2.36 (sd=3.85)	2.44 (sd=2.95)	4.78 (sd=10.44)	3.27 (sd=5.49)	4.19 (sd=6.14)	2.91 (sd=3.85)

Note: * Data from Jansen, Goodrum, and Spink (2000)

9.   MULTIMEDIA WEB TERMS

Table 10.6 presents the term-frequency for the top 25 most frequently occurring terms within each data set, after removal of stop words.

In previous studies of general Web searching trends, there is a documented shift away from entertainment to commercial, and increased information searching on a variety of topics (Spink, Jansen, Wolfram and Saracevic, 2002). These changes have paralleled the increased availability of commercial content on the Web (Lawrence and Giles, 1998).

Table 10.6 suggests that this does not appear to be the case with multimedia Web searching, as evidenced by the most frequently occurring terms, most of which are entertainment-related. Many terms are sexual in nature. Although this may cause offense for some, it is important for researchers and practitioners in the field of multimedia retrieval to clearly understand the motivation and information need of many users currently searching for multimedia on the Web. It remains to be seen whether or not Web multimedia searching follows the same trend as general Web searching, which is a shift to other topics.

The other notable area of interest is the frequency of term usage. The term frequencies between general and image searching are nearly identical. Audio and video frequencies are substantially higher. However, one might expect this given the clustering in the entertainment domain.

Table 10-6. Top 25 Most Frequently Occurring Web Terms in Each Data Set

General		Audio		Image		Video	
Total Terms	3,132,106	Total Terms	18,544	Total Terms	510,807	Total Terms	46,708
Term	Occurrences	Term	Occurrences	Term	Occurrences	Term	Occurrences
free	0.6%	mp3	1.0%	nude	0.6%	sex	3.7%
sex	0.2%	music	0.8%	sex	0.4%	free	1.2%
pictures	0.2%	you	0.6%	girls	0.3%	teen	1.0%
new	0.2%	sounds	0.5%	pictures	0.2%	nude	1.0%
nude	0.2%	free	0.5%	p***y	0.2%	f**k	0.9%
music	0.2%	sex	0.5%	naked	0.2%	porn	0.9%
school	0.2%	john	0.5%	teen	0.2%	girls	0.9%
how	0.2%	me	0.4%	women	0.2%	p***y	0.9%
lyrics	0.2%	song	0.4%	pics	0.2%	f***ing	0.8%
home	0.2%	love	0.4%	free	0.1%	c*m	0.8%
pics	0.2%	sound	0.4%	black	0.1%	gay	0.7%
download	0.2%	by	0.3%	girl	0.1%	lesbian	0.7%
online	0.1%	my	0.3%	porn	0.1%	video	0.7%
american	0.1%	on	0.3%	big	0.1%	black	0.7%
state	0.1%	songs	0.3%	hot	0.1%	anal	0.6%
county	0.1%	download	0.3%	t*ts	0.1%	hardcore	0.6%
university	0.1%	wav	0.3%	young	0.1%	big	0.6%
car	0.1%	world	0.3%	f***ing	0.1%	hentai	0.5%
Texas	0.1%	theme	0.2%	flag	0.1%	t*ts	0.5%
real	0.1%	orgasm	0.2%	sexy	0.1%	young	0.5%
games	0.1%	midi	0.2%	gay	0.1%	girl	0.5%
software	0.1%	star	0.2%	c*m	0.1%	videos	0.5%
art	0.1%	your	0.2%	a**	0.1%	movies	0.4%
map	0.1%	down	0.2%	world	0.1%	asian	0.4%
Florida	0.1%	pink	0.2%	map	0.1%	women	0.4%

Note: p***y, t*ts, f***ing, a**, f**k: expletives deleted

10.   DISCUSSION

The research reported in this chapter sought to identify the characteristics of AltaVista Web multimedia searching and measuring the effect of radio buttons on multimedia Web searching. The data shows that multimedia Web searching appears to require greater interactivity between the user and Web search engine, relative to general Web searching. The increase in Web query and session lengths and the increase in the number of results pages being viewed indicate this greater interactivity. Overall, the interactions between Web searchers and systems are still relatively simple, as evidenced by the low use of query operators.

However, the range of information needs appears to be broadening, based on the high percentage of unique terms and large number of terms not repeated in the data set. Other Web studies also report a trend toward a broadening of topics (Jansen and Spink, in press; Spink, Jansen, Wolfram and Saracevic, 2002). The increased interactivity is actually welcome news for Web search engine developers, as it indicates a move by Web searchers to more carefully refine their information topics.

There was a decrease in the number of pages viewed, especially between the first and second and the second and third results pages, with very few users viewing more than four or five pages of results. AltaVista users have a low tolerance for reviewing large numbers of results, although again the trend is to view more. Given that over 70% of Web users utilize search engines to locate other Web sites (Alexa Insider, 2000), the implications are rather clear for content providers. Certainly for those publishing multimedia content on the Web or engaged in Web e-commerce in the multimedia area, the need to be ranked within the top 10 or 20 results remains critical in order to direct visitors to one's Web site.

At the term level of analysis, the most frequently occurring terms represent a small percentage of overall term usage. The most frequently used term (*free*) accounted only for approximately 0.6% of all term usage. The use of sexual terms was extremely low, in the general set, and the diversity of terms was quite large. Even in the multimedia searching, with more target topics, the frequency of top term usage was quite low. Again, this diversity indicates that these Web users are searching for an increasing variety of information topics.

Generally, it appears that the use of separate Web searching interfaces may aid users in multimedia searching. Multimedia Web searching using AltaVista's "radio button" ontology is less complex in terms of query and session length than searching for multimedia content without such ontology. However, even with the use of the multimedia radio buttons and specific multimedia content collections, searching for multimedia is more complex than general Web searching. This indicates the need for and the possibility for further system improvements in this area.

Of the four types of multimedia Web searching (general, audio, image and video), image searching appears to be the more multifaceted task. The mean terms per query for image searching was notably larger (4 terms) than the other categories of searching, which were less than 3 terms. The session lengths for image searchers were longer than any other type of searching, although video sessions were also relatively lengthy. Boolean usage by image searchers was 28%, over four times the next highest category of general Web searching. These results certainly indicate the need for more efforts to increase the ease of multimedia searching.

11. CONCLUSION

Query analysis has formed the basis for the examination of much multimedia searching. Most studies in this area focus on image seeking and use in indexed image collections (Enser, 1995; Goodrum and Kim, 1998; Hastings, 1995; O'Connor, O'Connor and Abbas, 1999; Turner, 1994). These studies indicate that the number of terms by a single user searching for an image may be low, but the pool of terms employed across all users searching for images is quite large.

This contrasts to the mean number of terms used to find textual documents in structured databases (Spink and Saracevic, 1997) These textual studies identified a mean of 7±1.5 terms per query. Jansen, Spink, Bateman and Saracevic (1998), Jansen, Spink and Saracevic (2000), and Spink, Jansen, Wolfram and Saracevic (2002) found that queries on the Web averaged only 2.3 search terms. As discussed in this paper, this closely approximates the mean search terms employed by users searching for images on the Web. Limited studies have examined users' behavior when seeking images from the Web. This is an important area of research for the development of models of image information seeking and more effective Web-based image retrieval tools.

The results of our research provide important insights into the current state of multimedia searching and Web information system usage for users, Web search engines developers, and Web sites designers. Certainly, system design work needs to continue, especially in the area of multimedia Web searching. The short session lengths and short queries are challenging issues for designers of Web information systems. This approach does not seem to be a successful strategy to maximize either recall or precision, the traditional and limited metrics for information retrieval system performance.

There are several avenues for future research. Certainly, there is a need for more analysis in this field on a wider variety of Web search engines, ideally on the most popular search engines such as Microsoft Search, Google, America Online, or Yahoo!. However, access to the user data and the willingness of search engines to provide the access hampers this type of research. Additionally as Web search engines introduce additional searching interfaces changes, researchers should continue the evaluation of these changes to gauge their effect on Web searchers, using either transaction logs analysis or lab studies. Finally, we must continue the trend analysis of Web searching in order to predict future behavior and identify future user needs.

12.   REFERENCES

Alexa Insider. (2000). *Alexa Insider's Page*. Alexa Insider. Retrieved 30 March, 2000, from the World Wide Web: <http://insider.alexa.com/insider?cli=10>.

Barnard, K., Duygulu, P., Freitas, N. D., Forsyth, D. A., Blei, D. M. and Jordan. M. I. (2003). Matching Words and Pictures. *Journal of Machine Learning Research* (3), 1107–1135.

Chen, H. (2001). An Analysis of Image Queries of Art History. *Journal of the American Society for Information Science and Technology, 52*(3), 260–273.

Djeraba, C. (2000). When Image Indexing Meets Knowledge Discovery. In *Proceedings of 6th ACM SIGKDD International Conference on Know edge Discovery and Data Mining*, pp. 73–81. Boston, MA, USA. 20–23 August.

Enser, P. G. B. (1995). Progress in Documentation: Pictorial Information Retrieval. *Journal of Documentation, 51*(2), 126–170.

Fidel, R. (1997). The Image Retrieval Task: Implications for the Design and Evaluation of Image Databases. *The New Review of Hypermedia and Multimedia, 3*(1), 181–199.

Fidel, R., Davies, R. K., Douglass, M. H., Holder, J. K., Hopkins, C. J. and Kushner, E. J. (1999). A Visit to the Information Mall: Web Searching Behavior of High School Students. *Journal of the American Society for Information Science, 50*(1), 24–37.

Goodrum, A. and Kim. (1998). *Visualizing the History of Chemistry: Queries to the Chf Pictorial Collection*: Report to the Chemical Heritage Foundation Pictorial Collection.

Goodrum, A. and Spink, A. (2001). Image Searching on the Excite Search Engine. *Information Processing & Management, 37*(2), 295–311.

Greenberg, J. (1993). Intellectual Control of Visual Archives: A Comparison between the Art and Architecture Thesaurus and the Library of Congress Thesaurus for Graphic and Materials. *Cataloging and Classifications Quarterly, 16*(1), 85–101.

Gudivada, V. V., & Raghavan, V. V. (1995). Content-Based Image Retrieval Systems. *IEEE Computer, 28*(9), 18–22.

Hastings, S. K. (1995). Query Categories in a Study of Intellectual Access to Digitized Art Images. In *Proceedings of the 58th Annual Meeting of the American Society for Information Science*, pp. 3–8. Chicago, IL. October 9–12, 1995.

Jansen, B. J., Goodrum, A. and Spink, A. (2000). Searching for Multimedia: Video, Audio, and Image Web Queries. *World Wide Web Journal, 3*(4), 249–254.

Jansen, B. J. and Pooch, U. (2001). Web User Studies: A Review and Framework for Future Work. *Journal of the American Society of Information Science and Technology, 52*(3), 235–246.

Jansen, B. J. and Spink, A. (in press). An Analysis of Web Searching by European AlltheWeb.Com Users. *Information Processing and Management*.

Jansen, B. J., Spink, A., Bateman, J. and Saracevic, T. (1998). Real Life Information Retrieval: A Study of User Queries on the Web. *SIGIR Forum, 32*(1), 5–17.

Jansen, B. J., Spink, A. and Saracevic, T. (2000). Real Life, Real Users, and Real Needs: A Study and Analysis of User Queries on the Web. *Information Processing and Management, 36*(2), 207–227.

Jörgensen, C. (2003). *Image Retrieval: Theory and Practice*. New York: Scarecrow Press.

Keister, L. H. (Ed.). (1994). *User Types and Queries: Impact on Image Access Systems*. Medford, New Jersey: Learned Information. pp. 7–22.

Lawrence, S. and Giles, C. L. (1998). Searching the World Wide Web. *Science, 280*(3), 98–100.

Lawrence, S. and Giles, C. L. (1999). Accessibility of Information on the Web. *Nature, 400*, 107–109.

Lew, M. S. (2000). Next Generation Web Searches for Visual Content. *IEEE Computer, 33*(11), 46–53.

Lew, M. S., Sebe, N. and Eakins, J. P. (2002). Challenges of Image and Video Retrieval. In M. S. Lew, N. Sebe and J. P. Eakins (Eds.), *Lecture Notes in Computer Science* (Vol. 2383/2002, pp. 1–6). Heidelberg: Springer-Verlag.

Li, J. and Wang, J. Z. (2003). Automatic Linguistic Indexing of Pictures by a Statistical Modeling Approach. *IEEE Transactions on Pattern Analysis and Machine Intelligence, 25*(9), 1075–1088.

O'Connor, B., O'Connor, M. and Abbas, J. (1999). Functional Descriptors of Image Documents: User-Generated Captions and Response Statements. *Journal of the American Society for Information Science, 50*(8), 681–697.

Ozmutlu, S., Spink, A. and Ozmutlu, H. C. (2003). Trends in Multimedia Web Searching: 1997–2001. *Information Processing & Management, 39*(4), 611–621.

Porkaew, K., Ortega, M. and Mehrotra, S. (1999). Query Reformulation for Content Based Multimedia Retrieval in Mar, S. In *Proceedings of the IEEE International Conference on Multimedia Computer Systems*, pp. 747–751. Florence, Italy. 7–11 June.

Rasmussen, E. M. (1997). Indexing Images. *Annual Review of Information Science and Technology, 32*, 169–196.

Smeaton, A. F. (2004). Indexing, Browsing and Searching of Digital Video. In B. Cronin (Ed.), *Annual Review of Information Sciences and Technology* (Vol. 38, pp. 371–407). Medford, NJ, USA: Information Today.

Smith, J. R. (2003). *Webseek at Columbia University* [Web site]. Retrieved 16 July, 2003, from the World Wide Web: <http://disney.ctr.columbia.edu/webseek/>.

Spink, A., Jansen, B. J., Wolfram, D. and Saracevic, T. (2002). From E-Sex to E-Commerce: Web Search Changes. *IEEE Computer, 35*(3), 107–111.

Spink, A. and Saracevic, T. (1997). Interaction in Information Retrieval: Selection and Effectiveness of Search Terms. *Journal of the American Society for Information Science, 48*(5), 382–394.

Swain, M. J. (1999). Searching for Multimedia on the World Wide Web. In *Proceedings of IEEE International Conference on Multimedia Computing and Systems*, pp. 9032–9037. Florence, Italy. 7–11 June.

Turner, J. (1994). Indexing Ordinary Pictures for Storage and Retrieval. *Visual Resources: An International Journal of Documentation 10*, 265–273.

Turner, J. (1998). Words and Pictures in Information Systems for Moving Images. In *Proceedings of the 1998 Association of Moving Image Archivists Conference*, pp. 309–315. Miami, Florida, USA. 7–12 December.

Wang, J. Z. (2000). Simplicity: A Region-Based Image Retrieval System for Picture Libraries and Biomedical Image Databases. In *Proceedings of ACM Multimedia*, pp. 483–484. Los Angeles, CA. October 2000.

Section IV

CONCLUSION

Chapter 11

KEY FINDINGS, TRENDS, FURTHER RESEARCH AND CONCLUSIONS

1.   KEY FINDINGS

This chapter outlines the key findings and the Web search trends we identified during our multi-year research project. We discuss areas for further research and draw conclusions from our eight-year exploration, study and analyses of Web search beginning in 1997 to 2004 (Jansen, Spink and Bateman, 1998; Jansen, Spink and Saracevic, 2000; Spink, Jansen, Wolfram and Saracevic, 2002). Based on the knowledge, experiences, insights, and feedback from this stream of research, we also present possible future trends in Web search.

2.   SOCIAL AND ORGANIZATIONAL RESEARCH

A key finding of our book is that the overwhelming research focus in the scientific literature is on the technological aspects of Web search. The studies that do venture beyond the technological aspects are generally focused on the individual level of analysis. Despite the growth of the Web as a worldwide phenomenon, there are fewer studies that examine the social and organizational level of Web search, although there are some (Choo, Detlor and Turnbull, 2000).

This is surprising, given the impact that the Web has had in the areas of commerce, retailing, heath, and education, to name just a few. As Dr. Tefko Saracevic states in the Foreword of this book, "Within a decade the Web was a part of our social fabric – it affected every human activity in some way or other. It was adopted and adapted by the society-at-large".

Certainly, as data collection methods improve, we can expect more studies focusing on the organizational and social impacts and implications of Web. Research at the social level of analysis is certain a fruitful area, with questions ranging from commerce performance to trust of content to adverse consequences of the technology.

3.   COGNITIVE RESEARCH

Overall, from 1995 to 2004, Web search behavior studies at the cognitive level have increased in number and complexity, and they have become more international and interdisciplinary in nature. The range of studies has diversified to include cognitive and behaviors studies using Web transaction log analysis, experimental, and single Web site studies. In addition to viewing Web search behavior from a human information behavior perspective based on information seeking, the information foraging approach is producing a growing range of studies. There is also limited research focusing on theories and models of information seeking on the Web, with some notable exceptions (Choo, Detlor and Turnbull, 2000; Marchionini, 1995).

One major problem at the cognitive level of analysis is the lack of large-scale and in-depth studies using very large subject pools and subject pools that mirror the Web demographics. We also need studies of Web search that take a longitudinal and holistic approach of the information seeking process and the complex interactions among the searcher, the system, and the content.

4.   RESEARCH METHODS

There is a growing diversity of research methods that researchers use, ranging from Web transaction log analysis through experimental methods to surveys. The diverse disciplines that are investigating Web search behavior use the various methods common to their domains. Information and computer scientists have used Web transaction log analysis. Education and cognitive scientists tend to adopt experimental approaches. Commercial and non-profit organizations tend to use surveys. As of yet, there are few researchers who have used a diverse range of data collection and analysis methods to gain a more holistic insight into public Web search.

Certainly, one issue leading to this is the difficulty of data collection from the aggregate Web population. Improved methods of data collection for a large number of Web users would aid more in-depth and wider breath investigations of Web search. Better data collection methods would also help address the shortcomings of a very limited number of longitudinal studies. The longest study duration focusing on a Web search engine is about forty days (Silverstein, Henzinger, Marais, and Moricz, 1999), although longer studies have investigated searching on single Web sites (Croft, Cook and Wilder, 1995; Jones, Cunningham and McNab, 1998; Wang, Berry and Yang, 2003).

5.   COMMON SEARCH CHARACTERISTICS

Generally, we see some common characteristics of searching on all Web search engines, with some expected variations based on both particular engine and date. Perhaps the most telling in this regard is the most frequently occurring terms. Of the 105 terms on the most frequently occurring lists from the three search engines, 58 terms (55%) appear on at least two of lists. When combined with other evidence presented, such as term co-occurrence and topical classification, it appears Web searchers have some common topical interests that transcend particular systems.

Interestingly, the percentage that these terms represent of the total number of terms is decreasing. So, although the Web population has some common informational interests, their overall information needs are being more diverse. This may be in response to certain changes on the Web environment, including a greater quantity of and more diverse content, better searching and access technologies, or an increased user acceptance of the Web as a legitimate source of information.

6.   SEARCH TOPICS

This information diversity is reflected in research attempting to categorize Web queries and interests. Not only are Web searching interests becoming more diverse, but a significant finding of our research is that the major Web searching topics are changing. There was a decrease in sexual searching as a percentage of overall Web searching on both European and U.S. based Web search engines. The overall trend is towards the Web as a tool for information or e-commerce, rather than entertainment, medical or sexual searching. This trend is more pronounced with U.S. as opposed to European Web search engine users.

This analysis confirms survey and other data that the Web is now a major source of information for most people, there is increased use of the Web as an economic resource and tool, and people use the Web for an increasingly variety of information tasks. One must note, however, that our analysis is for Web search engines and may not reflect the topical interest supported by Web portals, niche search engines, and specialty Web sites (i.e. pornography sites, medical sites, e-commerce sites). Web searchers may fulfill their Web information needs via these non-search engine portals into the Web.

7.   QUERY LENGTH

There are certainly similarities among the users of the entire Web search engines that we researched; however, there also appear to be some search engine dependences. Query complexity, as measured by query length and use of query operators, appears to be increasing. At the very least, it is holding steady and not decreasing. The mean query length on the AlltheWeb.com search engine is about 2.4 terms per query. For the AltaVista search engine, average query length increased by about 0.5 terms from 1998 to 2002 (i.e., from 2.3 to 2.9 terms).

Mean query length also increased on Excite to over 2.5 terms per query. Generally, one could say the average query length appears to be increasing, albeit slowly. The majority of Web searchers certainly continue to use very short queries, and it appears that this is a factor that Web search engines and Web content providers must account for in providing relevant results for the foreseeable future.

8.   BOOLEAN OPERATOR USAGE

The use of query operators for Web queries has generally been about 10% of all queries. Query operator usage was almost non-existent on AlltheWeb.com, with usage well under 5%. For the AltaVista Web search engine, the usage of query operators has held steady at approximately 20%. However, the use of the PHRASE operator accounts for over 50% of query operator usage, with the AND operator the next most common, coming in a distant second. For the Excite Web search engine, the usage increased steadily from 1997 to 2001, at about 11% for both Boolean and other operators.

Similar to AltaVista, the PHRASE and the AND operators accounted for most of the total query operator usage. Although this low usage may be a problem for effective retrieval, there are more and more indications that greater usage of query operators may not increase Web search engine performance. Technology with term proximity, link, anchor text, and other ranking algorithms often produce results lists from simple queries (i.e., those with no operators) that are nearly identical to those same query terms with query operators.

9.   SEARCH SESSION LENGTH

Overall, it appears that session length is increasing, although slightly, with more searchers submitting more queries on the Excite and AltaVista Web search engines during the periods of data collection. The indications on AlltheWeb.com are counter to this, however, with more searchers with one session queries. Session durations for the vast majority of Web search engine users tend to be 15 minutes or less, although the average is a couple of hours. A substantial percentage of Web sessions are less than 5 minutes. We also see a growth in multitasking sessions, which are sessions that include two or more topics.

Generally, we can say that Web searching sessions do not lend themselves well to statistics such as averages. The averages hide the diversity of behaviors among Web search engines users. Some Web search engine sessions are very simple, with few interactions, and occurring quickly. Other sessions are complex, sometimes with multi-topics, a large number of interactions, and occurring over a long period. Many Web searchers appear to make relevance decisions in a matter of minutes or sometimes seconds. Others take a very lengthy period of time, a couple of hours. A large portion of Web search engine users will never look beyond the first page of results; others will view dozens of results. This wide diversity of searching behaviors, taken as a whole, is very complex and a challenge for designers of Web search engines and those providing Web content.

10.   PAGE VIEWING

There is an increase in the percentage of Web searchers viewing only the first results page. The viewing of results past the first page is decreasing. Although this may indicate increasing simplicity in interactions, there may be a relationship between viewing only the first results page and longer sessions and queries. The more complex and refined queries may be retrieving better results, so there is a decreased need to examine more documents. It may also be an indication of the increasing ability of search engines to relevance-rank Web documents more effectively.

For content providers, the need to appear in the top ten results has been, is, and will probably continue to be of critical importance. Additionally, the majority of Web searchers will spend not more than three minutes on a Web site before returning to the search engine. A sizeable percentage will spend less than 30 seconds. This is an extremely short duration for one to make a relevance judgment. In a time-critical situation such as this, the need for specific, fast loading and well-designed Web sites is a necessity.

11.   GEOGRAPHIC DIFFERENCES

There are both similarities and differences between usage on U.S. and European-based Web search engines. Searchers on both appear to be viewing fewer results pages. The use of Web query operators on both is fairly stable. However, the usage of these advanced Web query operators is much higher on U.S.-based Web search engines than on their European counterparts. In investigating this difference, we ruled out content collections (they are all immense), user bases (they all number in the millions), or algorithmic sophistication (they are all similar in performance tests). This leads us to linguistic differences; however, the majority of queries, at least on AlltheWeb.com, are in English. This difference in query operator usage is an area of potential future research.

12.   E-COMMERCE QUERIES

Certainly the Web has the potential to be a significant vehicle for business, and our research supports that the Web continues to become a key centerpiece for e-commerce. This commercialization will probably continue with the development of new tools and new ways of searching for e-commerce information on the Web.

However, searching the Web today for e-commerce information is somewhat akin to searching a library catalog and equally as frustrating. The Web also lacks a standardized approach to search engine functionality and terminology in this area, although major search engines are responding with product-specific search tools.

The e-commerce terminology on the Web is also incredibly varied and difficult for the typically Web user to implement with accuracy. As more Web users begin to ask questions rather than producing simple term queries, we need methods and approaches to analyze and process question queries in a "question and answer" format to diagnose the user's real information requirements to complete the cycle of e-commerce and facilitate the effective sale of goods and services over the Web.

13.   MEDICAL QUERIES

Overall, our studies show that a small percentage of Web queries are medical or health-related. The top five categories of medical or health queries were: (1) general health, (2) weight issues, (3) reproductive health and puberty, (4) pregnancy/obstetrics, and (5) human relationships. Over time, the medical and health queries may have declined as a proportion of all Web queries, perhaps as the use of specialized medical/health Websites and e-commerce-related searching on search engines has increased.

14.   SEXUAL QUERIES

Sexual information seeking is also declining as a percentage of total information seeking on the Web search engines. There appears to be differences in the quantity of sexual information seeking from search engine to search engine, and from one geographical region to another. We found that for sexual information seeking, an initial query that is sexual in nature can be followed by subsequent queries that are non-sexual in nature. Perhaps, this may be due to a curiosity factor, where some other information need draws a user to the Web but the user tries a sexual query to see what happens. Further studies focusing on these aspects of sexual information seeking would be of interest for various cognitive and social reasons.

15.   MULTIMEDIA QUERIES

Multimedia searching on the Web has generated significant interest because many people see the potential for significant value for both content providers and users. This has especially been true in the audio and video areas, where those in the music and movie industry have significant copyright concerns. There is also a strong user interest in these topics. For the most part, this issue does not seem to be a major portion of the searching on Web search engine, probably due to the existence of popular peer-to-peer file sharing applications and the introduction of specialty commercial music services. Major Web search engines appear to provide an ancillary service, in this regard, providing access to information and images of popular singers, movie stars, and models.

Certainly, multimedia searching does occur on Web search engines. Our findings show that Web multimedia searching is more interactive and more complex than general Web searching. Web multimedia searchers exhibit a broad range of information needs, but sexually-related topics are still the dominant ones. This is different than general Web searching. One could predict multimedia searching would follow the same path; however, this is not certain. The interest in sexually-related images could continue. Another of our findings is that image searching is more multifaceted than audio or video searching, with a high query operator usage (28% of image queries). This complexity may indicate the need for more specialized tools to support this mode of searching.

16.   TRAINING STUDIES AND SEARCH ENGINE EVALUATIONS

Overall, studies suggest that information task complexity and the quality of search terms affects search performance. However, we need further studies to model how people learn how to search, learn about Web search engines, and how this learning will impact user training courses and improve Web search interfaces and techniques. There are few studies in this area (Lucas and Topi, 2002). We will need more information on how searchers and search engines interaction as people use the Web for more addressing more complex information tasks.

Are people finding the information that addresses, or best addresses, their information needs? Much of the Web search evaluation studies draw on measures developed in the field of information retrieval. Few new user-based evaluation measures have been developed and tested that are based on more longitudinal, information behavior and cognitive variables within the complex Web environment. There are numerous and recurring "search engine shoot-offs" (c.f., SearchEngineWatch.com <http://www. searchenginewatch.com/>) and snapshot evaluations (Eastman and Jansen, 2003).

However, there are very few longitudinal evaluations of search engine performance, with exceptions such as Ding and Marchionini (1996), and Nicholson (2000). With the content collection of the Web continually changing, along with algorithmic modifications, search engine results can change within the span of a few minutes (Selberg and Etzioni, 2000).

17.　　WEB SEARCH TRENDS

A major finding of our studies is the existence of trends in the Web search phenomenon. Searching sessions are increasing in interaction. Queries appear to be slowly increasing in length. Information needs are broadening. The number of results pages viewed is decreasing. New information topics are emerging, as information and commerce areas are replacing previous top topics of entertainment and technology. The emergence of new technologies, such as niche search sites and multimedia-specific content collections, are altering Web search engine users' searching behaviors.

We need further large-scale and ongoing research to identify and track trends in public Web searching, at the individual, organizational, and societal levels. The Pew Internet and American Life Project <http://www.pewinternet.org/> is providing valuable snapshot and survey studies, but apart from our studies and a handful of others, few people have been able to gather sufficient data to determine Web search trends.

18.　　CONCLUSIONS

At present, most Web research funding is focused on the computing and technical aspects of the Web. The co-authors of this book have achieved their longitudinal and trends studies with little outside support, except the generous provision of large-scale Web transaction logs by some commercial Web search companies, for which we are extremely grateful. These transaction logs were never easy to come by. Due to the consolidation of Web search companies, transaction logs from Web search engines are becoming more even difficult to obtain.

Ongoing collaboration is needed between the commercial Web search companies and academic researchers to continue to identify and track trends in Web search. This type of ongoing trends analysis will provide advantages to the commercial, academic, industry and public sectors alike. The only way to achieve this is through the ongoing provision of Web search data by Web search companies and the increased funding of cognitive, organizational and social Web search research by government agencies, such as the National Science Foundation, industry groups, and non-profit organizations.

19.   REFERENCES

Choo, C. W., Detlor, B. and Turnbull, D. (2000). *Web Work. Information Seeking and Knowledge Work on the World Wide Web.* Kluwer Academic Publishers.

Croft, W. B., Cook, R. and Wilder, D. (1995). Providing Government Information on the Internet: Experiences with Thomas. In *Proceedings of the Digital Libraries Conference,* pp. 19–24. Austin, TX. 11–13 June.

Ding, W. and Marchionini, G. (1996). A Comparative Study of Web Search Service Performance. In *Proceedings of the 59th Annual Meeting of the American Society for Information Science,* pp. 136–142. Medford, NJ.

Eastman, C. M. and Jansen, B. J. (2003). Coverage, Ranking, and Relevance: A Study of the Impact of Query Operators on Search Engine Results. *ACM Transactions on Information Systems, 21*(4), 383–411.

Jansen, B.J., Spink, A. and Bateman, J. (1998). Real Life Information Retrieval: A Study of User Queries on the Web. *SIGIR Forum, 32*(1), 5–17.

Jansen, B. J., Spink, A. and Saracevic, T. (2000). Real Life, Real Users, and Real Needs: A Study and Analysis of User Queries on the Web. *Information Processing and Management, 36*(2), 207–227.

Jones, S., Cunningham, S. and McNab, R. (1998). Usage Analysis of a Digital Library. In *Proceedings of the Third ACM Conference on Digital libraries,* pp. 293–294. Pittsburgh, PA. June 1998.

Lucas, W. and Topi, H. (2002). Form and Function: The Impact of Query Term and Operator Usage on Web Search Results. *Journal of the American Society for Information Science and Technology, 53*(2), 95–108.

Marchionini, G. (1995). *Information Seeking in Electronic Environments.* Cambridge: Cambridge University Press.

Nicholson, S. (2000). Raising Reliability of Web Search Tool Research through Replication and Chaos Theory. *Journal of the American Society for Information Science, 51*(8), 724–729.

Selberg, E. and Etzioni, O. (2000). On the Instability of Web Search Services. In *Proceedings of RIAO 2000: Computer-assisted information retrieval,* pp. 223–236. Paris, France. April.

Silverstein, C., Henzinger, M., Marais, H. and Moricz, M. (1999). Analysis of a Very Large Web Search Engine Query Log. *SIGIR Forum, 33*(1), 6–12.

Spink, A., Jansen, B. J., Wolfram, D. and Saracevic, T. (2002). From E-Sex to E-Commerce: Web Search Changes. *IEEE Computer, 35*(3), 107–111.

Wang, P., Berry, M. and Yang, Y. (2003). Mining Longitudinal Web Queries: Trends and Patterns. *Journal of the American Society for Information Science and Technology, 54*(8), 743–758.

SUBJECT INDEX

AUTHOR INDEX

Information Knowledge and Science Management

Kluwer Academic Publishers – Dordrecht / Boston / London